# THE DREAM IN ISLAM

# THE DREAM IN ISLAM

*From Qur'anic Tradition
to Jihadist Inspiration*

❧◈❧

IAIN R. EDGAR

**berghahn**
NEW YORK · OXFORD
www.berghahnbooks.com

Published by in 2011 by

*Berghahn Books*

www.berghahnbooks.com

© 2011, 2016 Iain R. Edgar
First paperback edition published in 2016

**Library of Congress Cataloging-in-Publication Data**

Edgar, Iain R.
    The dream in Islam : from Qur'anic tradition to Jihadist inspiration / Iain R.
Edgar.
        p. cm.
    Includes bibliographical references and index.
    ISBN 978-0-85745-235-1 (hardback) — ISBN 978-1-78533-222-7 (paperback)
— ISBN 978-0-85745-236-8 (ebook)
    1. Dreams—Religious aspects—Islam. 2. Dream interpretation—Islamic
countries—History. 3. Ethnopsychology—Islamic countries—History. 4. Dreams
in literature. I. Title.
    BP190.5.D73E34 2011
    297.5'7—dc22

                                                                                2011016472

**British Library cataloguing in publication data**

A catalogue record for this book is available from the British Library.

ISBN 978-0-85745-235-1 (hardback)
ISBN 978-1-78533-222-7 (paperback)
ISBN 978-0-85745-236-8 (ebook)

*To my children, Nick and Sophie,*
*and*
*my grandchildren, Luke and Ollie*

# Contents

# Acknowledgments

This real journey into the Islamic dreamtime has been an immensely social experience, and I thoroughly enjoyed the variety of research subjects as well as the numerous friends and dreamers that I have encountered on this way. It would take up pages to thank all the people that have helped and inspired me during the research and writing process, and this book is a witness to them as much as it is an academic investigation into the dream in Islam.

Certain people have been of crucial help in various stages of my research. My dear friend and colleague Dr. Charlotte Hardman, social anthropologist in the Department of Theology and Religion, University of Durham, gave me crucial beginning contacts by organizing a conference on religion and violence in the aftermath of 9/11. Through this conference I was able to establish my contacts in the Sufi order of Shaykh Nazim, first in England and later in Northern Cyprus.

Furthermore, I am very grateful for the wonderful epilogue to my book by my Durham colleague Dr. Elisabeth Kirtsoglou, whose original thinking and quality of writing I have always admired. My good friend and colleague Dr. Steve Lyon of the Anthropology Department, University of Durham, has been a mainstay and an invaluable source of contacts, good will, encouragement, and support. Through him I met Mariam abou Zahab, French political scientist at IEP/CERI-INALCO, Paris, who provided many significant militant jihadist dream references and introduced me to the BBC Pakistani journalist, Rahimullah Yusufzai, who when I interviewed him in Peshawar provided significant information and analysis about the night dreams of the Taliban leader Mullah Omar.

Some people I met during my travel turned out to be invaluable, my great thanks to them: Mehmet Onal, Adnan Menderes University, Aydin, Turkey, taught me much about Islamic dreaming, and pressed me to focus not only on the Qur'an but also on the hadiths; Kayhan Delibas was my friend and translator in Aydin. In Pakistan, Ehsan Akhtar and his wife Catalina very warmly hosted me, and Muhammed Saeed gave me his fine translation service and companionship.

I would also like to thank Marion Berghahn, publisher of Berghahn Books, who has remained immensely supportive and encouraging, even when the book took longer than she (and I) expected. Thank you for your patience and sense of humor Marion! I extend my thanks to Kristine Hunt, who did the main editing and prevented many typographical errors.

This research would not have been possible without the help of the British Academy, who gave me a grant under its small research grants scheme and allowed me to travel and hunt dreams in Turkey, Pakistan, and North Cyprus for two months in 2005. The Department of Anthropology at Durham University contributed substantially by providing the research leave to write this book and for being a most stimulating department to work in.

A special thanks to my PhD student David Henig, who was always prepared to read drafts of this book and who made helpful recommendations. During the realization of this book, David and I became 'friends in Islam' as we spent valuable research time together in Bosnia: we interviewed the dream healer, Sadeta, in Sarajevo and we enjoyed many interesting conversations about Islam, Sufism and Islamic dream incubation, *Istikhara*. Thanks also to my PhD student Aurang Zeb Mughal for doing transliteration work on this book. Furthermore, I like to thank Christine Michaels for her gentle and subtly stimulating presence during the writing of this book. Finally, I thank my partner Gwynned de Looijer, who not only made me great cappuccino, but who also kept me focused, pressed me to check and double-check my references ("the Hebrew Bible is a big book!!"), and considerably helped and supported me in preparing the final draft.

# Preface to the Paperback Edition
## The Dreams of Islamic State

Since this book was first published in 2011, excellent studies of dreaming in Islamic societies have been published (or come to the author's attention), among them Amira Mittermaier's outstanding anthropological study of a contemporary poetry and dreaming group in Cairo,[1] Özgen Felek and Alexander Kynsh's edited collection of dreams and visions from a historical and cultural perspective,[2] and Elizabeth Sirreyeh's comprehensive historical and contemporary study of the history of dreaming in Islam.[3] Traditional dream interpretation practices continue to develop in Muslim lands; Muhammad alZekri's[4] book on the historical development of dream interpretation in Dubai shows the ever increasing importance of internet sources, while Mittermaier's elegant study of mixed contemporary Muslim and Freudian dream interpretive practices in Egypt[5] shows how apparently conflicting interpretive paradigms co-exist and mingle. The academic study of the role of dream interpretation amongst jihadists has not seriously developed during this time, hence my focus upon it in this preface.

Previous research, reported in this book and by Elizabeth Sirreyeh, has shown that jihadists attach great importance to dreams, to the point of taking them into account in personal and strategic decision-making. This preface asks whether the same is true of Islamic State (IS).[6] Using evidence from social media and IS publications, I review night dream accounts by IS members and supporters, seeking to assess the prominence, main themes, and reception of such accounts. Dreams appear to be at least as important to IS as to previous jihadist groups. Like other jihadists, IS activists consider dreams a potential window into the future and use them to make sense of the world, justify decisions, and claim authority. In at least one case (that of Garland attacker Elton Simpson), a dream may have informed the decision to take violent action.

Several studies over the last decade have shown that militant Islamists such as al-Qaeda and the Taliban make extensive use of reported night dreams to inspire, announce, and validate violent jihad.[7] In this preface I ask whether dreams play a similar role in IS. Using evidence from social media and IS publications, I review night dream accounts by IS members and supporters and the discussions they generate. This is the first academic study of dreaming in Islamic State.

As we shall see, IS members and sympathizers appear to attach considerable importance to dreams. Just as in other jihadist groups, dream accounts and discussions proliferate, and activists express belief in the predictive potential of night dreams. Dreams may also feature in decision-making processes at different levels in the organization, from Abu Bakr al-Baghdadi's decision to withdraw forces from Mosul, Iraq, in late 2014 to IS sympathizer Elton Simpson's May 2015 attack in Garland, Texas.

The preface has three parts. First I summarize what we know about the significance of dreams in Muslim societies generally, and in jihadist groups specifically. I then describe a sample of IS-related night dream accounts, before briefly discussing the connection between dreams and political action.

## The Significance of Dreams

### Dreaming in Islam

To understand the jihadist appreciation for dreams, it is important to realise that dreams are important in Islam more generally. The interpretive tradition regarding the "true dream" (*al-ruya*) is a fundamental feature of Islamic theology.[8] There are three dream reports in the Qur'an, two reported as received by the Prophet Mohammed. One of these directly relates to the decisive battle of Badr between the Muslims and the Quraish from Mecca in 624 CE.[9] The Joseph sura in the Qur'an contains the reported dream experiences of the Prophet Joseph, such as that of the seven fat and seven lean cows.[10] The true dream tradition is reported more extensively in the hadith, the recorded sayings of the Prophet Muhammed. The hadith Bukhari and Muslim Sahih, for example, each have a chapter recording the teachings of the Prophet Muhammed about true dreams that come from Allah.[11]

The Islamic tradition distinguishes between three types of dreams: the true dream (*al-ruya*), the false dream, which may come from the devil, and the meaningless everyday dream (*hulm*). True dreams are more likely to be experienced or received by pious Muslims, but potentially all Muslims can receive them. There is an extensive literature on the art and science of dream interpretation going back over a thousand years.

In the contemporary Muslim world, dreams command considerable popular interest. Arabic TV channels, for example, are replete with dream interpretation programs. My anthropological research over many years across four continents have shown that *Istikhara*, the ritual of incubating night dreams for guidance, is widespread in many if not most Islamic countries.[12] During my fieldwork research, especially in Pakistan, Turkey, Bosnia, and the UK, I rarely met a Muslim who didn't relate to his night dreams as a potential portal to the divine. Moreover, I found this dream tradition to be similar across all the main branches of Islam: Sunni, Shia, Salafi, and Sufi, as well as amongst the minority Alevi and Ahmadiyya sects.[13] In the Sufi mystical traditions, dreaming is most highly regarded.[14] While Sufis have traditionally paid the most attention to dreams, the more literalist Salafis appear to have become more interested in them over time. As a Salafi dream interpretation book states: "Salafis view the tradition of vision and dream interpretation as being rooted in Islam and having been inherited from the *Salaf.* Indeed, it has been inherited from the Prophets (peace be upon them), so any insinuation that Salafis are in some way opposed to vision interpretation in its totality would be incorrect."[15] Dreams thus have a different status in the Muslim world compared to Western societies. A longstanding Christian tradition dating in part to the fourth century CE viewed dreams as superstition, perhaps to prevent charismatic dreamers challenging the institution of the church.[16] Later, Freudian psychoanalysis considered dream content as mirroring, reassembling, and encoding personal experiences of the past. By contrast, Islamic dream interpretation has an important forward-looking component.[17] As Lamoreux writes, "Dream interpretation offered Muslims a royal road that led not inward but outward, providing insight not into the dreamer's psyche but into the hidden affairs of the world. In short, the aim of dream interpretation was not diagnosis, but divination."[18]

## Dreaming in Jihadism

For my previous research on al-Qaeda's dreams and interpretive practices as outlined in this book, I trawled books, newspapers, internet reports, and trial transcripts for dream accounts by militants to see whether there was a distinctive jihadist dreaming. I found a lot of material. Osama Bin Ladin himself brought up dreams in one of the first videos released after 9/11.[19] Elsewhere, I found dream accounts reported by numerous well-known militants: Richard Reid, the failed shoe bomber; the two core 9/11 planners Ramzi bin al-Shibh and Khalid Sheikh Muhammad; the "twentieth" suicide bomber, Zacarias Moussaoui; and several Guantanamo Bay detainees.[20] Scattered through autobiographies and biographies of various al-Qaeda linked militants, night dreams are prominently described and invoked as justifications for daytime decisions to wage violent jihad.[21] The famous jihadist website Azzam.com contained biographies of martyrs from Bosnia and elsewhere that include many examples of dreams of martyrdom, featuring either anticipatory illustrations of future paradisiacal states of being or of fallen martyrs describing paradise to the living.

I also conducted extensive fieldwork in Pakistan, Turkey, and Northern Cyprus. In Pakistan in March 2005, I interviewed Rahimullah Yusufzai (then a BBC journalist and now the editor of Pakistan's *The News International*), who was probably the only pre-9/11 journalist who had extensively interviewed the Taliban leader, Mullah Omar. This interview transcript is reported in full in chapter six. Yusufzai confirmed the importance of both inspirational and strategic planning dream accounts for the Taliban commanders and soldiers:

> I kept hearing these stories, no big military operation can happen unless he [Mullah Omar] gets his instructions in his dreams; he was a big believer in dreams; he told me he had been entrusted with a mission, a holy mission and the mission is to unite Afghan, to save it from divisions and to restore order and enforce Sharia law.[22]

And it was not just in the mountains of Afghanistan that radicals discussed dreams. Three years ago at a conference, an anonymous intelligence officer from a major western country (not the UK or US, but one from which many jihadists have left to go to Somalia and Syria) told me, "Everyone we are watching in our area is into dreaming as crucial to their jihadi membership, progress, and their final decision, via *Istikhara/* Islamic dream incubation, as to whether to go on militant jihad." Of course, not all Muslims who believe they have true dreams about jihad or martyrdom, become militants. For some radicalized individuals, however, a dream or series of dreams can be a catalyst for taking up arms. A short or long period of contemplation can be followed by a vivid command or message dream of the kind described by Yusufzai above.[23]

Not all dream imagery is as explicit as Mullah Omar's message dream. Often, the meaning of the dream is opaque or metaphorical and needs interpreting by the dreamer—possibly via one of a number of dream interpretation books (such as the well-known book purported to be written by the medieval Islamic dream interpreter Ibn Sirin), by a family member or an imam, or indeed through a dream interpretation website.[24] In radical circles or militant groups, that interpretation is often carried out by fellow activists and therefore susceptible to biased interpretation or outright manipulation.

## The Dreams of IS Members and Supporters

Let us now turn to the dreams of IS fighters and their many online supporters. In the following section, I present a sample of dream accounts collected from social media and IS publications.

### Twitter-based Dream Interpretation

A number of IS sympathizers discuss dreams on Twitter. J. M. Berger's article refers to the now-defunct Twitter handle "End of Time Dreams". (@entimdrms), which "serves as a broker between dreamers and allegedly authoritative third parties (more numerous and tweeting in Arabic) who interpret those dreams with a pro-ISIS bent".[25] The name of the handle is likely inspired by a hadith which states that at the end of time the dreams of the believer will come true.[26]

At the current time of writing, a similar-looking Twitter handle (@entdrm13) is active and providing the same kind of service as the original End of Time Dreams.[27] Berger writes also that "in a monitored list of 329 English-language accounts targeted by active ISIS recruiters, the 'End of Times Dreams' account cited previously was the second-most influential, based on a weighted count of interactions".[28] About half the posts by @entdrm13 are about dream accounts that seem to be offering positive expectations of IS advances on the battlefields of Iraq and Syria. Some of the dreams also refer to anticipated pledges of allegiance to IS by other jihadist groups:

> July 11: *seems to be a few dreams about the Kurds too, watch out for Kobani and Tal Abyad.*[29]

> July 11: *The brother had this dream yesterday so that leaves until next Thursday or Friday for it to occur: just had a dream that Hasakah has been liberated in Ramadan and ISIS is marching towards Kurds.* Abu Talha@akbanyash87.[30]

Here we see dreams presented as anticipatory or even in the prophetic tradition of true dreams:

> July 11: *recent rumours whether al shabaad will give bayat…here's two dreams. Also a dream from 2013 about a bayat from Egypt.*[31]

> *Dream: I saw al-Zawahiri in video giving a talk and you could see signs of regret on him. I give bayat to the amir of the lands between the two rivers (Iraq) and Somalia.*

> *Interpretation* (on site): *if the dream comes true then al Zawahiri will give bayat to the Islamic state after the mujahideen of Somalia give it (al shabaab) and Allah knows best.*[32]

We see here the classic Islamic theme of dreams shedding potential light on the future. Such posts probably serve to reinforce the sense among IS fighters that God and destiny is on their side in their holy war. They view the future as being known only to God, but also as divinable through true dreams. Let us now take a look at some slightly longer dream descriptions by IS fighters.

### Explicit Dreams: The "Critical Prophet"[33]

The following example was posted by a Russian-speaking IS fighter and was shared on social media on 1 July 2015 by several IS accounts, including @pravdaig ("Truth ISIS"). The timing of the dream was significant, because it reportedly occurred during a series of difficult battles for IS against the Syrian Kurdish People's Protection Units (YPG) during June and July. In mid-June 2015, Kurdish forces recaptured the Syrian border town of Tal Abyad—which is the focus of the dream—from IS in a significant defeat for the extremist group, because it deprived IS of a strategic border crossing key point for bringing supplies and foreign fighters into Syria.[34]

> THE DREAM OF A CERTAIN BROTHER!
> Assalam aleikum Muslim brothers and sisters and mujahideen! Recently, one of the brothers of the Islamic State dreamed a dream. In the dream, he saw the Communist Kurds took Tel Abyad and got as far as Ayn al-Isa. And he saw the Prophet of Peace [In Russian, the word "mir" can mean both "peace" and "world"] above them, who thrust his sword into the ground. And the brothers said to him, fight with us against them. He replied that he would not fight. When they ask him about the reason for his refusal, he replied that you are being profligate with food [i.e. wasting food], throwing food away and not giving it to the poor, you are not getting up for the night time namaz [prayers]. May Allah reward you with a blessing![35]

We can see that a dream image of what is presumed to be the Prophet Muhammed, though that is not certain, is taken as a true dream according to the hadiths as described beforehand. The fighter's supplication for help from the Prophet is refused due to IS fighters failing to do their charitable duty of feeding the poor. Fighters would likely interpret this dream as a command to give more food to the poor and to be more observant of prayer in the future.

### Opaque Dreams: "The Lion, the Tree and the Hypocrite"[36]

A Chechen IS fighter writes of a dream had by a fellow IS militant named Abu Yusuf about Omar al-Shishani (Tarkhan Batirashvili), an ethnic

Chechen from Georgia's Pankisi Gorge who had risen to become IS's military commander in Syria.[37] Al-Shishani was a greatly admired figure among Russian-speaking IS jihadists. To be fighting alongside al-Shishani is therefore a noteworthy event. The fighter who relates Abu Yusuf's dream goes on to say that, he, too, had the very same dream.

> One brother-mujahid (Abu Yusuf) had a dream: "I was standing on the front line, as if guarding the brothers. It seemed as if brother Adam was among them, and definitely Umar Shishani. Suddenly, I heard the noises of dogs, suddenly it became dark, and Umar and the other brothers were asleep. I was alert, and started to look attentively in all directions, and I saw a large animal akin to a lion, dull gray in color. Alongside it was a masked man, looking like the brothers, who petted the lion.
>
> I went up to Umar and said,
> "Umar, there is a lion and a suspicious man in a mask."
> He went with me, "show me," he says, and I showed him.
> I asked him, "Can you shoot them?" At that, Umar said, "Wait a minute and look at them."
> But suddenly they saw us, the man in the mask saw us first. And he swiftly ran at me, saying, now I will kill you.
> I asked Umar for permission to shoot.
> But Umar instead of speaking fell silent. The man in the mask ran very close. I wanted to shoot but it seemed I had not taken the safety off my gun. But Umar, defending me, started to shoot at him. I also opened fire and we started to shoot together and killed the one in the mask. But the lion was not dead. Then Umar said, "there's a tree, jump up on it." All the brothers jumped. Me and Umar remained on the ground.
> Umar said that these lions can climb trees. So be careful. We also climbed the tree. And the lion jumps after us and says to me in human speech, "if I catch you, I'll kill you." He jumps from side to side. I jump up after him. I jump, catch the lion's head and turn it this side and that. And I say to myself, 'I'm only afraid of Allah, not you.' And I actually killed the lion."
> Ma sha'llah. And at that time I dreamed the same dream. We explained the dream according to the Quran and the Sunna: the lion is the taghut, the man in the mask is a munafiq (hypocrite), the tree is IS.[38]

In these two contrasting dream accounts, we see the classic distinction between explicit and opaque dreams. The first dream gives a clear reprimand about the waste of food and failure to pray correctly, while the second dream is more metaphorical and open to interpretation. This distinction echoes the Freudian notion of manifest and latent dream content.[39] The command dream doesn't need interpretation, but rather explicitly advocates remedial action and explains military failure. The metaphorical interpretation of the second dream utilizes Qur'anic references, which is commonplace in Islamic dream interpretation books and dictionaries.[40] The second dream also shows Omar al-Shishani as a heroic and successful warrior leader saving the dreamer and the group from being devoured by the enemy lion and man (hypocrite).

There is an intriguing reference at the end of this dream account about the reporter (the author) and the reported (the dreamer, Abu Yusuf) having experienced the same dream. There is a Bukhari hadith that refers to this phenomenon but does not explicate it further.[41] We also know from bin Laden's first post-9/11 video that he had been worried prior to the attack that people would get wind of the plan as so many of his followers were having dreams of planes flying into tall buildings.[42]

### Dream Accounts as Authoritative Arguments

*Dabiq*, IS's main English-language magazine, is primarily concerned with reports of battlefield successes and effective rebel governance. But *Dabiq* also contains references to dreams. In one instance, *Dabiq* reproduced a dream account from a well-known hadith:

> When the Prophet (sallallahu alay-hi was sallam) migrated to madinah, At-Tufayl ibn amr Ad-dawsi (radiyallahu anh) migrated to the Prophet, and along with At-Tufayl migrated a man of his tribe. They later disliked residence in Madinah (because of disease and fatigue caused by its climate). The man fell sick and lost patience. So he took hold of a wide arrowhead and cut off his fingerjoints. The blood gushed forth from his hands, until he died. At-Tufayl said to him, "what did your Lord do with you?" He replied, "Allah granted me forgiveness because of my hijrah[43] to his Prophet." At-Tufayl said, "why do I see you covering your hands?" He replied, "I was told, 'we will not mend what you have damaged." At-Tufayl narrated this dream to Allah's messenger (sallallahu alay-hi was sallam). Then Allah's messenger prayed, "O Allah, forgive him also for his two hands" (Muslim Sahih).[44]

This dream narrative and its interpretation are included in a section devoted to "Hijrah and Forgiveness". This is a so-called "strong" (i.e. reliable) hadith, and its inclusion provides theological justification for IS's claim that emigrating to the Islamic State will lead inexorably to God's forgiveness of previous sins.[45] Indeed, just above the previous quotation is the reporting of the Prophet Muhammed saying, again from a Muslim Sahih hadith, "Are you not aware that Islam wipes out all previous sins? And that Hijrah wipes out all previous sins? And that Hajj wipes out all previous sins?"

### Paradise Revealed Through Dreams

IS's ideological literature is replete with the expressed belief that fighters who join IS and die on the battlefield become martyrs for whom a special place has been reserved in paradise. One example from *Dabiq* refers to a paradisiacal outcome for having gone on hijrah: "Because Hijrah for Allah's cause is a great matter, Allah revealed about it ... Allah is pleased with them and they are pleased with him, and he has prepared for them gardens beneath rivers flow, wherein they will abide for ever. That is the great success."[46] In an audio tape, IS leader Al-Baghdadi constantly refers to the future paradisiacal state of those who die in the cause of jihad:

> And He (the Glorified) said, And those who are killed in the cause of Allah—never will He waste their deeds. He will guide them and amend their condition, and admit them to Paradise, which He has made known to them. Indeed, Allah has purchased from the believers their lives and their properties [in exchange] for that they will have Paradise. They fight in the cause of Allah, so they kill and are killed. [It is] a true promise [binding] upon Him in the Torah and the Gospel and the Qur'ān. And who is truer to his covenant than Allah? So rejoice in your transaction which you have contracted. And it is that which is the great attainment.[47]

### Believing in the "Invisible" Paradise

Given this belief, it is not surprising that the dreams of IS fighters and other jihadis are often about Paradise. In the Islamic dream tradition, the only way to personally pre-experience heaven and hell is through the true dream or vision. In chapter nine of the hadith by Bukhari, there are several accounts of the prophet Muhammed's paradisiacal dreams offering information as to followers and their place there.

Kinberg's detailed study shows how dreams in Islam have historically been considered as a "communicative technology" between the living and the dead.[48] She defines two types of dreams: dreams that emphasize rewards bestowed upon the pious in the afterlife, and dreams in which the dead answer the questions of the living about the process of dying, or about the most rewarding deed. The dreams included in these categories share one common ethical purpose, namely to show believers the right code of conduct. In the first type, dreams illustrate specific rewards such as paradise with "its magnificent gardens and palaces, and its beautiful women who wait for the pious people to come."[49] Kinberg quotes many examples of this, one of which is that of a reported dream of the Prophet Muhammed:

> Likewise the Prophet informed his companions about ar-Rumaysaa and Bilaal being in paradise based upon one of the Prophet's dreams. Jaabir ibn Abdillah related that the Prophet said: I saw myself (in a dream) entering paradise, and saw Aboo Talhah's wife, ar-Rumaysaa. Then I heard footsteps and asked, "Who is it?" Somebody said, "It is Bilaal." Then I saw a palace with a lady sitting in its courtyard and I asked, "to whom does this palace

belong?" Somebody replied, "It belongs to Umar." I wanted to enter it and look around, but I remembered your [Umar's] sense of honor [and did not]. Umar said, "Let my parents be sacrificed for you, O Allah's messenger. How dare I think of my sense of honour being offended by you?"[50]

Thus, paradisiacal insight and knowledge of other worlds can be available via the portal of dreams. The example of Muhammed above is echoed in many biographies of fallen jihadists before the formation of IS and detailed and analyzed elsewhere.[51] One well-known example can be found in the famous "9/11 hijacker letter" which instructed the hijackers on what to do in the final days and hours before the operation, "You should know that the Gardens {of paradise} have been decorated for you in the most beautiful way, and that the *houris* are calling to you: "O friend of God, come," after dressing in their most beautiful clothing."[52]

Such beliefs are widespread among militant Islamists. For example, a Sunday Times journalist, abducted by jihadist insurgents in Syria in 2012, later said his guard had lectured him about the rewards of martyrdom, "we kept receiving sermons from the Koran. When you die you will be taken to paradise by a green bird. You will see Allah and his thrones, in a house made of gold and silver. Your family will meet you up there. You will have 72 wives."[53] The motif of "green birds" is commonly invoked in relation to martyrdom. For a recent example, on 21 July 2015, *The Guardian* newspaper reported the death-in-action of a 21 year-old British man from Cardiff, Reyaad Khan, who appeared in ISIS propaganda videos. Part of the report recounted, "On social media, an account believed to belong to a female British jihadi in Syria said on 17 July that 'Abu Dujana' (a name used for Khan) had been 'lost'. Employing a term used by jihadis to describe dead fighters, she went on to describe him as having become a 'green bird'."[54]

David Cook traces the dream-martyrdom connection back to the seventh century, when Muslims were also reporting dreams about martyrs, as recorded by Ibn Abi al-Dunya, a Muslim scholar of dreams (d. 994-95).[55] Cook, who maintains a database of some 5000 dream accounts from throughout Islamic history, concludes his survey of early Islamic martyrdom:

> All of these dreams—only a small selection of those available—are common throughout the Muslim martyrdom tradition. The general themes of the martyrdom literature serve to confirm the status of the martyrs after their death, to demonstrate their satisfaction with their fate and to influence others to follow them.[56]

Cook's conclusions about early Islamic martyrdom and dreaming closely resemble mine in relation to contemporary jihadists.

Dreams and visions are likely then to have kept their special place in the spiritual or ideological worldview of IS. A core part of such a role for the dream vision is to give information about future paradise and the place of fallen comrades; indeed such dreams are the key to the unseen, and presumed heavenly knowledge.

The evidence reviewed so far suggests that dreams interest IS members greatly and constitute an important part of their religious experience. But does it matter? Do these spiritual experiences have any practical implications?

## Dreams and IS Decision-Making

Previous research has shown that some jihadists take, or at least claim to take, dreams into consideration when they make decisions to join a group, become a foreign fighter, volunteer for operations, or (if they are leaders) pursue particular military strategies. There are several examples of jihadists claiming to make such decisions almost *entirely* based on alleged dreams.[57] Thus far there is limited evidence of this in relation to IS, but there are three important cases worth mentioning.

### Al-Baghdadi's Mosul Dream

The first is a very interesting, albeit somewhat unreliable, report of IS leader Abu Bakr al-Baghdadi allegedly taking a strategic military decision based on a dream. In March 2015, anti-IS news outlets reported that al-Baghdadi had had a dream in which the Prophet Muhammad ordered him to withdraw forces from Mosul.[58] The Kurdish Democratic Party website reported that "Baghdadi ordered his fighters to withdraw from the city, following his dream that he met the Prophet Mohammed, who ordered him to leave Mosul city." This was at a time when the Iraqi army had retaken Tikrit and there was speculation that it would move toward Mosul. The Kurdish website interpreted the report to mean that "fear is spreading among the militants in Mosul for the predictions of liberating Mosul."

While this one report is by no means conclusive regarding the current importance of dreams within IS, the account is entirely within the realm of the possible—in the past other militant leaders, such as Mullah Omar, have openly claimed to have made military decisions based on dreams. In such cases, we can never know whether the leader's dream experience is genuine or fabricated, but it is worth bearing in mind that in Islam it is considered a serious sin to lie about a dream; indeed a special part of hell is reserved for such sinners.[59] Even if this report was fabricated by anti-IS Kurds, it still shows how dream reports can be part of the current Middle Eastern propaganda war.

## The Dream of Elton Simpson

The second data point concerns Elton Simpson, one of the two perpetrators of the gun attack on the Muhammad cartoon exhibition in Garland, Texas, in May 2015. According to the researcher Amarnath Amarasingam, who studied Simpson's conversion statement and interviewed his family, Simpson may have been spurred to act based on a dream. Here is Amarasingam's analysis:

> According to some in his *baqiya* family,[60] with migration to Syria no longer viable, a few factors came together pushing Simpson to act. First, there is the increasingly vibrant narrative coming from the Islamic State that Muslim youth who cannot migrate to Syria must commit acts of violence in their home countries. Second, Simpson became aware of an event in Texas, organized by so-called anti-Islam activist Pamela Geller to draw the Prophet Muhammad. Given the brand of Islam Simpson had adopted by this point, he clearly saw the event as a legitimate and timely target.
>
> Then there is the dream. As some members of his online family told me, Simpson had a dream some months ago "about a woman in a hijab looking down at him on the road." For those who see themselves on the path of jihad, this dream is often seen as an indication that the women (or "virgins") of paradise are awaiting him. In other words, it is a sign that martyrdom is near. Simpson followed the signs that he believed were being sent to him and acted accordingly. For his *baqiya* family, however, it came as a shock. He left no clues and didn't really discuss it with them, leaving behind only a tweet pledging an oath of allegiance to the Islamic State. "The brother was beautiful," said one of his online friends, "We always exchanged hadith and always laughed and joked. I will miss him. I wish I told him how much I loved him for the sake of Allah."[61]

We also know that Simpson discussed his dream with IS-affiliated Twitter users. Berger writes that Simpson had been in contact with the above-mentioned "End of Time Dreams" Twitter handle days before his attack:

> Significantly, "End of Time Dreams" conversed over Twitter with Elton Simpson, one of two Americans who attacked a "Draw the Prophet Mohammed" contest in Garland, Texas. While a complete record of the exchange was unavailable, due to Simpson's account having been suspended, it appeared "End of Time Dreams" arranged for a dream to be interpreted at Simpson's request several days before the attack took place.[62]

Simpson, it would seem, was emotionally affected by this paradise virgin dream and may have been triggered by it. We cannot be sure how important the dream was compared to other factors, but we cannot exclude the possibility that the dream mattered.

## Muslim Dost's Caliphate Dream

The third data point was presented in a *New York Times* article as a dream experienced in Guantanamo Bay prison, by the deputy of the IS supreme commander in Khorasan and Afghanistan, Hafiz Saeed Khan:

> The most prominent of Mr. Saeed's Afghan deputies is Abdul Rahim Muslim Dost, a 55-year-old former poet and essayist with an extremist past. Mr. Muslim Dost, who lived most of his life in Pakistan, was detained by the security forces there soon after the Sept. 11, 2001, attacks, officials said. He was accused of having ties to Al Qaeda, and the United States military sent him to the prison camp at Guantánamo Bay, Cuba. He was released in 2005, and joined the Pakistani Taliban before defecting to the new Islamic State branch.
>
> In a video pledging allegiance to the Islamic State's leader and self-declared caliph, Abu Bakr al-Baghdadi, Mr. Muslim Dost said he had seen a vision of the Islamic State while he was imprisoned at Guantánamo. He dreamed of a palace with a large closed door, which he said was "the house of the caliphate." Above the door was a clock that pointed to the time: 12 minutes before 12 o'clock.
>
> "It came to my mind that the caliphate would be founded after 12 years, God willing," he said in his pledge. "This interpretation of my vision was made real."[63]

These three examples alone do not tell us much about the extent to which dreams inform IS decision-making. More research is needed here. It is worth bearing in mind that we are at a very early stage in the process of documenting the IS phenomenon. We may know a lot about the group's propaganda, military exploits, and governance efforts, but we have only rudimentary knowledge of the personal trajectories of IS fighters, especially their leaders. As more in-depth descriptions of life within IS emerges, I expect to see more evidence of dream-inspired action.

## Conclusion

We have seen that dreams understood as true by the believer can transform perceptions of earthly defeat into the will of God and the call to greater righteousness. Dreams can augur victory, legitimize defeat, and inspire or demoralise armies. Dreams and their interpretations are strategic military goods, and may be manipulated strategically; dreams confirm and legitimate radical group membership, the path of holy jihad, and the destined entry to paradise, with all sins forgiven. Dreams are a form of metaphysical currency to be shared and reflected upon and redeemed in action.

IS follows in this tradition and resembles al-Qaeda and the Taliban in their ascribing importance to the Islamic dreamland. The examples presented here reflect the traditional Islamic separation of dreams as either clear messages or metaphorical ones, and the tendency to see some dreams as offering information about future paradisiacal realms. Dreams may even be critical tipping points in the move from contemplating jihad to actually killing people, as in the case of Elton Simpson.

However, this article only constitutes a preliminary study and more research is needed on the importance of dreaming in IS. Key questions to explore include the role of the dream in the recruitment, inspiration, and day-to-day guidance of IS members of different ranks in the organisation. Are "lone wolf" fighters in developed countries more prone to relate to their dreams than fighters on the Middle Eastern battlefields? And how do such "lone wolf" fighters interpret special dreams without the support of real-life comrades? Are particular dream imagery sequences linked to being primary, secondary, or ancillary drivers of radical conversion to militant jihad? Do IS fighters dream of their leader, al-Baghdadi, or other commanders—even fallen ones, such as Omar al-Shishani—and if so, how, and with what outcome? How do IS followers deal with dreams thought to be prophetic that don't seem to come true in real life? These questions can be addressed by compiling and examining more written dream accounts, by analysing memoirs of IS fighters, and by interviewing IS defectors and former foreign fighters.

The recent Quilliam Foundation analysis of the propaganda war between IS and the West describes the radicalization process as being from "tacit supporter to active member"[64] Their analysis weighs the evidence of the radicalising effect of the internet and social media, and refers to Jacques Ellul's work on propaganda immersion;[65] yet, how that total propaganda immersion influences dreaming, and how that subsequent dreaming influences behaviour, if at all, is not considered.[66] As David Anderson, the official reviewer of the UK's terrorism laws, put it: "A lot of people talk a good game about terrorism. The knack is to identify those who are going to do something about it."[67]

Maybe intelligence agencies will one day use dream reports as part of a predictive technology to identify individuals and groups who reach over and across the line between contemplation and action. Such agencies may even develop algorithms to identify nefarious activity thinking found within dream content reports. However, I have no doubt that countless non-violently motivated Muslims will continue to interpret their dreams as containing divine wisdom and guidance.

## Notes

This preface is based upon a journal article titled, "The Dreams of Islamic State", previously published in *Perspectives on Terrorism* 9.4 (Terrorism Research Initiative: 2015). I am very grateful to Thomas Hegghammer, the editor of this special edition of the journal on Islamic State, for his very considerable editing work.

1. Amira Mittermaier, *Dreams that Matter: Egyptian Landscapes of the Imagination* (Berkeley: University of California Press, 2011).
2. Özgen Felek and Alexander D. Kynsh, eds., *Dreams and Visions in Islamic Societies* (New York: SUNY, 2012).
3. Elizabeth Sirriyeh, "Dream Narratives of Martyrdom: Constant and Changing Roles Past and Present," *Dreaming* 21, no. 3 (2011): 215–33.
4. Muhammad alZekri, *Women Dreaming in Arabia: Exploring the Cultural Heritage and Society of Dubai (Space, Knowledge and Communication, Volume 1* (Bonn: Scientia Bonnensis, 2014).
5. Amira Mittermaier, "Muslim and Freudian Dream Interpretation in Egypt," in *Dreams and Spirituality: A Handbook for Ministry, Spiritual Direction and Counselling,* eds. K. Adams, B. Koet and B. Koning (London: Canterbury Press, 2015).
6. Islamic State (IS) is known by seveal names and anacronyms, such as 'The Islamic State of Iraq and Levant' (ISIL), 'Islamic State of Iraq and Syria' (ISIS), and Daesh. I have used the term 'Islamic State' (IS) throughout this preface.
7. Iain R. Edgar, "The Inspirational Night Dream in the Motivation and Justification of Jihad," *Nova Religio* 11, no. 2 (2007): 59–76; Iain R. Edgar, "The "True Dream" in Contemporary Islamic/Jihadist Dreamwork: A Case Study of the Dreams of Taliban Leader Mullah Omar," *Contemporary South Asia* 5, no. 3 (2006): 263–72.
8. Iain R. Edgar and Gwynned de Looijer, "The Islamic Dream Tradition and Jihadi Militancy," in *Jihadi Culture,* ed. T. Hegghammer (Cambridge University Press, forthcoming); Elizabeth Sirriyeh, *Dreams and Visions in the Word of Islam: A History of Muslim Dreaming and Foreknowing* (London: I.B. Taurus, 2015); Özgen Felek and Alexander D. Knysh, eds., *Dreams and Visions in Islamic Societies* (New York: SUNY, 2012); Louise Marlow, ed., *Dreaming Across Boundaries: The Interpretation of Dreams in Islamic Lands* (Cambridge, MA: Harvard University Press, 2008); Nile Green, "The Religious and Cultural Roles of Dreams and Visions in Islam," *Journal of the Royal Asiatic Society* 13, no. 3 (2003): 287–313; John Lamoreux, *The Early Muslim Tradition of Dream Interpretation* (New York: SUNY, 2002): 16; Henry Corbin, 'The Visionary Dream in Islamic Spirituality,' in *The Dream in Human Societies,* eds., G. Von Grunebaum and R. Callois (Berkeley: University of California Press, 1966).
9. The Qur'an, *Al Anful* (Riyadh, Saudi Arabia: Abulqasim Publishing House, 1997): 43.

10. The Qur'an, *Sura Yusuf,* (Riyadh, Saudi Arabia: Abulqasim Publishing House, 1997): 308–25.
11. Bukhari, *The Translations of the Meanings of Sahihal-Bukhari,* trans. M. M. Khan (Lahore, Pakistan: Kazi Publications, 1979); Muslim Sahih, *Sahih Muslim bi-Sharh al Nawawi,* 18 vols. (Beirut: Dar al-Kitab al-Arabi, 1987).
12. Iain R. Edgar and David Henig, "*Istikhara*: The Guidance and Practice of Islamic Dream Incubation Through Ethnographic Comparison," *History and Anthropology* 21, no. 3 (2010): 251–62.
13. Jens Kreinath, "Visual Encounters with Hızır and Other Muslim Saints: Dreaming and Healing at Local Pilgrimage Sites in Hatay, Turkey," *Contemporary Middle East and Central Asia* 2, no. 1 (2014): 25–66; Marzia Balzani, "Dreaming, Islam and the Ahmadiyya Muslims in the UK," *History and Anthropology* 21, no. 3 (2010): 293–305.
14. Sara Sviri, *The Taste of Hidden Things* (Inverness, CA: Golden Sufi Centre, 1997); Sara Sviri, "Dreaming Analysed and Recorded: Dreams in the World of Medieval Islam," in *Dream Culture,* eds. D. Shulman and G. Stroumsa (London: Routledge, 1999); Mark Sedgwick, *Sufism* (Cairo: American University, 2000); J. Spencer Trimingham, *The Sufi Orders in Islam* (London: Oxford University Press, 1971); Llewellyn Vaughan-Lee, *Catching the Thread: Sufism, Dreamwork and Jungian Psychology* (Inverness, CA: Golden Sufi Centre, 2003); Robert Rozehnal, "Flashes of Ultimate Reality: Dreams of Saints and Shrines in a Contemporary Pakistani Sufi Community," *Contemporary Middle East and Central Asia* 2, no. 1 (2014): 67–80.
15. Shaykh Abu 'Ubaydah Mashur bin Hasan Aal Salmaan and Shaykh Abu Talhah 'Umar bin Ibraheem Aal 'AbdurRahmaan, *Introductory Salafi Themes in the Interpretation of Visions and Dreams,* ebook found at salafimanhaj.com/pdf/SalafiManhaj_Dreams.pdf.
16. Steven Kruger, *Dreaming in the Middle Ages* (Cambridge University Press, 1992).
17. Sigmund Freud, *The Standard Edition of the Complete Psychological Works of Sigmund Freud,* trans. J. Strachey (London: Hogarth Press and the Institute of Psychoanalysis, 1953); Sigmund Freud, *The Interpretation of Dreams* (New York: Basic Books, 1955); Ellen Basso, "The Implications of a Progressive Theory of Dreaming," in *Dreaming: Anthropological and Psychological Interpretations,* ed. Barbara Tedlock (Cambridge University Press, 1987): 86–7.
18. Lamoreux, *Early Muslim Tradition*; op. cit. note 3.
19. Andy Lines, "Sick Videotape Proves bin Laden Was the Evil Mastermind behind the Horrors of Sept. 11," *The Mirror* (London), December 14, 2001; also John J. Lumpkin, "Pentagon Releases Video of bin Laden Joking about September 11," *The Independent* (London), December 14, 2001.
20. Phil Hirshchkorn, "Shoe bomber denies role in 9/11 attacks," CNN, http://www.cnn.com/2006/LAW/04/21/moussaoui.trial; Yosri Fouda and Nick Fielding, *Masterminds of Terror: The Truth Behind the Most Devastating Terrorist Attack the World Has Ever Seen* (London: Mainstream Publishing, 2003); Katherine Donahue, *Slave of Allah: Zacarias Moussaoui vs. The USA* (London: Pluto Press, 2007); Edgar, "Inspirational Night Dream", 74–75, op. cit. note 2.

21. Stewart Bell, *The Martyr's Oath: The Apprenticeship of a Home Grown Terrorist* (Mississauga, ON: Wiley, 2005): 76–7; Fouda, *Masterminds of Terror,* op. cit. note 15.

22. See chapter 6, this volume, 79–94.

23. See chapter 6, this volume, 82–3.

24. Ibn Sirin, *The Interpretation of Dreams* (London: Dar Al Taqwa, 2000); Ibn Sireen, *Dreams and Interpretations* (New Delhi: Abdul Naeem for Islamic Book Service, 2000); i.e. http://www.myislamicdream.com.

25. J. M. Berger, "The Metronome of Apocalyptic Time: Social Media as Carrier Wave for Millenarian Contagion," *Perspectives on Terrorism* 9, no.4 (2015): 61–71. The Twitter handle Entimdrms is now unavailable (https//twitter.com/entimdrms/status/593175693720211457).

26. Bukhari, *Translations of the Meanings,* 9.87. 144, op. cit. note 6.

27. Twitter handle: entdrm13, https://twitter.com/entdrm13

28. Berger, "Metronome of Apocalyptic Time", 68, op. cit. note 20.

29. entdrm13, Twitter post, July 11, 2015, https://twitter.com/entdrm13

30. Ibid.

31. Ibid.

32. Ibid.

33. Joanna Paraszczuk shared and translated this dream account for me, as well as writing the contextual paragraph introducing the dream account.

34. "ISIS unexpectedly attacks Tal Abyad, seizes a district," *Daily Sabah,* June 30, 2015, http://www.dailysabah.com/mideast/2015/06/30/isis-unexpectedly-attacks-tal-abyad-seizes-a-district.

35 Joanna Paraszczuk translated this dream account.

36. Joanna Paraszczuk shared and translated this dream account for me, as well as writing the contextual paragraph introducing the dream account.

37. Al-Shishani was reported killed by the US in March 2016; Melanie Eversley, 'Islamic State Operative al-Shishani Believed Dead', *USA Today,* March 15, 2016.

38. Joanna Paraszczuk, "I Dream of Umar: Jihadi Dreams and Cult Figures", *From Chechnya to Syria* (blog), April 21, 2014, http://www.chechensinsyria.com/?p=21759.

39. See chapter 8, this volume, 111–18.

40. See chapter 7, this volume, 95–110.

41. "Interpretation of Dreams", Sunnah.com, http://sunnah.com/bukhari/91.

42. Lines, "Sick Videotape", op. cit. note 14.

43 IS seems to define 'hijrah' as a "path to jihad", especially to travel and join IS.

44. *Dabiq* 3 no 24.

45. *Dabiq* 3 no 27.

46. Umm Summayyah Muhajirah, "The Twin Halves of the Muhajirin", in *Dabiq* 8 no 32; The Qur'an, *Sura At-Tawbah* (Riyadh, Saudi Arabia: Abulqasim Publishing House, 1997):100.

47. Pieter Vanostaeyen, "A New Audio Message by Abu Bakr al-Baghdadi ~ March Forth Whether Light or Heavy", *Pietervanostaeyen: Musings on Arabism, Islamicism, History and Current Affairs* (blog), May 14, 2015, https://pietervanostaeyen.wordpress.com/2015/05/14/a-new-audio-message-by-abu-bakr-al-bagh

dadi-march-forth-whether-light-or-heavy/. The Qur'an, *Sura At-Tawbah*: 111, op. cit. note 39.

48. Leah Kinberg, "Interaction between This World and the Afterworld in Early Islamic Tradition," *Oriens* 29/30 (1986): 285–308.

49. Ibid., 296–7.

50. Abu Ameenah Bilal Philips, *Dream Interpretation According to the Qur'an and Sunnah* (Kuala Lumpur: A.S. Noordeen, 2001): 53.

51. Edgar and de Looijer, "Islamic Dream Tradition," op. cit. note 3.

52. David Cook, "Suicide Attacks or 'Martyrdom Operations' in Contemporary Jihad Literature", *Nova Religio* 6, no. 1 (2002): 32–3.

53. John Cantile, "Are You Ready to Die?", *Sunday Times,* August 5, 2012.

54. Ben Quin, "Briton Reyaad Khan Believed Killed in Air Strike", *The Guardian,* July 21, 2015, http://www.theguardian.com/uk-news/2015/jul/21/briton-reyaad-khan-believed-killed-air-strike-islamic-state-syria.

55. Cook, "Suicide Attacks", op. cit. note 45.

56. Ibid., 7–44.

57. For examples, see the dream accounts of Zacarias Moussaoui who was "inspired" in dreams to fly a plane into the White House in Washington, DC; see Donahue, *Slave of Allah,* 80–1, op. cit. note 15; and also chapter 5, in this volume: 69–70). Richard Reid, the shoe bomber, talks of dreams that he understands as guiding him in his choice of targets; see Hirschkorn, "Shoe bomber denies role", op. cit. note 15. Mullah Omar, Taliban leader, is reported as founding the Taliban and developing his campaign strategies through his true dreams; see chapter 6, this volume: 79–94). Dreams are reported as an important recruiting strategies in bringing many young women to fight in the siege of the Red Mosque in Islamabad in 2007; see Barbara Plett, "Jihadis tap anti-Musharraf feeling," *BBC News,* July 14, 2007, http://news.bbc.co.uk/2/hi/programmes/from_our_own_correspondent/6897601.stm; Misbah Abdulbaqi, "Pakistan's Red Mosque: Start of Unrest: The Full Story Behind the Red Mosque Crisis", http://www.onislam.net/english/politics/asia/433784.html. Yaroslav Trofimov, in *The Siege of Mecca,* writes of hundreds of the followers of Juhayman bin Seif al-Uteybi (the leader of the failed siege of the Grand Mosque in Mecca, Saudi Arabia in 1979) started having dreams of Muhammed Abdullah al-Qahtani, as being the true *Mahdi*: "Militants from as far away as Lebanon who never encountered Mohammed Abdullah in person claimed to have had the same dream"; Yaroslav Trofimov, *The Siege of Mecca* (London: Penguin, 2007): 50–1. An American jihadist in Somali, Omar Hammami, describes dreams as influencing his jihadist decision-making to continue fighting; see Abu Mansuur al-Amriiki, *The Story of an American Jihadi: Part One*: 88, ebook found at https://azelin.files.wordpress.com/2012/05/omar-hammami-abc5ab-mane1b9a3c5abr-al-amrc4abkc4ab-22the-story-of-an-american-jihc481dc4ab-part-122.pdf.

58. Gianluca Mezzofiore, "Isis chief Baghdadi 'Prophet Mohammed dream' rumour spreads amid tension before Mosul battle," *International Business Times,* March 16, 2015, http://www.ibtimes.co.uk/isis-chief-baghdadi-prophet-mohammed-dream-rumour-spreads-amid-tension-before-mosul-battle-1492161;

"Leader of IS 'Abu Bakr al-Baghdadi': I met the 'Prophet Muhammad' and he ordered me to leave Mousl", *AhlulBayt News Agency* (ABNA), March 15, 2015, http://en.abna24.com/service/middle-east-west-asia/archive/2015/03/15/676921/story.html; "Leader of IS 'Abu Bakr al-Baghdadi': I met the 'Prophet Muhammad' and he ordered me to leave Mosul", *Friends of Syria* (blog), March 18, 2015, http://friendsofsyria.info/index.php/2015/03/18/leader-of-is-abu-bakr-al-baghdadi-i-met-the-prophet-muhammad-and-he-ordered-me-to-leave-mosul/.

59. Bukhari, *Translations of the Meanings*, 12. 427, op. cit. note 6..

60. Amarasingam writes that *baqiya* means: "For this study, I interview current and former fighters, the friends and family of these jihadist volunteers, and members of the close-knit transnational virtual community of Islamic State supporters. They call themselves the '*baqiya* family.' *Baqiya* means enduring, and is often used as a war cry by members of the Islamic State". Amarnath Amarasingam, "Elton 'Ibrahim' Simpson's Path to Jihad in Garland, Texas", *War on the Rocks* (blog), May 14, 2015, http://warontherocks.com/2015/05/elton-ibrahim-simpsons-path-to-jihad-in-garland-texas/2/.

61. Ibid.

62. Berger, "Metronome of Apocalyptic Time", op. cit. note 20.

63. Mujib Mashal, "Afghan ISIS Branch Makes Inroads in Battle Against Taliban," *New York Times,* October 13, 2015, http://www.nytimes.com/2015/10/14/world/asia/afghan-isis-branch-makes-inroads-in-battle-against-taliban.html.

64. Charlie Winter, *The Virtual 'Caliphate': Understanding Islamic State's Propaganda Strategy* (London: Quilliam Foundation, 2015).

65. Jacques Ellul, *Propoganda: The Formation of Men's Attitudes,* trans. Konrad Kellen and Jean Lerner (New York: Random House Vintage Books, 1973).

66. Ibid.

67. Alan Travis, "MI5's battle to identify radicalised Britons likely to turn to terrorism," *The Guardian,* February 27, 2015, http://www.theguardian.com/uk-news/2015/feb/27/mi5-struggle-identify-people-britain-likely-turn-terrorism-isis.

꧁ ꧁ ꧁

# Foreword

*Anthropological Skepticism Encounters Dreamed*
*Realities Following Fieldwork in Pakistan*

Edgar's timely and creative contribution to the study of dreams among Muslims and possible Islamic foundations is important for a number of reasons. Not least of which is the fact that talking about dreams is a way of communicating things about the world around dreaming. There are individual approaches to dream interpretation, and one must be cautious subscribing to an overly prescriptive and simplistic understanding of what dreams "mean" in any given context, nevertheless, there are broad cultural patterns in which those individual idiosyncrasies exist. Edgar's concentration on dreams places him in a fairly unique position in the world. He is fluent, on the one hand, in the major dream theories in Western philosophy and psychotherapy, and on the other he is open minded and curious enough to explore radically different approaches to the same subject matter in the Muslim world. The subsequent body of work is, to my knowledge, unparalleled in the social sciences or humanities today. I can think of few comparable studies that bring the same high level of scholarship to the study of what may be one of the single most significant elephants in the room, when it comes to trying to understand how millions of people in the Muslim world engage with their dreams and by extension, with their daily lives.

The following cases should illustrate the extent to which Pakistani Muslims may be powerfully motivated by dream narratives and dream experiences. They are both drawn from field research conducted in a rural village in northern Punjab, throughout 1998 and 1999. In both cases, it was clear that the Pakistani informants assumed that dream narratives about God, the Prophet Muhammed, and the Qur'an should be trusted as a faithful account of the dream experience. As must be abundantly clear in a Western European context, such assumptions are far from universal and speak both to the effectiveness of dream narratives among Pakistani Muslims as well as their very great potential for exploitation by those people who are not averse to lying about even the most sacred subjects.

## Case 1: Feeding People

Throughout the agricultural villages of Attock District in northern Punjab, I had the occasion to observe and participate in a series of common public feasting events known locally as *deg*. *Deg* is the name for the cauldron in which rice is cooked in Punjab. The number of these large cauldrons prepared at a particular *deg* is used as the indicator of how big or impressive the event is. So if a family hosts a small *deg*, they might prepare only two cauldrons (normally one with savory rice and one with sweet rice). A medium-sized *deg* might have six to ten cauldrons of rice prepared and last half a day. The *deg* in question here involved twenty-five cauldrons' worth of rice being prepared at the base of the mountain next to the village. The cooks were hired in especially for their high-quality reputations and cooked from sunrise till sunset. During that time several hundred people at any one time were gathered in the area eating as much rice as they could manage. Children collected rice to take back to the ladies in their homes. Although village women did work outside, during events such as a large *deg* with a great many unknown men in the area, they appeared to be more inclined to restrict their movements. Anyone in the area was invited to participate in the *deg* by eating as much rice as they could. So all truck drivers on the way to or from the nearby cement factory stopped and ate. The workers in the nearby poultry farm took their lunch breaks at the *deg* and helped themselves to as much food as they could eat at a single sitting. I returned throughout the day and ate all three meals from the *deg*—a behavior pattern that I was told was not only common but expected. The host of this extraordinary event spent the entire day eating sparsely some distance away from both the cooks and the main crowds. He met with guests who came to pay their respects to him and surveyed the progress of the cooking. His younger brothers acted as co-hosts at this event and also appeared to capitalize on the networking potential offered by the event.

I have previously analyzed these events in terms of their role in political rivalries between landlords (Lyon 2004a: 145–62, and in a revised form Lyon 2004b). The political significance of such public feeding is highly significant and should be understood in conjunction with the focus on the dream narrative aspect presented here; however, for the sake of brevity I shall dispense with a detailed summary of *deg* as opportunities for expressions of political rivalry and concentrate on what I have subsequently understood to be a critical inspirational dream that underpins the largest *deg* in the village's history.

On the day of this large *deg*, one of the burning gossip items doing the rounds was the cause for such an audacious *deg*. Villagers were genuinely impressed and somewhat perplexed by the landlord's decision to host such a massive *deg* that lasted from sunrise till sunset. As his close friend, people assumed that I knew the reason, and so I ended up addressing the question repeatedly throughout the day. At the time, I asked the landlord why he chose to do something on such a grand scale, and he gave me what I thought was a playful but deceptive explanation. He told me that Allah had come to him in a dream and told him to feed his village. Quite frankly, I dismissed the explanation out of hand. It clearly made no sense and was a very flimsy rationale upon which to take such a costly and time-consuming decision. Nearly ten years on, I have come to the conclusion that while my analysis of the political significance of such feasting rituals was both useful and productive, it neglected something rather interesting about a critical element in the underlying inspiration for the decision.

In hindsight, I believe that the landlord must have been as puzzled by my blatant dismissal of his dream narrative as I was by his attempt to explain an obviously politically motivated event by way of what seemed to me to be an entirely unverifiable instance of fantasy. My own agnosticism dismissed the possibility of an actual god (by whatever name) entering a person's dream and directing them to act in a particular way. However, to assume that my friend would lie about such a dream was, I now realize, doing him a great disservice. I am certain that many Pakistani Muslims are capable of lying about epiphanal religious experiences, and some may openly and boldly claim to have spoken to Allah or another metaphysical being very cynically and with no internal conviction that such a conversation took place. It was unkind of me to think such a thing of my friend, and I have, many years after the fact, apologized to him for this lack of confidence in his integrity. Nevertheless, I stand by my skepticism and insist that it is both healthy and necessary. Some people lie, and we cannot always know who those people might be. Yet, there is something very powerful about dreams that involve Allah, the Qur'an, and the Prophet Muhammed. I have come to the conclusion that while there must be many people willing to lie about such dreams, they are a minority, and what seems to be far more common is a widespread fear that such lies will invoke the anger of Allah and must be atoned for sooner or later. Indeed, I met a man who was convinced that Allah would not allow anyone to lie about such matters. Should a man lie about such dreams, then ill health and poor luck shall certainly befall him and possibly his family.

Consequently, I have reassessed the significance of that landlord's dream in light of the work of Edgar (2004a; 2006; 2007), which motivated me to ask more questions about dreams more recently with old friends in Pakistan. It is likely that the landlord did not lie about his dream experience, and while the narrative he told me may have been embellished and reconstructed into a more coherent script, it was not done so with the intention of twisting or altering the message from God. In fact, subsequent conversations with the landlord in 2007 led me to believe that he must have been intensely pleased to have been, in his view, visited by God in a dream. So much so, that I see no inconsistency in suggesting that the public feasting would not have taken place as it did in the absence of the dream. To be sure, the landlord had hosted numerous such *deg* in the past and would certainly have hosted some *deg* at some point that year, but the dream seems to have been pivotal in shaping the specific shape and direction of that event. In this instance, I suggest the dream served more than a simple justificatory function (though even if this were the case, it would be important), but a motivational function as well.

## Case 2: Dreaming of the Qur'an

The second case study was, like the first, serendipitous. I had no research agenda to concentrate on dreams nor was I particularly concerned with matters that are by their very nature hard to observe and hard to produce data around. The case has been selected because in a way it serves a form of control in what is, at best, a weak natural experiment. Despite the weakness, this case, like the first, is highly suggestive of the extent to which Pakistanis are inclined to accept certain kinds of dream narratives at face value. They will of course understand that dreams might be modified in the narration and the re-narration, but underpinning such modifications, there seems to be a disarming confidence that dream experiences and narratives about Allah, the Qur'an, and the Prophet Muhammed are only possible with the approval of God. This case involves a dream I had that I told to a friend. The friend was a young landlord in his early twenties. He, like the landlord in the previous case study (his cousin), was a good friend during my extended stay in the village and has remained a good friend to this day. He is noticeably less devoutly religious than his cousin and is openly disdainful of the Wahabism that holds some sway in the region.

In my dream, I was drinking tea in the local tea shop called, rather grandly, the "hotel" by villagers. The hotel is small and has only three walls. Customers sit in *charpais*,[1] smoke hookahs or water pipes (locally called *chillum*), and drink the milky tea freshly prepared while they wait. In my dream, I was sitting on a *charpai* drinking tea when suddenly I fell into a trance, and a white glow emanated from around my body. In the trance I began to recite the Qur'an in Arabic. I remained in the trance until I completed the Qur'an and then woke up from my trance with no knowledge of what I had done and no sudden ability to speak Arabic. I interpreted this, rightly in my view, as a response to continual attempts to persuade me to become a Muslim. I can say in all honesty that not one week went by over the total of three years that I lived in Pakistan that someone did not attempt to convert me to Islam. For the most part, such conversion attempts are done with good humor and are kind. Occasionally the conversion attempts are aggressive and uncomfortable. The steady diet of people attempting to persuade you that the Qur'an is the true Book of God and that Hazrat (Prophet) Muhammed was the last prophet of the one true God is not what attracted me to Pakistan and remains one of my least favorite aspects of spending time in Pakistan. It is, however, a ubiquitous part of life there, and if one doesn't develop coping strategies for politely resisting conversion then life may not be as good as it could be.

The night I had the dream came after a particularly intense week of conversion attempts. It was the week of the Prophet Muhammed's birthday, and I had stayed up through most of the night at the top of the nearby mountain at the shrine of Baba Shaikh Daud (see Lyon 2004) listening to a circle of men praying and reciting the Qur'an from start to finish. While listening, I lay back and watched the stars and saw perhaps the most spectacular green comet I have ever seen in my life. Assuming others had seen it, I said something along the lines of, "Wow, that was pretty." No one else had apparently seen the comet, and so I had to explain what I had seen. This was taken by some members of the circle to be a direct sign from God that I should convert to Islam on the spot. I declined, but it was one of the higher-pressure conversion attempts I have experienced. The following day, two young men were teaching me how to say the Kalmah—the declaration that all Muslims must pronounce as one of the five pillars of Islam. I was not converting but wanted to break down the words and try to memorize it. They took me syllable by syllable through the Kalmah until I could say it smoothly from memory. They then clapped in glee and announced that I was officially a Muslim and they gave me an Islamic name (Saddiq). To this day, there are people in the village who refer to me as Saddiq Khan and believe that I have converted to Islam in my heart but that out of respect for my mother, I have not made it public to the world. It was following these two events, which were interspersed with countless other less-memorable conversion attempts, that I had the dream of reciting the Qur'an.

I did not see the dream as a mystery that needed explaining but rather as an entertaining dream that my friends might enjoy. I assumed erroneously that they too would assume that my dream was part of the psychological process of working through the tensions of living in slightly unusual conditions. So I shared my dream with the young landlord who, as I said, was not overtly religious and was in my experience remarkably tolerant and relaxed about religion. I recited the dream to him only slightly embarrassed. I do not normally tell my dreams to people, but this one happened to be rather vivid and seemed to speak to my situation explicitly. My friend became noticeably nervous and spoke very quietly. He whispered to me that I must not tell anyone else the dream. He explained to me that I could not have had that dream if it had not come from God. God would not have allowed me to dream the whole of the Qur'an in Arabic like that unless he wanted me to become a Muslim. I reminded my friend that I do not speak Arabic and have not memorized the Qur'an, so it was not possible that I had genuinely dreamed the whole of the Qur'an in Arabic—I thought that is what I did, but it must have been gibberish since I did not have the requisite knowledge to have such a dream. He dismissed my naiveté out of hand. If God wanted me to dream about reciting the Qur'an in Arabic, then there could be no naysaying such a capacity. My friend understood that I had no intention of converting and so instead urged me, for my own sake, to remain quiet on the matter. No doubt, he worries for my soul in the long run, but perhaps he believes that ultimately God will not give up on me and I will some day become a real Muslim.

I chose to follow my friend's advice and must admit that I mostly put the dream out of my mind, apart from noting the dream and my friend's reaction to the dream narrative in my field notes. What strikes me so clearly now a decade later is that my friend did not seem to consider that I might invent a dream narrative to stimulate a particular conversation. I freely admit that I am not above such harmless (in my view) deceptions, but it did not occur to me to do so at the time, and now that I understand how seriously the people around me took such dreams, I would hesitate very long before knowingly inventing such dreams.

## Assumptions of Validity and Meaningfulness

If we assume that dreams are meaningful only to the person experiencing them and dismiss an absolute frame of reference that might imbue dreams with universal validity, then we risk misinterpreting part of the decision-making process for many Pakistani Muslims. Conversely, if we assume that Pakistani Muslims always believe their own and others' dreams, we risk a great deal more. People manipulate social and cultural systems for numerous reasons, and decision making is complex and at times seemingly contradictory. Somewhere in the midst of the quagmire of dream interpretation among Muslims and particularly Pakistani Muslims, it behooves us to take seriously the concepts and attitudes that our informants take seriously. Evans-Pritchard studied witchcraft among the Azande because that seemed to be a priority for his informants (1937), but when he worked with the Nuer, he shifted his focus to cattle and segmentary lineages (1940, though of course he continued to investigate religious issues in part because of personal interests; see Evans-Pritchard 1956).

My own body of research has largely been driven by the preoccupations of my informants. I lived with a landlord family who spent a considerable amount of time in land disputes and local political networking, so those became my preoccupations as well. Dreams were not openly discussed very often around me, and so I neglected them. It is clear that this was an unfortunate oversight. There can be no doubt that dream incubation (*Istikhara*) plays a significant role in certain kinds of decision-making processes. Similarly, there seems little doubt that dreams of specific religious themes are less likely to be the subject of intentional deception (though again, one must be cautious in denying deception in others). What remains unknown is the extent to which uncontrolled dream experiences play a role in key life decisions. Dream experiences offer one of the few examples of extra-cultural sensation that must be reframed upon waking or it remains effectively unknowable. It is the transformation of this potentially random factor to alter decisions that is both fascinating and instructive. Anthropologists have long known that people make ostensibly "bad" decisions that would appear to be detrimental to the decision maker. It is likely that repeated bad decisions that interfere with a decision maker's capacity to survive must be subject to something akin to natural selection and so will disappear. A great many bad decisions, however, are isolated events that have no such dire consequences. In effect, we need more comprehensive theoretical frameworks from which we might disaggregate the complex sets of attitudes, histories, behaviors, beliefs, and cultural systems that feed into decisions to try to make sense of the apparently irrational and unpredictable decisions taken by the people with whom we work.

To be sure, the point is not to posit that Pakistanis are prone to believing the incredible and Western Europeans are not, but rather to explore the role of the incredible, irrational (for lack of a better word) forces that impact on our decision making. In all places, presumably individuals will be more or less affected by the emotional content of dream experiences, and those will influence certain types of decisions. As a young man, I dreamed that a friend had insulted me and was very cross with him the following day—despite the fact that he had not insulted me at all outside of the dream. It was irrational, and I hope that such events are rare, but there is no denying that people have emotional reactions to dreams, and in transforming those into narratives, they can take on a level of coherence that might affect behaviors, including decision making. In the two cases I have presented here, it is useful to go beyond the idiosyncratic effects of dreams and examine the extent to which there is a culturally identifiable dream repertoire that interacts with dreams both experientially and discursively. Whatever one dreams while asleep must then be constructed into some form of narrative. Such narratives do not merely recount the experienced dream but also construct it, even if only partially. To the extent that people attempt to recount their dreams accurately and sincerely, it is possible to identify cultural rhetorics at play and potentially more radical elements that force the narratives to take different shapes. These radical elements, I suggest, may help explain some of the decisions taken by people that strike others as odd or unusual. In a culture that dismisses dreams as the by-products of chemical flows in the brain that generate more-or-less random images, one would expect the dream not to play an explicit role in decision making; however, in cultures where certain dream images and events are thought to originate from outside the individual, one would expect such dreams to play a more prominent and acknowledged role in decision making. A role that would not only influence the decision maker but would be a respected and understood strategy in the process by others.

## Conclusion: The Justificatory and Motivational Power of Dreams

The decisions that people make are affected by cultural systems, available information, physiological capacity, social status, and beliefs about all of those things. The apparent rationality or irrationality of the bases for decisions is critical in assessing a decision, and such an assessment is problematic if attempted cross-culturally. Although I am not an expert on contemporary Britain, it seems to me as a resident that attempting to justify a decision on the basis of a dream would invite scorn in many circles. That is to say, dreams as justification, which I have already suggested must be treated as rational, in Britain lack the shared cognitive environment in which such evidence may be accepted as reliable. There is therefore an absence of collective public treatment of the dream as a place where "real" information can be obtained. While I lack the necessary empirical data to confirm this, my assumption is that dreams may nevertheless serve a motivational function in contemporary Britain. In other words, people may take decisions based in part on emotional responses shaped and influenced by dream experiences. To admit to such motivation would be tantamount to declaring oneself an irrational decision maker, however, so I suggest that there is a fundamental difference in the ways in which people must address the role of dreams in decision making, at least publicly.

In contrast, rural Punjabis seem to be more inclined to accept certain kinds of dreams as legitimate grounds upon which to base a decision. Edgar's body of work on the subject would suggest that such phenomena are not confined to rural Punjab and that dreams may play important motivational and justificatory functions more generally among Muslim populations. Clearly, dream interpretation publications enjoy widespread popularity across the Muslim world, but that is not, in and of itself, evidence that dreams are taken seriously. Daily horoscopes are a feature of countless newspapers in North America and Europe, but that does not render them trustworthy in the eyes of most people,[2] so we must be cautious about assuming that Muslims treat such publications are more than entertainment. There are, however, enough ethnographic accounts of the seriousness with which many Muslims regard what are classified as true dreams (in addition to this book, see Edgar 2006, 2007) that it is safe to conclude that dreams are not merely entertainment for many (and possibly most) Muslims.

Edgar's latest installment on these matters is both welcome and necessary. For while it is easy for me to suggest that dreams play such an important part in the life of Pakistani Muslims and we must pay greater attention to the cultural dream vocabularies, I have not adequately demonstrated such a claim, and it is unlikely that I would be competent to do so. My interests in the political scheming of the political world will always blinker my access to the realm of dreams. I fear that regardless of how powerful I intend my suspension of disbelief to be, I will continue to slip into looking for more material explanations for all matters of a spiritual or metaphysical nature. Thankfully, Edgar has done what I, and many other anthropologists, cannot. He has taken seriously what matters to his informants because he takes it seriously himself. He is steeped in a tradition that exists and has existed in Europe for some time, but which has, for various reasons, dropped out of the dominant mode of discourse about unconscious realms. He is also steeped in a tradition of pragmatic and empirically verifiable social science, which means that he has somehow managed to reconcile the doubting Thomas and the enthusiastic believer that must both reside, comfortably by all outward signs, within him.

Steve Lyon
Senior Lecturer in Social Anthropology, University of Durham

# Notes

1. *Charpai* perhaps needs no translation for a British audience, but for the sake of clarity, a charpai is the four-legged cot, sofa, or bed that serves so many functions across South Asia.
2. Even those who subscribe to astrology and accord it a certain degree of external, universal validity are often disdainful of the daily horoscope found in newspapers.

⚜ ⚜ ⚜

# Introduction

> The Prophet (Muhammed), now quite ill, is carried into the Mosque on
> the shoulders of two companions. He tries to lead the prayer, but is too weak.
> He delegates his duties to Abu Bakr. And as he leaves, proclaims: "[When I
> am gone] there shall remain naught of the glad tidings of prophecy, except
> for true dreams. These the Muslim will see or they will be seen for him."
> (Lamoreaux: 2002: 84)

Islam is the largest night dream culture in the world today. In Islam, the
night dream is thought to offer a way to metaphysical and divinatory
knowledge, to be a practical, alternative, and potentially accessible source
of imaginative inspiration and guidance and to offer ethical clarity concerning action in this world. Yet dreams, even purportedly true dreams,
are notoriously difficult to validate and, sometimes, to interpret. This book
explores some key aspects of Islamic dream theory and interpretation,
and as well as exploring the role and significance of night dreams to contemporary Muslims in general, it considers many examples of the inspirational guidance claimed by many of the best known al-Qaeda and Taliban
leaders and jihadist activists. I thematically analyze these jihadist dream
narratives.

The foreword and introductory essay by Dr. Steve Lyon contains two
fascinating examples of the power and significance of night dreams in
the Pakistani village that he studied in 1999, which he has subsequently
realized were significant aspects of cultural creativity in such a Muslim
community. Chapter 1 introduces the metaphysical theory and practice of
dream interpretation in Islam. I also reflect on the "true" dream tradition
in other cultures and on how reported night dream narratives are ideologi-
cally significant in contemporary global conflict with examples from Israel/
Palestine and Kosovo. I introduce many examples of contemporary reported true dreams among Muslims from several countries where I have
been privileged to undertake fieldwork, in the United Kingdom, United
States, Bosnia, Turkey, Pakistan, and Northern Cyprus. These examples
illustrate that Muslim reported experience of sacred and perceived true
imagery in night dreams is a contemporary and not solely historical phenomena. Moreover, it appears widespread throughout the Muslim world

with a confirmatory study by Amanullah (2009) in Malaysia. A focus on night dreams is most explicit amongst Sufi groups, and indeed in such contemporary Sufi groups as the Golden Dawn centers in California and the United Kingdom, a Jungian-oriented dreamwork practice is clearly central to their overall spiritual practice.

While, broadly speaking, in Western Christianity dream interpretation became after a few centuries relegated to superstition (Kruger 1992), this has not apparently happened in Islamic cultures. Indeed while all other forms of divination are regarded in Islam as unlawful (*haram*) as the future belongs solely to the will of Allah, dream interpretation, due to the prophetic example of Muhammed, is generally considered acceptable and even possibly very beneficial.

Indeed as the opening quotation in this introduction shows, while major prophecy ended with the death of the Prophet Muhammed, the seal of the Prophet, minor prophecy and guidance can come in the form of true dreams, "glad tidings." Such a metaphysical belief and perception, rooted in the remarkable dreaming abilities of the Prophet Muhammed, gives an occasional powerful role to the phantasmagoric experiences of the night dreamer. A salutary corrective to this potential Pandora's box that this high valuation of dreams denotes is the elaborate art, even science, of dream interpretation in Islamic cultures that has grown up over the centuries and that this book intends to unravel as far as possible.

Chapter 2 considers the methodological issues in researching dreams and reflects particularly on the evidential sources used for this study. I have previously written a book (2004a) on the methodological issues concerning researching the inner world of the imagination and the dream. The collection of primary sources was by participant observation and unstructured and semi-structured interviewing. Secondary sources used were books, articles, the web, and a trial transcript.

Chapter 3 introduces the little-known (outside of Muslim societies) dream incubatory practice of *Istikhara*. Almost no studies of this widespread divinatory practice has been made to date, though Aydar (2009) has written a thoughtful study on the practice in Turkey. I particularly encountered *Istikhara* in my fieldwork in Pakistan in 2005 and was surprised by how commonplace and accepted this practice was by men and women, young and old, and how diverse were the concerns of such a dream incubation practice, whose roots must surely go back to the well-known dream incubation practices of ancient Greece and even before (Bulkeley 2008). While *Istikhara* was most commonly used around marriage choice, I found it was also used for business and even political decision making. Moreover, I have now found its use is not uncommon among Pakistani communities in the United Kingdom. This chapter unearths many earlier references by social anthropologists to the use of *Istikhara* across Islamic cultures in Northern Africa such as Morocco, Senegal, and Sierra Leone. I also present a recent (Edgar and Henig 2010) case study of *Istikhara* gathered in Sarajevo, Bosnia, with my PhD student colleague David Henig. Interestingly, the data from this case study involves opposing reported local sorcery as well as a focus on assisting supplicants in making marriage choices.

The fourth chapter presents, illustratively, the rich history of night dreaming in the Sufi tradition, history, and narrative. I have found among the Sufi communities that I have encountered and spent time with that a very high value is placed on the potential spiritual significance of night dreams by both members and their leaders, the shaykhs. Islam contains as a central narrative that the empirical world that we assume is reality is but a way station toward hidden future, yet metaphysically present, other worlds, particularly heavens and hells. Such coexisting existential possibilities are continuously reiterated in the Qur'an. These unseen worlds— discovered by the Prophet Muhammed in his famous night journey, in either a vision or dream, from Mecca to Jerusalem, the *Laylat ul-isra wal miraj*—are universally and even necessarily accessible to humans through the medium of night dreams, the only virtually universal experience that humans have of an altered state of consciousness separate from, but often related to, this world. All humans dream at night, and dreams seem to have some necessary but still unproven function for human well-being. Evolutionary psychologists consider their value to be in offering opportunity and "space" for rehearsing future strategies, while cognitive psychologists focus on their value being in the unconscious categorization of the day's experiences (Foulkes 1985).

The enigma of the dream is that while the human ego experiences the night dream, it does not, unless the dreamer is a lucid dreamer or a practitioner of Tibetan dream yoga, generate the content of the night dream, and this has led human societies to speculate on the significance and import of at least some night dreams. Islam has hierarchically codified this metaphysical terrain underpinned by the very significant role that night dreams appear to have had in Islamic history, inspired by the example of the Prophet Muhammed. It is the Sufis, the mystical seekers of inner knowledge and illumination, who have become most conversant with dream interpretation and their reported holy guidance received through night dreams. A very little and playful example from my experience of a Sufi community: A visiting shaykh told me how he had dreamed the night before of the Prophet Muhammed feeding him a piece of bread; this shaykh told the senior shaykh in the community of this dream, and the next day at the senior shaykh's birthday party, the senior shaykh playfully put a little piece of bread into the first shaykh's mouth. This action can be read as a ludic play on the power relations between the two shaykhs, an affirmation of the senior shaykh's status as the "friend of God." Also I present a mini-ethnography of dreaming in a UK Sufi community. This chapter should perhaps be read in tandem with Dr. Lyon's mini-ethnography of two dream examples he studied in a Pakistani village that is contained in the foreword and introductory essay.

Chapters 5 and 6 really enter the hornet's nest, or even metaphorically the gateway to hell, of the Islamic night dream. Following 9/11, I read the odd newspaper snippet about Osama bin Laden relating fearfully to his followers that the secret of 9/11 might be disclosed due to so many of his followers having dreams of planes flying into tall towers. I also read a report that Mullah Omar, the Taliban leader, had founded the Taliban following a commandment from a sacred figure in a night dream. Moreover, Richard Reid, the notorious shoe bomber, had talked of being guided in his militant jihad to his planned terror plan, in one of his final three e-mails to his sister. My curiosity led me to study the role of reported true inspirational dreams among contemporary al-Qaeda figures and related militant jihadist groups. I present this material gleaned particularly from newspapers, trial transcripts, and books, albeit with necessary source critical awareness. In particular as part of my British Academy–funded fieldwork study of the role of night dreams generally in contemporary Islamic cultures, I was privileged to interview Rahimullah Yusufzai, the very well-respected Muslim Pakistani BBC journalist who lives in Peshawar and who was virtually the only foreign journalist who had access to Mullah Omar before the events of 9/11. Chapter 6 reports and extensively quotes from my interview with Yusufzai. This interview confirms the centrality of the inspirational role that Mullah Omar's reported dreams, whatever their actual veracity, had and possibly have today on the Taliban leaders and foot soldiers. I contextualize this interview by drawing on contemporary academic and journalistic analyses of the rise and development of the Taliban in Afghanistan in the last fifteen years. I did not interview any militant Islamist fighters or jihadists directly.

In this chapter I thematically analyze this material and conclude that several themes run through these dream narratives: their legitimating function for militant jihad, for their followers, and for the Islamic *Ummah* in general; the dreams' role in experientially connecting the dreamers to the Golden Age of Islam; the militant jihadists' focus on the manifest content of dreams; the interpretation of dreams within the Islamic dream tradition with a focus on understanding dream material similarly to how daytime reality is understood; the relationship between night dream data and future divined events; and the strategic role of night dreams in warfare.

That militant jihadists believe that some of their night dreams are inspired by Allah sits ironically, even tragically, with the Christian guidance reported by the then US president George Bush and the then UK prime minister Tony Blair. But then, as in World War I, the various European armies were each and every one blessed by the Christian establishment as being "just wars." If there are worlds beyond our empirically experienced one and if there is a transcendent being, he, she, or it is certainly incomprehensible to myself!

Chapter 7 is a detailed study of a selection of the most commonly used dream dictionaries in the Islamic world and so gives us a clear, contemporary insight into how dreams are currently being understood and interpreted in Islamic cultures today. The work of the historical figure of Ibn Sirin is the mostly commonly used Islamic dream dictionary, the first port of call for millions of Muslims worldwide, even being reported as the most popular book purchase at the 2007 Algerian book fair! The work attributed to Ibn Sirin is partly based on earlier dream dictionaries from before Islamic times, such as that of Artemidorus (1992), the ancient Greek dream interpreter. Clear similarities as well as differences occur. While Ibn Sirin is the named author and is thought to have died in 728 CE, Lamoureaux (2002: 19–25) has made an extensive study of the dream interpretation texts and concluded that Ibn Sirin is not the actual author of this most famous Islamic dream dictionary. Lamoreaux writes that later dream interpretation authors drew on anecdotal traditions of Ibn Sirin's dream interpretive practices, and he has subsequently been credited with having divine powers in this field. Moreover, hundreds of dream manuals have been ascribed to him in a variety of languages. Lamoreaux concludes that there is evidence that Ibn Sirin took a great interest in dream interpretation, that there are traditions that state that the prophet Joseph initiated Ibn Sirin in his dreams into a mastery of dream interpretation, and that Ibn Sirin "put into circulation" (Lamoreaux 2002: 24) a significant tradition of dream interpretation in Islamic lands. I have studied three contemporary versions of Ibn Sirin's work published in London, Karachi, and Delhi and find them almost indistinguishable.

In all probability, the codification of the human interpretation of dreams goes back to the beginnings of human history, and Islamic dream dictionaries draw implicitly upon ancient Egyptian, Assyrian, Jewish, and Christian interpretative traditions. These dream dictionaries show the complexity of dream interpretation in Islam. For instance, the spiritual and professional status of the dreamer is very significant, as is the time of the night of the dream and the season in which the dream occurs. Also, idiomatic word play is significant, and to cap it all, dreams can mean the opposite of what they appear manifestly to signify!

Chapter 8 analyzes the differences and similarities between classic Western psychoanalytical dream interpretative practices and Islamic approaches. In Islam there is a strong interpretive tradition in which the dream specialist defines directly the meaning of the dream for the dreamer. In the Western dreamwork movement, an offshoot of humanistic psychology, the dreamer is their own expert, and the role of the group leader is definitely facilitative rather than directive. It is a crucial difference, but both traditions deeply respect the potential value and insight of some dreams. I suggest that the Jungian dreamwork tradition, with its concept of the collective unconscious and its related therapeutic practice of active imagination, is closest to the Islamic dream interpretative model.

My conclusion in chapter 9 weaves the material and themes of the previous chapter into an analytical "flying carpet"! Particularly I argue from my textual studies and ethnographic fieldwork that there is a commonality across Islam and among many, if not most, Muslims as to the creative and dynamic role of the imaginal (non-egoic imagination, the Sufi concept of *alam-al-mithal* as defined by Corbin 1966) from which arise some night dreams and some human visions, *al-ruya*.

## Acknowledgements

I think that all publications are works in progress, and even a book is the same. Some of the ideas contained in this book have had embryonic outings in some of my earlier publications and in earlier forms: Edgar 1995; 2002; 2004a and 2004b; 2006, 2007, 2009, and Edgar and Henig 2010.

CHAPTER 1

# Context and History

*Dreams as Perceived Metaphysical and*
*Divinatory Knowledge in Islam*

Islam was both born in and gave birth to spiritual dreamtime. The Prophet
Muhammed is said to have received *ruyan* (the plural of *ruya*) or "true
dreams" from Allah for six months before the beginning of the revelation
of the Qur'an. Bukhari, compiler of the best-known hadiths (sayings and
actions of the Prophet Muhammed) reports the words of Muhammed's
wife, Aisha, stating the "commencement of the divine inspiration was
in the form of good righteous [true] dreams in his sleep. He never had
a dream but that it came true like bright day light." Indeed, it is said
that 1/46th of the Qur'an was given to Muhammed in dreams (Bukhari
1979: 9:87).

Sara Sviri (1999: 252) sets out the key significance of the role of
dreaming in medieval Islam: "While prophecy has ceased, Muhammad
being the seal of the Prophets, messages of divine origin can still be communicated through dreams, albeit on a smaller scale than prophecy." The
same point is made in a hadith included in Bukhari (1979: 9:99): "Nothing is left of prophetism except *Al-Mubashshirat*," which the Prophet
explained as being "the true good dreams that convey glad tidings." In
mainstream Islam, then, there is no future revelation to come other than
through the oneiocratic vehicle of true dreams. This gives such dreams a
special charisma, power, and authority, and means that—for all Muslims,
and particularly for those followers of Islam with a mystical facility—the
dream is a potential pathway to the divine. In sleep or in deep contemplation, the mystically attuned have access to the noumenal, not just the
surreal.

Indeed as Kinberg (2008: 30) writes, dreams have a special authority
in Islam as they communicate truth from the next world (*dar al-haq*).
They provide information as to the "relationship between acts in the present world and rewards in the next, helping to decipher the enigma of

divine retribution." Dreams offer knowledge for the community, "thus [becoming] the ultimate source for profound knowledge, authoritative enough to settle major communal disputes." In Kinberg's (2008: 32–33) work she particularly describes how renowned Muslims had dreams showing the primacy of the Qur'an in general over the hadiths. She also describes recorded dreams that proclaim the value of studying the Qur'an and singing it in a certain way, promising rewards for such people.

## The Dreaming Self in Islam

In his *Epistle on the Nature of Sleep and Dreams,* the Islamic philosopher Ibn Ishaq al-Kindi (d. ca 866) argues that while asleep, the psyche is liberated from the senses and the sensible (*al-hissiyya*), and has direct access to "the form-creating faculty" (*al-quwwa al-musawwira*). In general, he states the truth (*al-Haq*) can only be discerned by the pure heart once the many veils covering it have been removed by spiritual and religious practice. In dreams, however, the liberated soul has potential access to the truth as the material world with its many desires is dormant.

Three kinds of dreams are recognized in Islam by the Prophet and by later dream writers such as Ibn Sirin: First come true spiritual dreams, *ruyan* inspired by God; second come dreams inspired by the devil; third are largely meaningless dreams from the *nafs* (Ego, or the lower self as described in Islamic psychology). This third kind of dream, *hulm,* could be caused by what had been eaten and by what was desired by the dreamer, so producing "a medley of dreams, muddled, jumbled dreams, mere hallucinations, and nightmares" (Gouda 1991: 4).

One of the most significant dream narratives in the history of the Prophet Muhammed is his night journey to the Al-Aqsa mosque site in Jerusalem (*Laylat ul-isra wal miraj*), in which he is believed to have seen the secrets of the cosmos. Within Islam there is a range of understandings as to the nature of this sacred journey. Many Muslims perceive it to be a divine dream or vision. Some Muslim sects view it as a concrete trip. Gouda (1991: 3) describes this journey as follows:

> The vision in question was the ascension of the Holy Prophet: he was transported from the sacred Mosque (of Makkah) to the Al-Aqsa (the farthest) mosque (of Jerusalem) in a night and shown some of the signs of God. The Hadeeth gives details of this night journey wherein the Prophet was first transported to the seat of the earlier revelations in Jerusalem and then taken through the seven Heavens, even to the Sublime Throne, ... and initiated into the spiritual mysteries of the human soul, struggling in space and time.

The role of inspirational dreams in the revelatory development of the nature of the Islamic religion was not, however, confined to Muhammed. For example, a companion of the Prophet, Abdullah Ibn Zayd, dreamt the *Adhan,* the five-times-daily Islamic call to prayer, at a time when Muhammed and his followers were seeking a way of defining their new faith.

The appearance of the Prophet Muhammed in a dream is of particular importance. The hadiths say that if the Prophet appears in a dream, then it is a true dream. For example, a hadith reported by Bukhari (1979: 9:104) relates that the Prophet said, "Whoever has seen me in a dream, then no doubt, he has seen me, for Satan cannot imitate my shape." Nile Green (2003: 287–313) writes in his excellent overview of dreams and Islam, "Yet dreams of the Prophet have formed one of the earliest and most lasting expressions of Islamic piety ... whilst dreams of the Prophet continue to be important to believers in this modern day." Many people I spoke to confirmed this. For non-Muslims, the conviction that to dream of the Prophet is to have received a true guidance from God could be seen as opening a Pandora's box. However, there are safeguards: The Prophet must be complete in his shape, and no true dream can advocate behavior contrary to the teachings of the Qur'an and the hadiths. An imam in Peshawar gave two examples of this from his own experience. The first involved a lawyer who went to him for help in interpreting a dream of the Prophet rolled up in a carpet. The Imam responded by saying, "You are a corrupt lawyer," presumably as the body and energy of the Prophet were circumscribed. The second example was of a man who had a dream in which the Prophet had said he could drink alcohol. The imam asked him if he was a drinker, and the man said "Yes," to which the imam replied that it was not the Prophet he had seen, but a self-justification for his drinking alcohol.

It would be incorrect to consider that only the appearance of the Prophet complete in a night dream should be taken as true. As we will see, many Muslims consider that other figures from the Islamic narrative are deemed as sacred figures. In Shia Islam, Ali and the Twelve Imams are so considered. Particularly striking in Shia Islam is the widespread practice of visiting Ali's grave at Najaf to pray and to receive healing and guidance dreams (Sindawi 2008: 179–201). A follower of a shaykh will usually consider his appearance in their dreams to be true, as was the case among the Naqshbandi Sufis I studied in the United Kingdom. Also Kinberg (2008: 29) quotes a well-known tradition in Islamic dream lore, ascribed to the reported dream interpreter Ibn Sirin (see later) that the appearance of a dead person in a night dream should always be taken as a true dream. Their truthfulness is because they reside in the "world of truth" (*dar al-haq*).

Interestingly, auditory communication in dreams is given a higher status in Islamic dream theory than visual experiences. Kahana-Smilansky (2008: 116) explains this perception, writing about self-reflection and conversion in early Islamic autobiography. She elaborates on the tenth-century neo-Platonist philosopher, al-Sijistani, and his view

> that knowledge received by auditory experience is more noble and exalted than visual experience, because verbal communication originates in the intellectual realm (the Primal One), while the visual imagery characterizes a lower level of consciousness.

She further asserts that this view of the primacy of auditory dream content was "commonly accepted in medieval Islam" (2008: 116). She quotes a Qur'anic verse (42:51) supporting this view, "The Prophet said:... 'sound dreams are the speech of the Lord to the believer,' though such speech is 'not direct but from behind a screen'." Overall, she stresses the role of historically recorded dreams as being decisive moments in the evolution of the individual after long periods of doubt, turmoil, and self-reflection.

The status of perceived sacred images in dreams is problematical. For example, in medieval Islam, an epistemological classification and understanding of a dream image involved an applied understanding of hierognosis. Hierognosis refers to the hierachical classification of the different orders of visionary knowledge displayed both in dreams and waking realities. Therefore dreams would be interpreted by reference to the status of religious imagery appearing in any dream. Hence, the appearance and message from the dream of the Angel Gabriel would have a higher potential truth value than a message received from the dream image of a local saint. Dream interpretation involved particularly the assessment of whether the dream image and its apparent meaning emanated from angels or demons (Meier 1966: 422); demons being able, in dreams, to manifest themselves as angels. The assessment of the dream image hinged on the context of the dream and particularly on whether the dream advocated moral or immoral choices, as angels would be unable to advocate "evil" as the concept of "evil" was understood in Islam.

Anyone, then, may have a true dream, though it is more likely to be experienced by a pious person, or by one who is perhaps going to become more pious on account of the dream. In this sense, Islamic dream theory and practice enshrines the possibility of every believer having true dreams, and indeed in Islamic eschatology, all believers will receive true dreams prior to the end time.

The sometimes lack of certainty as to whether a dream or a waking vision is being described (*ruya* can refer to either a true dream or vision) is in part due to the Sufi tradition within Islam in which the concept of the "imaginal world" is developed proposing a discernible world called *alam al-mithal* outside that of sensibility and intelligibility. This imaginal world is defined as "a world of autonomous forms and images" that is apprehended directly by the imaginative consciousness, through vision and dream particularly, and is held to validate suprasensible perception. This imaginal world should not be confused with an "imaginary" world, which refers to something unreal. Human access to this imaginal, or imaginative, realm is the essential and interactive way of divine transmission (Green: 2003: 287–313). Nile Green summarizes this imaginative pathway excellently drawing on the work of Ibn Arabi, one of the foremost Islamic philosophers of the *alam al-mithal:*

> He [Ibn Arabi] in this way considered the use of the imagination to be the essential part of the journey into God, as the supreme human faculty capable of bridging the existential gap between human and divine knowledge ... for Ibn Arabi regarded visions as, at the same instant, both descending from God to man as a private revelation and ascending from man to God as a creative visual encounter with the divine. Every original and creative act of man ... was to be seen as a divine act of self-manifestation.

While it is beyond the scope of this book to address in depth the philosophical history of the construction and understanding of the self, it is important to conceptualize the Islamic perception of how the true dream is "downloaded" into the human mind. The concept of the *alam al-Mithal,* the imaginal, is crucial. Sviri (1999: 256) develops this idea with reference to the work of the Islamic philosopher Abu Hamid al-Ghazali (d. 1111). Al-Ghazali, Sviri writes, bases his understanding of true dreams described in "the final part of the *Ihya,*" on the distinction between "the world of possession and (sense) perception" (*alam al-mulk wash-shahada*) and the "world of the angelic kingdom and the unseen" (*alam al-malakut wal-ghayb*). True dream visions emanate from this latter world of the angelic kingdom and the unseen and relate "to a mode of inner seeing (*Mushahada*) that is independent of the outer senses." Further, Sviri writes:

> A veridical dream vision, which is by definition a weak version of prophecy, may be granted to the pious and righteous during their lifetimes. Al-Ghazali explains that in a state of outer and inner purification, the veil covering the heart is lifted and a vision of the future is revealed to the heart's eye. The heart, he explains, is like a mirror upon which forms (*suwar*) and meanings (*ma'ani*) are reflected. The source of these preserved forms and meanings is the (Preserved) Tablet (*al-lauh al-mahfuz*), the heavenly book that records all created and preordained phenomena from the beginning of creation to its end. In the process of dreaming, it is suggested, a double act of mirroring is taking place: the Tablet mirrors the incorporeal forms that exist in the

unseen, and the unveiled heart, in contemplating the Tablet, mirrors the images reflected there. When the heart is not obscured by the veils of desires and sense perception, visions from the world of the unseen may thus flash and become reflected upon its clear surface. This is best achieved in sleep, since in sleep the senses lie dormant and do not distract the heart. ...

Imagination, according to al-Ghazali, is the faculty which, through imitation (*hikaya*), represents the non-corporeal meanings reflected upon the heart by means of producing analogous images (based on sense perception), which are then stored in memory (*hifz*). These images require interpretation, since they are no longer the original forms and truths (*haqa'iq*), but only their symbolic representations. (1999: 256–57)

This summary by Sviri of al-Ghazali's inner philosophical cosmology of transmission via the true dream of the unseen to the seen memory is complex and not verifiable within the Western empirical philosophical tradition. Moreover, it depends upon a mystical or symbolic Islamic perception of the heart as being not just an organ of the body but as being a mystical and receptive center of consciousness. For example, Said Nursi (see later in this chapter), the Turkish Islamic intellectual leader, writes extensively about the spiritual functions of the heart for "contemplation (*mushahada*) and spiritual witnessing (*kashf*)" (Kuspinar 2008: 126–32). It is impossible to understand the theory of Islamic true dreaming without understanding the importance of the heart (*kalb*) or inner heart (*sirr*) as an organ of spiritual and symbolic perception and engagement. Again, quoting Kuspinar, writing about the work of Said Nursi,

Nursi gives among others the example of the faculty of imagination, which, he says, works under the command of the heart and enables the heart to travel all around the world in joy, provided that the latter, that is, the heart, is fostered and flourished by the love (*muhabba*), contemplation (*tafakkur*), and remembrance (*zikr*) of God. (2008: 131)

This Islamic dual conception of the heart is central to understanding the nature of dreaming in Islam.

In his detailed study of dream interpretation in the early days of Islam, Lamoreaux (2002: 108) significantly asks the question as to whether dream interpretation is a duty of Muslims and whether it is sanctioned in the Qur'an. He concludes that while there are several significant dream narratives in the Qur'an, particularly the Joseph sura (Qur'an 12.6), there is nothing that enjoins Muslims to undertake dream interpretation as such. However, all the principle hadiths (i.e., Bukhari, Muslim) do contain a longer or shorter chapter on dream interpretation and its significance for the Prophet Muhammed, and to the practice of Islam itself. Lamoreaux shows that almost all the hadiths concur that the meaning of the phrase "glad tidings" in sura 10.64 refers to true dreams (2002:

110). The full phrase in question is "those who believe and fear (god) ... they will have glad tidings [*al-bushra*] in the life of this world and in the next." This hadith, based on understanding of the 10.64 Qur'anic verse, is part of the theological structure of Islamic dream interpretation and underpins the authority of the Islamic oneirocritical tradition.

## Said Nursi

In the contemporary Nur community mainly based in Turkey—founded by Bediuzzaman Said Nursi, who died in 1960, and which numbers perhaps six million followers—some dreams are important. Said Nursi writes:

> Experiencing them numerous times, true dreams became for me like decisive proofs at the degree of "absolute certainty" that Divine Determining encompasses all things. Yes, especially the last few years, these dreams have reached such a degree that it has become certain for me that the most significant events and unimportant dealings and even the most commonplace conversations I will have the following day are written and recorded before they occur, and that by dreaming of them the night before, I have read them not with my tongue but with my eyes. Not once, not a hundred times, but perhaps a thousand times, the things I have said in my dreams or the people I have dreamt of at night, although I had not thought of them at all, turned out exactly or with little interpretation the next day. It means that the most insignificant things are both recorded and written before they happen. That is to say, there is no chance or coincidence, events do not occur haphazardly, they are not without order. (Landau 2008: 153)

For Said, precognitive dreaming seems to have been highly developed and presumably influenced his philosophical reflections on the paradox of free will and determinism. Yet, Said Nursi affirms the value of the revelation of the Qur'an even over true dreams, thinking that even prophetic interpretation of dreams can be incomplete. An example from my readings of the Qur'an (Qur'an: 8.43) would, for instance, suggest that the dream of the Prophet Muhammed before the battle of Badr when he saw the Meccan army as smaller than it was in reality, so giving hope to Muhammed and his followers, shows that even a Prophet may not fully understand every aspect of a dream. Nursi seems to suggest (Landau 2008: 159) that dreams are like moonlight, which is the light of the reflected sun, while the Qur'an is the light of the sun itself. Nursi prefers to be "a servant of the Sun" and not a "lover of the night." Dreams to Nursi can be "the snare of the saints" and he advises caution in interpreting dreams (Landau 2008: 159). Certainly though, Landau writes about Nursi's powerful advisory dreams after his death, being seen by some of his followers, or followers to be (Landau 2008: 160).

## Abu Ja'far al-Qayini and His Dreams
## of the Prophet Muhammed

There are myriad traditional and contemporary "sightings" of the Prophet Muhammed in night dreams recorded, some of which are reproduced in this book; perhaps one of the most remarkable is Lamoreaux's (2008: 78–98) description and analysis of the dream conversations of Abu Ja'far al-Qayini and the Prophet Muhammed. The text is at least a thousand years old and contains the record of many conversations held in dreams between the Prophet and al-Qayini. Abu Jafar al-Qayini's reported dream interviews were presented by Lamoreaux, and he was the first to translate the two remaining manuscripts that reported this dream interview. The manuscripts date from the sixteenth century CE and al-Qayini lived around 1000 CE. Apparently the original source of the text was from one Abu Mansur al-Turaythithi who traveled with al-Qayini to Mecca from Qayin, a town two hundred kilometers south of Nishapur.

My experience of Muslims who have dreamed of the Prophet Muhammed identify him often quite easily; al-Qayini has a dream on 27 October 996 CE. He is climbing a mountain with much exertion, and reaching its summit he sees a man praying:

> I came round and knelt in front of him, until there was between me and his knee but a single span. I looked at his face and beard. And lo, he was thickly bearded. I looked at his cheeks. And lo, in them was just a touch of white. I looked at his lips. And lo, they were thick.
>
> I thought to myself: these are the characteristics of the messenger of God. ... I bowed my head and spoke not a word, neither did he speak. I then glanced up at him a second time, examining him closely, and I was persuaded that he was the messenger. ... timidly and reverently, I asked: Are you the messenger of God? He said: Yes, I'm the messenger of the Lord of the Universe. (Lamoreaux 2008: 81–82)

The subsequent dream interview in which al-Qayini asks questions of the Prophet Muhammed covers many subjects: asking for blessings for a friend; divisions among the Muslims, the seventy-two sects of Islam; the nature of dreams of the Prophet; differences between Islamic legal schools; the problems of the authenticity of the transmissions in the hadiths concerning the sayings and behaviors of the Prophet, etc.

Regarding the vexed issue of the authenticity of the hadiths, al-Qayini questions the Prophet about how he has been unfairly criticized by his teachers:

> Many of the leading scholars of prophetic traditions. ... used to disparage the trustworthiness of our reverent and pious elders and declare the pro-

phetic tradition they transmit to be weak. And yet, many of the contemporary *ulema* prevent me from doing the same, saying:

> "This is slander. Don't disparage them ... don't call them weak transmitters. ... Don't do this, even if the leading scholars of prophetic tradition did so." [The Prophet replied]: This isn't slander. It were a question of people other than the transmitters of Prophetic tradition, it would be. But, as it is, it's only through the chain of transmitters that scholars of prophetic tradition can declare accounts sound and distinguish between those that are sound and those that are not. (Lamoreaux 2008: 82–83)

A second example should suffice to get the tenor of these dream interview dialogues. Al-Qayini asks the Prophet Muhammed as to the "meaning of the well known prophetic tradition, that, after Muhammed's death, the Muslim community would fracture into seventy-three divisions, all but one of which were destined for Hell." Muhammed replies that the first part of the saying is correct, while the second part is in error. "Yes, all of these divisions will divide my community, but the mercy of God ... and my intercession shall encompass them all." Al-Qayini replies, "God is most great! You've given me great joy! May God grant you the means to accomplish this!" (Lamoreaux 2008: 83)

We can easily see here where power, authority, knowledge, true vision, and wisdom are deemed to reside. Al-Qayini asks and the Prophet Muhammed declares that which is the real situation. The negotiation of power, status, and authority is completed as soon as the dream ego of al-Qayini decides that it is the Prophet Muhammed sitting in prayer at the top of the mountain. In this interview there is a relative absence of contextual information in terms of the processual performance, though in al-Qayini's dream he has a picture of the Prophet. The focus is of course on the audible aspect of the interviews. Body posture, except at the beginning, and all the subtle clues as to meaning and sincerity prevalent in real-world interviewing are not really available in this example; however, al-Qayini is surprised by some of the Prophet's answers and clearly expresses feelings such as joy and bewilderment. There is no need for rhetorical persuasion by the Prophet except that the Prophet's answers are clear and unequivocal.

The Prophet's performance (or rather the dreamed image of the Prophet in al-Qayini's dream) and wisdom appeals to a higher-level knowledge of the inner meaning and future destiny of peoples as with his answer concerning the seventy-three sects of Islam. The context of the ascription of such wisdom to the supernatural dreamed image of the Prophet is located in the whole tradition of Islam and the Prophet Muhammed, part of which we have seen expressed and revealed in dream imagery and subsequent narratives. There is no doubting the impact on al-Qayini, and the appeal resides partly in the aesthetic of meeting the Prophet on the mountaintop in the dream and in his appearance.

## Dream Interpretation in Islam

Dream interpretation in Islam, even given the apparently simple tripartite classificatory system, is extremely sophisticated and takes into account factors that include the piety and spiritual rank of the dreamer, his/her social position, the time of night, and the time of year of the dream. Islamic dream dictionaries, unlike their Western counterparts, may contain many interpretations for the same symbol. For example, if a poor person dreams of honey, this can be a sign of illness as only then will poor people buy honey, whereas for a rich person to dream of honey is a favorable sign. I was told by Islamic religious scholars in Turkey that only a prophet can definitively distinguish a true from a false dream; even spiritual leaders such as shaykhs may disagree about interpretations. Also, Gouda's example of the pomegranate makes clear how multiple meanings of a dream symbol can depend on the social status of the dreamer:

> The interpreter should bear in mind the dream's compatibility with the status and vistas of the subject. For instance, a pomegranate would have different interpretations for a ruler, a merchant, a learned man, a hermit, a single man, and a pregnant woman. For the Sultan it could mean a dominion or a city to be added to his realm or area of influence. Its peels are the walls or fences of that city, its pips the inhabitants. For the merchant it would refer to his home, where his family dwells, his bathroom, his hotel, his ship full of merchandise and money plying the sea, his shop with plenty of clients, or his purse full of money. For the learned man or hermit it would refer to his book or Quran; its peels would be its pages and its pips the book's scriptures, which advocate reform and perfection. For the bachelor it could mean a wife with all her beauty and wealth or a maiden or a slave girl whom he would deflower, tasting all the pleasures of this delight, to borrow the expression of the ancient Arabs. For the pregnant women the pomegranate could represent a girl in her womb. (1991: 16–17)

A core difference I have found between Islamic and Western dream theories, particularly those of Gestalt and the Dreamwork Movement, is found in the tension between authoritative and facilitative interpretation. Islamic dream interpreters tend to tell the believer what the dream means based on their understanding of the Qur'an and the hadiths, which are perceived to contain all that humans need to know to live well, while certain Western dream interpretative traditions are much more facilitative. For example, I had a dream while I was in Turkey: I was a chauffeur of a car, dressed in black and picking up three females all dressed in white;

two of the females were children. I also knew these women in reality. My efforts at self-interpretation were focused on my understanding of roles and relationships and exploring my subsequent feelings with respect to these people. However, an Islamic scholar to whom I told the dream explained that because the women were all dressed in white and I was dressed in black, the dream meant that they were "good" and I was on a wrong path. I was quite shocked by the directive form and content of this interpretation. In contradistinction, in my long experience in dreamwork groups in the West, the principle was to consider the dreamer the expert with respect to their own dreams. Moreover, the role of the group leader was wholly suggestive and facilitative.

However, a report from the Egyptian weekly newspaper, *Al-Ahram* (22–28 June 2006, issue 800) demonstrates the popularity of dream interpretation. Dream interpretation programs seem extremely popular across the 150 Arabic television stations, and successful dream interpreters seem to have a celebrity status. This report also refers to the possible existence of a tension between modernist, more Freudian approaches to dream interpretation and those more traditional Islamic approaches:

> Dream interpretations have become a fixture of Arab satellite television. Some decipher dreams through the Freudian model, others eschew the father of psychoanalysis and focus on religious explanation. Call it obsession—it is more that than passion, anyway—but enquiring about the meaning and implications of dreams has become all the rage.

> The new talking-point for Arab audiences is the interpretation of dreams. The viewers are curious and yearn for someone in the know to explain the meaning of a particular recurring nightmare or a strange fleeting dream. Others find the entire experience very entertaining; they stay glued to their television sets for as long as the professional dream interpreters are on air.

> The intensity of the popularity of dream interpreters is such that they are treated as celebrities; many are virtually household names. Indeed, professional dream interpretation has become an especially lucrative trade. Like any other trade or profession, those dream interpreters with the largest following tend to be the most accurate, convincing and charismatic.

## The True Dream across Cultures and Throughout History

Anthropologists and dream researchers can and have studied the meaning, use, and occurrence of dreams that are considered revelatory in indigenous societies, especially in shamanic societies. In such societies, the dream is often seen as a profound resource for divination, healing, success in hunting, and all aspects of life both for the individual and the group;

indeed there are shamans who believe that nothing happens in waking reality before it has been performed first in the dream space. Krippner and Thompson (1996) found that among the Northern Iroquois and the Yuma North American Indians, "dreaming life was considered to be more 'real' and/or more important than waking life." The Hindu Upanishads "value dreaming above reality" (Tedlock 1987: 2–3) and the Dream Yoga of Tibetan Buddhism (i.e., Tulku 1999) offers a little-known way of enlightenment that seeks to illuminate its practitioners through developing an uninterrupted consciousness throughout both daytime reality and the dream state. In world history, the night dream has a potentially elevated status as a uniquely authentic but often problematic realm of experience.

Hence, dreaming is highly significant in many of the main world religions. Indeed, Taylor (1992) writes of the "startling agreement" among the "sacred/mythic narratives of the world" as to the "direct access to the divine" to be had through dreams. The importance of the dream within both Judaism and Christianity is frequently evident in both the Hebrew and Christian Bible (for a recent authoritative summary of these dream narratives, see Koet 2009: 17–31). "God" is said to communicate with the prophets through the medium of the dream and likewise speaks to men and women, such as Mary and Joseph, in the Christian Bible. Knafo and Glick write, "from Abraham to Joseph, dreams became another main channel of divine communication."

The study of core significance in dreams has been a hallmark of the International Association for the Study of Dreams. Hartmann (2008), for example, has focused on the study of the power of the "central image" (CI) in a dream. He has focused on how powerful the emotional content of such central images are, and he concludes that the emotional power of the CI is related to the participants' sense of the meaning, impact, significance, and importance of their dream. My own more solely qualitative study (1995) has developed related but perhaps more unfathomable concepts related to dream impact: beauty and awe, power, impact, manifest "message," and relevance to self. In Islam, particularly, we will see that the relationship of the dream content to future events is crucial, a feature displayed throughout dream traditions across indigenous cultures. Truth claims about dreams are not then confined to Islamic cultures.

While a study of powerful dream reports across history and religions offers an accumulation of significant narratives, anthropologists also can discern the communicative context in which dreams are told and interpreted and analyze the dream theory of the culture considered. This communicative theory of dreaming (Tedlock 1987) has to consider the dream narration as a communicative event involving three overlapping aspects:

the act and creation of narration, the psychodynamics of narration, and the culturally bounded group interpretive framework. Such a theory considers the analysis of dreaming as more than hermeneutics. Dreaming is also a social and cultural process or activity with expressive and instrumental outcomes. The communicative theory of dreaming alerts us to the importance of the psychodynamics of the social setting and the interpretive framework of the participants. And the Islamic dream interpretative tradition permits the interpretation of the night dream, on occasion, as being a true dream.

Dream interpretive theories are often developments of preceeding societies' theories, as is the case in Islamic dream theory, which has strong roots in, particularly, the dream theory of the ancient Greeks, notably contained in the *Oneiocritica* by Artemidorus. Islamic dream theory also has roots in the dream traditions of ancient Egypt and Assyria, and from Judaic and Christian theories of dreaming. For example, Macrobius, a Late Antique dream theorist, presents five different and hierachically ordered categories of dreams ranging from the true and the revelatory (*oraculum and visio*) to the false and mundane (*visum and insomnium*). Yet mediating this opposition of true and false dreams, Macrobius (Kruger 1992) suggests a middle type of dream (*somnium*) in which truth is represented in fictional, allegorical, and metaphorical form. The Islamic theory of true and false dreams is congruent with, and possibly derived from, earlier dream interpretative theories. Arguably then, what is most distinctive about Islamic dream theory and practice is not its tripartite classification but the prophetic example and its historical and cultural location in the Islamic worldview.

Dreams, however, are typically offered by charismatic leaders as a self-justifying and legitimating device, claiming them to be revelations from beyond this world. I would contend that a reported dream has a potentially special role in the legitimating role of charismatic leaders precisely because dreams are unverifiable, ontologically derived, and numinous. In Islam, particularly in the Persian Safayid dynasties (1501–1732) as described by Quinn (2008: 221–32) and the Mamluk period in Egypt and Syria (thirteenth to sixteenth centuries CE) (Frenkel 2008: 202–20), dream narratives are used to give a divine mandate to their political power. A dream cannot be precisely verified, tested, or observed or even its actual narrative contested; it just is as reported. And it can be seen to partake of the numinous quality of "other worlds." Knudson suggests that the intrinsic "beauty" of dream imagery in highly significant dreams may account for their long-term impact on the dreamer, while Knafo and Glick—grappling with the same issue of the numinous power of such dreams—suggest dreams "are on the edge between reality and fantasy, and future and past." Burridge (1969: 111) confirms the powerful role of night dreams in his study of charisma:

> At the start the personal qualities of the prophet seem to matter little. What is important is that his message should appear to come from a source beyond commonsense experience. It must be a revelation. Usually the message is claimed, or presumed, to have been revealed in a dream or a vision or some other mystical experience. Whatever the cultural idiom, the message is taken to be beyond man's wit to devise. It is a divine revelation. It transcends the capacities of a man acting alone.

Even Saddam Hussein seemed to have used the dream to assert divine guidance in his invasion of Kuwait. As Thomas Friedman wrote in the *New York Times:*

> Last week a Kuwaiti newspaper now publishing in Saudi Arabia reported that President Saddam Hussein of Iraq had dreamed that the Prophet Muhammed appeared before him and said Iraq's missiles "were pointing in the wrong direction." Middle East experts were quoted as saying that this dream indicated that the Iraqi leader could be preparing for a withdrawal from Kuwait. But the White House spokesperson, Marlin Fitzwater, asked for his reaction, responded: "No comment on dreams. I have enough problem dealing with reality." (28 October 1990)

Later in the same report he quotes a White House administration Arabist saying, "Saddam lets it be known that he had a dream, and we joke about it. But it sounds very different to Arab ears."

Night dreams can then be used by charismatic leaders to legitimate their actions and/or show that they are influenced by their dreams.

## Promised-Land Dreams in Palestine and Kosovo

We will see later how the Al-Jazeera journalist, Yosri Fouda (2003: 109) quotes Osama bin Laden saying that the 9/11 attacks were to avenge the occupation of Israel by the United States. Palestine is the hub of conflict in the Middle East, and even beyond, and the Genesis promised-land dreams (i.e., Jacob's ladder dream Genesis 28:11–19) are a significant part of the Zionist charter myth. Malinowski writes of a charter myth as being a myth of origin for "a primitive people" that:

> conveys, expresses and strengthens the fundamental fact of local unity and of the kinship unity of the group of people descendant from a common ancestress ... the story of origin literally contains the legal charter of the community. (1954: 114)

In appendix one of Fouda's book, he quotes an al-Qaeda statement justifying their jihad against the West and Israel:

> Muslims believe in all the prophets ... and if there is a promise in the Torah that Moses' followers have the right to Palestine, then we think that the Muslims should have that right. Therefore, the historical claim for the right to Palestine cannot be overlooked by the Islamic nation.

And yet, with a profound and unacknowledged irony, both Zionists and the Islamic militant jihadists appear to claim divine authenticity and legitimation for their nationalistic, territorial, and spiritual ambitions from "unseen" and so unverifiable dreams. With regard to Israeli and Zionist claims to Palestine, for example, Jacob's ladder dream at Bethel (Gen: 28:11–19) is the remembered occasion when Jacob is recorded as "seeing" angels ascending up a ladder and "heard" God give the land on which he lay to him and his descendants, promising this territory in perpetuity. Today, the F16 fighters flying over Gaza gain their political mandate, implicitly and in part, from the memory and subsequent political use of this recorded and remembered dream imagery. The Zionist argument for the territorial statehood of Israel is at the end of the day, in part, based on a recorded dream recounted over two thousand years ago. Faisal Bodi, a Palestinian journalist, writes in the UK *Guardian* newspaper (3 January 2001, 18) of Golda Meir, the former Israeli prime minister, who famously stated, "This country exists as the accomplishment of a promise made by God himself. It would be absurd to call its legitimacy into account." Bodi continues, "That Biblical promise is Israel's only claim to legitimacy." Part of that promise is found in Jacob's dream report mentioned above. As Knafo and Glick (2000: 28) write, the Patriarch's dreams (in Jacob's dream, for example) are the foundation dreams of Judaism and further, that those Genesis dreams "play a major part in highlighting the concepts of the Chosen Nation, the coming back from exile, the Promised Land" (Knafo and Glick 2000: 25). While I argue that dreams are part of this Zionist charter myth, I am aware that the Zionist promised-land claim is based on more than dream reports but also elaborately uses the Hebrew Bible to make their case; however, I focus here on the dream narrative.

Nor is Israel the only Western state so formed in the imagination of its citizens. Jonathan Steele wrote in the UK *Guardian* newspaper (29 June 1998) how the territorial mandate of the Serbian state is imaginatively based on a reported dream. In this case, the dream is recorded as occurring to the Serbian prince Lazar the night before the historically decisive battle of Kosovo Polje in 1389 CE. In this dream, a falcon apparently offers the prince a choice of achieving either a heavenly or an earthly kingdom. Choosing a heavenly kingdom, Prince Lazar subsequently lost the battle to the Ottomans the next day. The story of Prince Lazar, his dream, and the battle was enshrined and its memory kept alive in the Kosovo Epic cycle of poems/songs. These epic poems, which in part refer to a dreamed reality unseen by another, are core texts that, in part, underpin the present myth of Serbian national identity. Indeed Steele, in the same report, records how Milovan Djilas, Yugoslavia's "best-known dissident," wrote: "Wipe away Kosovo from the Serb mind and soul and we are no more. If there had been no battle at Kosovo, the Serbs would have invented it for its suffering and heroism." Even though the Serb myth of the tragic defeat at Kosovo only became politically invented and significant in the nineteenth century, it too is a key element in the collective memory and political authorization of the Serbian state. Malcolm writes further:

> Of all the elements of the Kosovo myth which was formed in the nineteenth century, none has been more powerful than the "Kosovo covenant." This is the idea that Lazar was offered a choice between an earthly kingdom and a heavenly one, and that he choose the latter; because of this decision, described as a covenant with God, the Serbs are often said to consider themselves as a "heavenly people." (1998: 80)

Malcolm also quotes a Serbian historian who writes in similar vein:

> 'The Kosovo covenant—the choice of freedom in the celestial empire instead of humiliation and slavery in the temporal world— ... is still the one permanent connective tissue that imbues the Serbs with the feeling of national unity.' (1998: 80, quoting Batakovic 1992: 35)

The savagery inflicted by such Serbian nationalism in this decade leading also to the Kosovo conflict is again based at least in part on a recorded dream. So two contemporary nations, Serbia and Israel, invoke memories of recorded dreams as a part of their claim to a promised land and a chosen people.

Of course, state genocide and ethnic cleansing is a complex historical and cultural phenomenon, and the dream will have gone through many a permutation before it becomes what social anthropologists, following Malinowski, describe as a "charter myth."

## Significance of Night Dreams to Muslims

My fieldwork confirmed the significance of dreams to Muslims in general by using extensive and random, even serendipitous, interviewing of people from all walks of life. Ask a Muslim about dreams, and usually you will be told of a significant dream that has influenced their life through focusing their attention on a possibility not previously recognized by their conscious mind.

However, from West Africa to the Philippines, the tripartite schematization of dreams explained above is part of the worldview of the majority of Muslims, not just the especially pious. Muhammad Amanullah (2009) studied a dozen staff in the religious studies department of a Malaysian university: the majority reported true dreams, and more than 50 percent believed that they had seen or felt the Prophet in a dream. Hoffman (1997) has shown how night dreams and visions are surprisingly common among both Muslims and Coptic Christians in Egypt. She writes, "In the course of my research I collected many stories in which dreams played a major role in guiding people to a particular spiritual guide" (1997: 53).

Allen (2006) has recently written a study of dream talk among Palestinian refugees in the Shatila refugee camp in Lebanon, showing the importance of this practice among women in kindling hope and offering possible imaginary excursions into an envisioned less-despairing future scenario. Dream talk then can help "by building affective bridges to the future" (2006: 14). Allen considers dream talk as the interpretative process of the dream with local dream interpretation specialists. In her analysis, dreams and dream talk are sites of agency and positive vision work in which "hopelessness could be engaged and temporarily transformed" (2006: 13). Moreover, such dream talk generates "'webs of trust' amongst the listeners" (2006: 18). Furthermore, she argues against the possible thesis that such hopeful dream talk is mere denial of a massively oppressed present outcast situation by arguing that such embodied dream talk is a counter to reality and can generate a potentially transforming optimism that has real-world outcomes: for instance, the occasional experience of daily joy (2006: 24). Such a view is congruent with the prophetic example of Muhammed, who always advocated a positive interpretation of a dream as a means of co-generating a more fruitful future through what psychology calls a self-fulfilling prophecy. Basso (1987: 86) similarly wrote of dreams and their interpretation being a part of the "self becoming." He attempted to marry Western and non-Western concepts as to whether and how the dream may portray or orient the dreamer to his/her future. Through his analysis of dreaming among the Kalapalo Indians of Central Brazil, he suggests that "dreaming is also a performative event because it causes the future by revealing the dreamer's life as it is encapsulated in current aspirations, moods and inchoately understood motivations and fears of an individual" (1987: 101). Dreaming then may assist the dreamer in his or her orientation to their future and so is not separable from the creation of that future.

A moving example from Allen's 2006 ethnography that encapsulates much of the above is the recounting of the death of a young, unmarried woman's mother in the aftermath of the Sabra and Shatila massacre. In this young woman's report, she, in her very real grief, has a dream in which a shaykh takes her to a bomb shelter; she expects to see her mother's body as there were many enshrouded bodies there, but instead she sees the face of an unknown man. Her daytime grief increases, and she seeks advice from a shaykh who says that this unknown man she has seen in her dream is God's gift to her from her mother, and if she should meet this man and he proposes to her, she should accept the marriage proposal. She meets him in reality a week later, and they become engaged in a year and married after a further three years (26). Allen concludes that we need to "attend to the structures and practices of hope that are already operating within" (38).

Among the dream examples that I have gathered in my research include the following. A hospital medical consultant was expecting a baby and was watching her dreams to help her name her offspring. To see a flower in a dream would provide a girl's name; a quality, such as strength, would suggest a boy's name. An academic told me how at very difficult periods of her life, she had dreamed of the Prophet Muhammed and angels, and these images had sustained her:

> The Prophet was very beautiful and dressed in black; she was looking down at him and was very upset at the time; the implicit message was "Do not be afraid, you will succeed." His body language made her feel this way.

> My second dream that she told me came after her father had just died; she did *Istikhara* [Islamic dream incubation] and saw golden angels on white clouds; they gave her prayer to her father and she felt it was answered.

> Her third dream was at a time when she was stressed and depressed, and she saw grown golden angels on white clouds; they threw her a lifejacket and gave her a golden triangular necklace.

I asked a gardener in a small town if he had ever had a memorable dream and he said, "Yes. Once I had a dream of crying and the next day I killed my neighbor over a land dispute and spent eight years in jail for murder." A Muslim drycleaner in the United Kingdom told of his mother, who had dreams in which the Prophet advised her about how to pray. In Pakistan, I found that all but one person I spoke to (a national poet) fervently believed in the power of dreams. Everywhere I went with my dream questions, people from all walks and classes of life would tell me how dreams had changed their lives. A textile shopkeeper in Peshawar spoke of how his life had been transformed by a dream of the Prophet who had advised him to pray five times a day. I recorded this dream from memory as follows:

In his dream five years ago, he was on a journey and saw a house of clay and was thirsty; he saw a pond full of water; he drank water but was still thirsty; he saw an old man, a very respectable man who comes out of the house and asks him "Why are you drinking so much water?" He replied that he had been drinking water for a while but was still thirsty. Then he asked him to make a vessel and wash his hands, face, and feet, then start praying; after saying his prayers, the old man asked him how he was feeling. Still thirsty? The dreamer replied: "Now I am okay, I am not thirsty; I am satisfied." Since then he has prayed five times a day and is happy; before he was a Muslim but didn't always pray.

A close companion told me how his illiterate father had been made literate following a dream. A close relative of a very senior Afghani politician and religious leader described how this relative had been advised by dreams while in prison under the Communists. A fifteen-year-old young man from Birmingham, UK, whom I met in a madrasah in Peshawar, told how he had moved to Pakistan to study to become an imam partly through a dream.

Dreams can facilitate conversions, either into Islam or into militant jihadism. An example of the first type of conversion is a Chilean man[4] whom I met in Islamabad, who had previously been a television shop owner in Chile. He told me he became Muslim following a dream in which he saw the first words of the Qur'an written in the skies. He moved to Pakistan with his family and was studying Islam in a Karachi madrasah. His mother had married a Muslim preacher, and his son had trained as a *hafiz* (one who can recite all the Qur'an). An example of the second type of conversion is Abu Mussab al-Zarqawi's sister's dream of the former leader of al-Qaeda in Iraq, which is said to have been one of two reasons why he converted to jihadism. This dream is discussed later in this book.

A recent anthropological study of female adult conversion to Islam in the United States confirms the crucial significance of night dreams in the conversion process. Fatimah is an American woman and recently divorced mother who has been very unhappy for some time, is seeking an awakening of faith, and has encountered Islam/Sufism. She tells the story of her dream:

That night I went to bed and I had this dream that was just really incredible. I woke up in the morning and I *knew* that I had to convert to Islam. That this was definitely my way. So I went to tell him [a man who held lectures about Islam and Sufism at the spiritual center where Fatimah was staying]. Well, he said, "You are lucky. It happens that there is one other man here today, you have to have two Moslims present to be witnesses." And they were here just because his son fell off of the tree and broke his arm. So he told me basically to go and make the ritual cleaning and put on some clean cloth and come out after lunch and he would do it. He was very nice because he made it a very special moment. So when I went in after lunch and into the room, there was the boy who had broken his arm and he was the boy that had been in my dream the night before. There had been two children in my dream and he was one of them. And in the dream he had been carrying a white sword. He came into the room with his arm in a sling carrying a white plastic sword. So you know I thought this is definitely what I need to be doing. (McGinty 2006: 63)

Fatimah's eyes fill with tears as she narrates her dream experience that triggered her conversion. This dream is experienced after two years of seeking a spiritual way forward in her life, and she wakes from it with a keen sense of spiritual certainty. For her, this certainty is confirmed by the coincidental and precognitive experience of seeing the boy with the white sword in reality the next day. This fusion of inner and outer experience is a key element in her conversion.

Muslim children also report true dreams. In her study of the dreams of Christian, Muslim, and secular children, Adams (2004) reports the dream of a Muslim girl:

Rasha, a Muslim girl, dreamt that she and a cousin were going on Hajj. She travelled by car and watched her cousin travelling by boat and they saw Mecca and the Kaaba before the boat turned round. Although the dream did not contain any images of the girls performing Hajj, Rasha felt that the dream was a message from Allah instructing her that she should go on Hajj (pilgrimage to Mecca) in the future.

Hence, Islamic consciousness, of all ages, seems to be replete with the possible occurrences of sacred imagery in night dreams.

CHAPTER 2

# Methodology

Previously, I have considered the role of dreams in politics (Edgar 2002: 79–92). Also, in my book on imagination-based research methods, I discussed the problems that may occur when one wants to use and validate dreams as data (Edgar 2004a: 60–80). While we cannot ever know directly another person's dreams, as social scientists we can study the worldly usage and indeed the politically legitimating function of dreams. How do dreams inspire and evoke emotion and novel insight? How and when do Muslims believe them to be true dreams from Allah? How do dreams play a role in the legitimation of (jihadist) action or in the authorization of political and religious leadership?

Night dreams can be seen as a technology of the sacred: While dreams are experienced by the ego, the ego generally does not generate or control them (unless the dreamer is an experienced lucid dreamer or a student of Tibetan dream yoga [Tulku 1999]). Social scientists traditionally have seen dream narratives and their impact on the "real" world as particularly problematic. However, the social anthropologist Waud Kracke (2003: 212) persuasively argues that this inability to know another one's dream is similar to the inability of knowing for certain another person's mental or emotional state. It is in an overall philosophical and epistemological context that dream researchers work. If social science research ignores the sometimes powerful visual nature of inner realities, then the study, for instance, of altered states of consciousness (ASC) and exceptional human experiences (EHE) becomes fraught and open to the accusation that all inner realities are fantastical and worthless to be used as evidence.

Therefore, it is interesting to see how in a different culture, Islam, the dream has a distinct role and function. In this book, I touch upon different settings within Islamic culture, in which the imaginary fields of dreaming are considered a natural source for guidance in reality. As this book will argue, in Islamic dream culture, inner worlds and experiences evidently influence Muslims' outer worlds and experiences.

Methodologically, I used various approaches throughout the book, depending on the subject, topic, and objectives of my research. First, I would like to address several general methodological issues and pitfalls of which a researcher of dreams and dream interpretation needs to be aware. Second, I wish to consider the different dream interpretation methods that are used in an Islamic context. And finally, I will address the aforementioned different approaches I used in this book.

## Methodological Issues in Dream Work

In chapters 3, 4, 5, and 6, the reader will encounter transcriptions of interviews, collected dream data from direct and indirect contact with dreamers, reports, trial transcripts, dream narratives, and dream rhetorics. In working with people's dreams, the dream researcher needs to be aware of several methodological issues.

### Access

There are issues of access to the hinterlands of the imaginative self. Dream researchers need to be aware of the how dreams are transformed into oral and written texts and contingent meanings. A process of transformation exists between the perceived internal image—the dream image—of the dreamer and its translation into a social and personal meaning for the individual dreamer. Therefore, the researcher needs to pay attention, not only to the dream and its perceived interpretation, but also to this individual process of transformation.

### Dream Interpretation Consists of Several Stages

There is the dreamer's recollection of the dream and subsequently the filtering of the original imagery into what Kracke (1987: 36) describes as "language-centred thought processes." This filtration of imagery into thought is an act of translation, which begins the construction of meaning. It does this by relating the visual imagery to the cognitive categories of the dreamer's culture. Such cognitive categories carry implicit ways of ordering and sequencing time and space, person and action that inevitably begin to define and delimit the possible readings of the text or narration. Hence, the dream researcher needs to be aware of the stages of interpretation as well as the socio-cultural influences on that interpretation process.

## Socio-cultural Considerations

Brown (1987) showed how the Sambian people of New Guinea sorted their dream imagery into three kinds—public, private, and sexual—and so related them differently and to different people depending on the kind of imagery. In this sense, the dream and its presentation cannot strictly be isolated from the social context in which they arise.

Certainly, almost all humans think imaginatively, remember, and daydream in pictures on occasions. REM sleep studies have demonstrated that all humans dream each night. Moreover, all cultures have distinctive approaches to understanding their night dream imagery, from the general forgetfulness of the Western perspective—with the exception of some psychoanalytical practitioners—to the common spiritual approaches found in religions such as Islam, Tibetan Buddhism, and Hinduism, which all grant some dreams a superior ontological status to that of daytime reality. Hence, the dream researcher needs to take the specific socio-cultural and religious background of his research topic into account.

## The Validity of Imaginative Accounts

As we already encountered in chapter 1, and will become even more clear in this book's section on militant jihadism, dreamwork research needs to critically assess the validity of imaginative accounts. However, one does not need to discount their overall integrity. Validity in dreamwork research refers to the authenticity of the attribution of cognitive meaning to visual experience, rather than in the authenticity of the reported dream image. The reported dream or daydream image is never precisely accessible, but some of the most dangerous situations in the world today are partly generated and sustained by peoples' belief in reported dream accounts. Imagination and dreaming are a part of our cultural experience, and we need to overcome some of the perceived problems in relation to traditional ideas of validity, for otherwise the qualitative research enterprise will be limited. Failure to include such a significant subject in the qualitative research enterprise will surely limit our understanding of different cultures and their motivational wellsprings. The fact that Moussaoui's trial transcript shows how his dreams (and bin Laden's interpretations of them) moved him from someone contemplating militant jihad to actually embarking on such a violent enterprise may appear very otherworldly to some positivistic researchers. However, in light of my research's evidence, such inner imaginative decision making does occur and is highly congruent with broader Islamic theological perspectives on the possibility of humans experiencing truly divine dreams that change their lives and the lives of those around them.

## Representativeness and Extrapolation of the Data

How representative are dream images and their participants' and researchers' understanding of them? Although my studies do not claim to offer a definitive account of the attitudes to dreaming of all Muslims, they do offer an indication of the *kinds of issues* that can be addressed and the *possible repertoire of perspectives* about dreaming and its relationship to reality that are likely to be found among Muslims in general. However, as a researcher I need to be cautious to extrapolate specific data obtained in specific geographical parts of the world.

So, it is not the representativeness of the hidden dream or day image that is the issue, but rather how representative is the social, cultural, religious, and personal interpretation of the dream. And that is evident from the reported dream narratives and the observed actions of the dreamer. From the wide range that my data and studies cover—geographically, subject-wise, and methodologically—I might argue that most Muslims are oriented to understanding night dreams within the Islamic tripartite perspective of true, false, and meaningless dreams.

## The Influence of Group Dynamics

Group dynamics is an important issue the researcher needs to consider when he or she evaluates groups in which dreams are discussed. The Prophet Muhammed is said to have started the day asking who has had an important dream (Lamoreaux 2002). Fisk reports a similar phenomenon regarding Osama bin Laden and his followers (2005: 34–35). The dynamic interactions and concealed and revealed expectations held by group members and their leaders are crucial to what is said and how it is heard, explained, and remembered.

## Power Strategies behind Dream Reports

The narrative of the dream can be significantly different from the original experience of the dream material. As we mentioned above, even in its remembering, the dream imagery is processed into the categories and forms of our culturally constructed existence. Moreover, a dreamer can, consciously or subconsciously, incorporate all kinds of strategies that might interfere with an accurate account of the dream material: association, embellishment, censorship, the desire for privacy and exhibition, all of which influence the rhetorical rendering of the tale of the dream. Also, the dynamics of the dream audience—the degree of trust, prior friendship, shared values, and length of time together—all contribute to the "narrating" and hence the "narrative" itself. Therefore, the researcher needs to be aware of the fact that there is no final or original or definitive dream text, but rather one of many possible renderings in a powerfully defining group and cultural context.

## The Environment In Which the Dream Account Is Given

Trust and confidentiality are key to a dreamer's emotional openness, without which, little of interest will emerge. Safety through emotional trusting is all. Safety, trust, and confidentiality are to be considered, not only when using primary sources, but also when making use of secondary sources. To whom did the dreamer tell his or her story, and what was the setting in which the account was given? Hence, the researcher needs to consider the overall ethics of the approaches.

## The Researcher's Attitude

I have already indicated that the development of trust and the creation of strong feelings of safety are paramount in dream research. The bona fide attitude of the researcher comes across to the research subject. The researcher needs to show respect for the value of the dream. Sensitivity to personal self-disclosure is necessary. Often, I have found that respondents will only tell you their most significant dreams once a special rapport and trust is developed. For instance, in chapter one, we encountered an art historian who told me her dreams of the Prophet Muhammed and of angels. She only told them to me after dinner, and said beforehand that she had only previously told them to her family. In Islam, it is a sin to lie about a dream. Also the hadiths advise people only to tell their good dreams to those they love and trust. In such case, self-presentation can be very important. Sometimes the willingness to share one's own dreams is crucial, both with respect to developing trust but also to experience a different perspective. The latter I clearly acknowledged in the early stages of my fieldwork, when a Muslim religious scholar interpreted one of my own dreams in a radically different manner than I expected: It made me realize how directive dream interpretation was in Islamic culture compared to the more facilitative approach usually found in the West. Moreover, I found particularly in my studies of *Istikhara*, Islamic dream incubation, that part of the process of decision making will not be disclosed to the researcher if he has no knowledge of or skill in dreams and dream interpretation. The influence of those involved in such choices, particularly mothers, daughters, and imams/*pirs* on *Istikhara* dream interpretations is little studied, perhaps for those reasons.

## Dream Interpretation Methods in Islam

The methods used in Islam to interpret a dream are extremely complex and consist of several different considerations.

### The Status of the Interpreter

In Islam, officially only a prophet—preferably Muhammed—is thought able to precisely interpret a dream, especially a true dream (*al-ruya*). Therefore, most of the lore of dream interpretation in Islam is based on the teachings of the Qur'an and the hadiths. However, there are many versions of the hadiths and only certain ones are considered highly reliable (e.g., Bukhari).

The first principle of dream interpretation is that it is permissible for others besides the Prophet to interpret dreams. However, when others interpret dreams, such as shaykhs, they run the risk of disagreeing among themselves. Hence, interpreting a dream is a tricky business. Therefore, the fourth principle of dream interpretation states that the interpretations of ordinary humans—i.e., in contradistinction to prophets—are no more than educated guesses, based on knowledge of symbols. Even the great interpreters such as Ibn Sirin would sometimes be unable to interpret a dream. The apocryphal story of the dreamer in the Middle Ages in Damascus who had a dream and went to the twenty-four best dream interpreters for an interpretation, only to find they all gave a different interpretation and they all came true, is a salutary reminder of just how difficult a business dream interpretation is.

However, in my research I have found that in daily life, many interpreters of dreams exist. *Istikhara* is practiced in many Muslim communities. Also, popular dream dictionaries provide categories and classifications of dream interpretation, from literal and symbolic dream interpretation based on the Qur'an and the hadiths to lists of dream symbols. Little, if anything, is known about how imams interpret dreams in the United Kingdom. There is little doubt though, that UK imams will interpret dreams within the Islamic dream interpretation tradition as a whole.

## Status of the Dream

The second principle of dream interpretation is that only good dreams may be interpreted. Islam knows a tripartite classification of dreams: either true, false, or meaningless. A dream of the Prophet Muhammed is always assumed to be a true dream, subject to the preceeding proviso. False dreams and meaningless dreams are left uninterpreted. After a false dream from *Shatan,* the dreamer is bidden to spit three times to his left and pray to Allah.

The third principle of dream interpretation in Islam is that good dreams should be interpreted positively. In order to secure this principle, the Prophet Muhammed ordered that dreams could only be interpreted by scholars or loved ones. It is the responsibility of the dreamer to only tell his dream to those who are most likely to give it a positive interpretation.

## The Status of the Dreamer

The meaning of a dream is contingent upon a host of factors, particularly the characteristics and spiritual development of the dreamer himself. In regard to the dreamer's actions in real life, the fourth principle of Islamic dream interpretation states that the dreamer is permitted to carry out in real life what he has seen as good in the dream.

## Mode of Interpretation

In contradistinction with Western dream interpretation, Islamic dream interpretation is much more scripturally based and therefore more directive towards the dreamer. Also, the manifest content of the dream often leads to a very straightforward and literal interpretation. Moreover, some dreams are better left alone and not interpreted at all (false and meaningless dreams). However, to establish whether a dream needs interpretation, the key directive is that it cannot advocate immoral action as defined by the Qur'an and the hadiths.

## Methods Used in This Book: An Overview

Most of the research for this book has been conducted between the years 2004 and 2008. In order to obtain an overview of the various dream forms that exist in Islam, I not only chose to look at different forms of dream interpretation but also researched the influence of geographical location and social context. It is with great joy that, during these years, I conducted extensive fieldwork in the United Kingdom, United States, Pakistan, Turkey, Northern Cyprus, and Bosnia. During this fieldwork, I interviewed Muslims from all walks of life. Usually I used semi-structured interviewing methods and adopted a serendipitous sampling procedure. I regularly interviewed members of a Sufi Nasqbandi order before and after their *Zikr*, and met their imam again in Northern Cyprus, where I interviewed Shaykh Nazim. Shaykh Nazim had become of interest to me, because he was seen in dreams by many of his followers (as I learned during my research in the United Kingdom).

I found that Muslims, once they knew of my interest in dreaming, would generally happily share their dreams and their interpretations. Because of the Muslim enjoinder only to share their dreams with someone they trust and who has knowledge, I was privileged to be so seen, especially as I was introduced and hence perceived as a researcher with a genuine interest in Islam and its dreaming tradition. As a result of my extensive fieldwork, I am pleased to have obtained primary data that offers a set of information that is credible and consistent with the findings of other Islamic dream-focused researchers. Below, I will address the research methods I used while studying *Istikhara*, Sufism, militant jihadism, and the role of dreams in the al-Qaeda 9/11 attacks and the foundation of the Taliban leadership in Afghanistan. Moreover, in chapters 1, 7, and 8, I used different comparative methods, which I will discuss below. However, first, it is important to stress certain general methodological remarks about studying the dream in Islam as a Western non-Muslim scholar.

## Inherent Limitations

From the eleventh century onwards, European Western scholars have developed an interest in the languages, texts, and religious experiences of Islam. Since the twentieth century, the social sciences and religious studies have given strong and new impulses to Islamic research. However, the enormous growth of factual knowledge about Islam has sometimes led to prejudices due to misinterpretations and one-dimensional evaluations of Muslim life. Some of these prejudices and misinterpretations have led to the current negative Western attitude towards Islam.

In this book, I have tried to stay away from the complexity that characterizes Islam today, without simplifying the subject of the dream. There are over seventy officially recognized Muslim sects, and their members live all over the world and speak many different languages. This book covers different geographical areas: the United Kingdom, Pakistan, Turkey, Northern Cyprus, and Bosnia. Also, it alludes to Western forms of Sufism in the United States. It is important to realize that religious experiences concerning dreams as well as people's values regarding the dream might be very different in these different social contexts. In order to do justice to the complexity of the Muslim dream experience, more in-depth research is needed in the economic, political, social, ethnic, and cultural aspects of the diverse forms of Muslim life. For the purpose of this book, however, I have limited myself to focus on people's accounts of their dream experiences, how they perceive the dream might be interpreted according to Islamic tradition, and the direct influence these dreams and interpretations have had on the course of their lives.

Second, my knowledge of the Arabic language is limited. Therefore, I have either relied upon others or have used translations of the Qur'an and hadiths, of which the reader can find an account in the bibliography. I am very grateful to have experienced people's willingness to discuss certain aspects of the Prophet Muhammed's dream interpretation with me at length. For instance, in my work on dream dictionaries, I found Philip's evaluation of the legislative dream rather confusing, for in Western eyes many of these so-called legislative dreams contain no legal aspects or ruling. Discussions have made clear to me that part of the legislative aspect of the dream is the fact that the Prophet Muhammed understood them as statements about future events and that he took action based upon the dream content.

Third, especially in the United Kingdom, Pakistan, and Northern Cyprus, my research might be colored along gender lines. As a Western non-Muslim man, I experienced some difficulty in speaking freely to women about their dreams. Sometimes this difficulty was simply geographical: I stayed in different quarters (as is the case in my research with Shaykh Nazim). The few examples of female dream experiences that I can give in this book—with perhaps the exception of the *Istikhara* examples—came from Western Muslim women or from the wives of my initial informants.

A fourth inherent limitation is the fact that part of my research is established without being able to have direct contact with informants. Most clearly, this is the case with the 9/11 attackers, militant jihadists, and the section on Mullah Omar. Due to this lack of direct contact, certain limitations and risks need to be mentioned here. First, there is an inherent risk of distortion in communication. This distortion might occur intentionally or unintentionally. An example of the former might be the fact that certain newsgathering has its own political agenda and therefore has a stake in portraying certain facts according to their own interests. An example of an unintentional distortion might be an interviewer's interpretation of his interviewee's words, without checking whether he has rightly understood its contents. Also, in working with texts instead of living communities or individuals, one runs the risk of obtaining only part of the information. In itself, written material always is an interpretation and might not fully contain people's beliefs and practices. Moreover, a written account does not in itself have to reflect what people do in real life. Hence, if a researcher is not able to question one's subject directly, he runs the risk of missing crucial information that might shed light on certain specific aspects of the written text. However, as any other scholar working with texts, I have obtained a certain healthy text-critical attitude towards my sources, especially newspaper articles. However, this critical attitude does not have to lead to a total discarding of my sources. In working with these sources, I have adopted an emic perspective: without taking the source—the newspaper—at face value, I believe I can still work with the factual dream information it contains. This dream information often can be factually checked, like in the case of Richard Reid's last e-mails to his sister, Osama bin Laden's first video interview, and Zacarias Moussaoui's trial transcript. Hence, these reports can give us an excellent ethno-historical insight into the mind of these people and how their dreams developed into actions in reality.

In conclusion, my methodological approach, in which I use textual and source-critical analysis, interview techniques, participant observation, and ethnography in a multi-sited social context, has its risks. However, in the diversity of methods, one is able to compare communities, peoples, their ways of life as well as the role and function of their sacred texts. However, the multi-site, multi-source approach has a downside in its loss of descriptive detail of its diverse social contexts and material evidence. Hence, I have chosen to focus on the dream without an in-depth investigation into the religious and socioeconomic differences between participants, and have found that the Islamic dream tradition has significant similarities in the way the role and function of dreams is perceived. The main driver of this level of similarity is the Qur'an, which together with the hadiths witnesses to the Prophet Muhammed's conviction of the importance of dream awareness and interpretation.

Below, I will address the different methods used according to their subject matter. This section's function is to describe to the reader how I gathered my data, what different sources I used, and how these different sources are evaluated over against and alongside of one another.

## Istikhara

For the section on *Istikhara*, several research methods were used. First, a literature review provides the reader with the results and findings of current research in the topic of Islamic dream incubation. This review contains both Western and Muslim sources on *Istikhara*. Next, I analyze the textual sources, which guide Muslims to use *Istikhara* as a way of interpreting dreams. This textual analysis shows that neither the Qur'an nor the hadiths textually support the practice of *Istikhara* as dream incubation. However, the *Istikhara* prayer has developed into a practice that includes the interpretation of dreams. This practice then is connected to certain recommendations in the hadiths.

Next, I recount my experience of the BBC 4 radio program *Beyond Belief*, in which I and the other guests were asked to comment on a pre-recorded report of a UK woman who based her life decision of marriage choice on dreaming and *Istikhara*. Next, the reader finds a case-study into the semi-professional practice of a seventy-year-old *Istikhara* healer in Bosnia. From this interview it becomes clear that, even though major similarities in *Istikhara* practice can be observed in the United Kingdom, Pakistan, Turkey, and Bosnia, there are also differences. This interview and case study clearly demonstrate that at least in Bosnia, *Istikhara* is also used to ward off sorcery, a function I never encountered elsewhere. Moreover, I used serendipitous interviewing techniques in different social contexts. From this an image emerges of *Istikhara* being done on particularly marriage choice, job choice, and migration to another country. But also advice is asked in making business and political choices. More research needs to be done into the role of gender in *Istikhara* practice: from my data it surely is suggested that *Istikhara* is predominantly done by women. However, in the case of political and business decision-making, I have also found evidence that men do *Istikhara*.

## Sufism

My studies into dream interpretation in the Sufi tradition first focuses on a literature review on Sufism and its practices, of course with a special interest in the role and function of dreaming. This has led me into the Sufi tradition's history. My text-based historical study of the meaning of dreaming for Sufi thought gives examples of the importance of the dream for great Sufi-oriented philosophers like al-Ghazali and Ibn al-Arabi. Textual evidence is found in secondary sources and through the analysis of their hagiography.

Next, I briefly touch upon Sufism in the West, as I analyze a lecture given in London on the practice of the Golden Sufi Center in the United Kingdom. Similarly, I describe the Western "New Age" synthesis of Jungian dreamwork and Sufi practice in the Golden Sufi Center in the United States: a brief analysis is given of their main beliefs and practices with regard to Sufi orders, inherently demonstrating the radically different approach between these groups and more Islam-oriented Sufism.

This chapter next uses participant observation in a Sufi Naqsbandi order in a major UK city. I took part in their *zikr* and subsequent meetings,
both at the mosque and in their imam's private home. I extensively interviewed members of this Sufi group. Through this research I came across
the phenomenon of members dreaming about their shaykh, who resides
in Northern Cyprus. Thanks to a British Academy small research grant, I
was able to conduct further research into this phenomenon in Northern
Cyprus. At the community and home of the Naqsbandi leader Shaykh
Nazim, I conducted further interviews and used participant observation.
Also, I interviewed the shaykh directly, and not only did he give me his
opinion of dream interpretation, but his approach made me aware of the
differences in Muslim and Western dream interpretation, on which I will
elaborate in chapter 8 of this book.

## Militant Jihadism and the Dreams of Mullah Omar

My work on militant jihadism is based upon analysis of contemporary
websites and newspaper reports. In the former section on inherent limitations, I already touched upon the limits and risks of such an approach.
Text-critical analysis has been done in order to retrieve socio-religious
and motivational information from these sources. Next, this information
is critically evaluated over against secondary literature and other informed
sources on jihadist ideology. Thereby my main focus has been to evalu-
ate the role and function of dreams in the foundation, development, and
justification of jihadist thought.

In the chapter on Mullah Omar, I also analyze secondary sources that
report on the function of dreams in the life of Mullah Omar and his followers. Moreover, I critically assess the role dreams may have played in his
coming to power and the foundation of the Taliban. I base my research
on the reports of my main informants, Mariam abou Zahab and Rahimullah Yusufzai. Mariam abou Zahab is a French political scientist who has
extensively worked on these issues in both Pakistan and Afghanistan. She
put me in contact with Rahimullah Yusufzai, the BBC correspondent in
Peshawar, Pakistan, who was in direct contact with Mullah Omar and
whom I interviewed in Pakistan. This interview is used in transcription,
where after it is analyzed and contextualized through the use of contemporary literature on the subject.

## Dream Dictionaries

In my analysis of different dream dictionaries, I have chosen to focus on
the content more than on the form. I have used comparative analysis on

how these different dream dictionaries, which all have different geographical and social backgrounds, work with the Qur'an and the hadiths as the most insightful sources for dream interpretation. As a basis to explore the field of dream dictionaries I used Gouda's *Dreams and Their Meanings in the Old Arabic Tradition*. I extensively use the insights of this book throughout this whole study, as it was this book that made me aware of the existence of such an elaborate dream culture in Islam.

Three out of the six dream dictionaries analyzed describe themselves as standing in the tradition of Ibn Sirin. In the introduction, I already described the difficulties that are attached to such a reception. However, it is interesting to see how the three Ibn Sirin dictionaries have minor differences, not so much in interpretation, but more in structure, use of language, and emphasis of certain topics.

The dream dictionary published by British publishing house Dar al-Taqwa is the only one that stresses Ibn Sirin's "presumed" authorship, makes comparisons to dreamwork in Western psychology, and relates to the use of symbols in Christianity. Furthermore, this dictionary is sympathetic towards Sufism, which it considers the only satisfactory response to philosophical questions concerning inside and outside worlds. Hence, its elaborate introduction and sensitivity towards comparative traditions give the reader the impression that this dictionary is focused on a wider, possibly even non-Muslim audience.

The second Ibn Sirin dream dictionary, published by Pakistani Publishing House Darul-Ishaat, covers the same contents but uses more Arabic terms and seems to address a more specifically Muslim audience. Moreover, it contains chapters 26, 27, and 28, which according to the Dar al-Taqwa dictionary cannot be ascribed to Ibn Sirin.

The third dream book claiming to be authored by Ibn Sirin, published by Abdul Naeem in New Delhi, has many similarities to the other books but can be broadly compared to the Pakistani dictionary.

The three other books I further analyzed are; Fareed, *Authentic Interpretation of the Dreams, According to Quraan & Sunnah;* al-Jibaly, *The Dreamer's Handbook, Sleep Etiquette & Dream Interpretation in Light of the Sunnah,* and Philips, *Dream Interpretation according to the Qur'an and Sunnah.* Fareed's book on dream interpretation is highly polemical against Sufism, which he considers to have "exploited dreams enormously" (2003: 12). Also, his reasons for writing such a dream book are almost militant, using polemical language like "the banner of Sunnah is raised [in this era]" and writing on his hope to be rewarded "on the Day of Judgement" (2003:11). Also, the author seems to take a rigorous "Sunnah" view, in the sense that he appears only to accept dream interpretation on the basis of scripture: any interpretation not based on the Qur'an and

Sha'ria is considered invalid. An equally negative attitude towards Sufism is recognized in al-Jibaly's work, which is more than any other analyzed dream dictionary preoccupied with the act of sleeping and dreaming. An extensive part of the book contains sleep etiquette and getting ready to sleep. The work seems to stress the need of purification and cultivation (2006: xix), which basically rejects any innovations (*bid'ahs*). Hence, al-Jibaly's book seems to be in line with the inner Muslim polemics we find in Fareed. Finally, Philips's book wants to be the academic answer to dream interpretation books that claim authorship of Ibn Sirin. Moreover, he claims that Ibn Sirin never wrote a dream interpretation book. Philips ascribes authorship of the Ibn Sirin dream interpretation book to al-Akili. His conclusion is in great contrast to the reverence we encounter in the Ibn Sirin dictionaries: "*Ibn Seerin's Dictionary of Dreams* is not only un-authentic, it is misleading and cannot be relied upon by sincere Muslims for guidance" (2001: 11). The book focuses on the English-speaking world and wishes to provide "an authentic and comprehensive analysis of this intriguing subject [ i.e., the dream]" (2001: 8). In light of Philips's aspirations to provide the reader with what he believes is an authentic account of Islamic dream tradition, he assembles major hadith narrations on the topic.

Hence, it will be clear to the reader that, even though many similar stories from the Qur'an and the hadiths can be found in all dream dictionaries that I have studied, scrutiny is needed with regard to the socio-religious background of each individual dictionary. Having said that, I believe the analysis of the respective dream dictionaries can still be fruitful to retrieve an insight into the world of Islamic dreaming and the importance of the Qur'an and the hadiths in dream interpretation.

## Western and Muslim Dream Interpretation

In this chapter, I make a literature review of Western psychological and psychoanalytical theories of dream interpretation, particularly Freudian, neo-Freudian, Jungian, Gestalt, and the perspective taken by the Western dreamwork movement. I make a comparative analysis of these approaches with Islamic dream interpretive practices, highlighting significant differences partly through data collected from Muslims about their dreams, collected during my current studies.

From 1990–1995 I studied for a PhD in sociology and social anthropology (Edgar 1995) in which I co-led a weekly dreamwork group and subsequently made follow-up interviews with members to ascertain the impact of the dream group upon their lives. I remained a member of this group for a further four years, meeting regularly. I read Western dream interpretative theory widely. In this dreamwork group, we took a Western dreamwork movement perspective in which the dreamer is the interpreter of their dreams, aided and facilitated by the group members and leaders. Idiomatic punning and wordplay was found to be particularly efficacious in terms of discovering meaning from dream imagery by group members. From my extensive fieldwork studies of Sufism and *Istikhara*, I became aware that the dream culture(s) in Islam had significant differences and similarities to those of Western psychology. I was able to compare my practice within the Western paradigmatic dreamwork traditions with my participant observation and interview data about dreams from Islamic countries. With my theoretical and practitioner experience of Western dreamwork theory and practice, I was able to discern and compare the striking differences and similarities between Western and Islamic dream-work theory and practice.

꠹꠹ ꠹꠹ ꠹꠹

CHAPTER 3

# *Istikhara*

## *Islamic Dream Incubation*

An important part of dream lore in Islam is the (outside of the Islamic community) relatively little-known phenomena of *Istikhara*. *Istikhara* has one main practice with either a focus on consequent daytime guidance or guidance through dream symbolism. Different authors stress the importance of daytime guidance while others stress guidance experienced through dreams (Aydar 2009: 123–36; Gouda 1991: 7). In this chapter I am focusing on *Istikhara* as dream incubation and the dream's interpretation in the Islamic tradition. My recent studies of the role of night dreams in Islam (Edgar 2004b, 2006, 2007) has shown that *Istikhara* is a significant feature particularly in marriage choice but also sometimes in political and business decision making. Also, *Istikhara* was found in these studies to be practiced by young and old alike.

Pre-Islamic dream incubation practices, particularly for healing, occurred among the Ancient Greeks in their Aesclepian temples (Bulkeley 2008: 157–59; Aydar 2009: 125). Hippocrates and Galen, two of the most famous physicians of antiquity, were both trained in these dream incubation temples and wrote of the "medically predictive value of dreams" (Bulkeley 2008: 158).

Pnina Werbner, Keele University, learned about Sufi cosmology from a senior Sufi, Hajji Karim, a follower of the now deceased Naqshbandi shaykh, Zindapir. Here Karim talks about *Istikhara*:

> The *pir* [shaykh] knows if a person is ready to embark on the journey [spiritual ascent] just by looking at the person, he has inspiration or revelation from God (*ilham*); otherwise, he can seek *Istikhara*, indirect signs (a form of divination). There are two forms of *Istikhara*: either the Saint reads a passage from the Qur'an and then falls asleep. At the start of his sleep he sees colours and signs which he can interpret as positive or negative. Certain colours such as green and white are positive; others such as black, red, or yellow, are negative. The other method is to read the opening *Surah* [chapter] of the Qur'an and repeat the words (after the third or fourth line) again and

again while praying. In this wakeful repetition, the head will tilt to the left or the right and this will indicate whether the answer is positive or negative. (Werbner 2003: 193–94)

In this excerpt we see that a shaykh can perform *Istikhara* for a follower and the same use of color symbolism is made. Also prayer and reading from the Qur'an is used among the Shia. I have not encountered the divinatory method of reading the inclination of the head before. Interestingly, Werbner's studies confirm the central role of dreams and visions among Sufis and their shaykhs' reliance upon them:

His life, as told by him or about him by his disciples, has been the life of a friend of Allah, and as such it has been a life motivated by and moved teleologically through the guidance of divinely inspired dreams and visions. ... He [Zindapir] has been guided, like all Sufi Saints [major shayks] only by religious imperatives known to him through visions and dreams. (Werbner 2003: 61)

In his study of "Saints, Jnun (Jinn) and dreams" Crapanzo, a social anthropologist, (1975: 148–49) refers to the Moroccan practice of *Stikhara,* which refers to intentional dream incubation at a sacred site, such as a saint's tomb. He reports that such practices are important among members of the Hamadsha sect and ordinary Moroccans. Likewise, Nile Green (2003: 307) refers to the practice of *Istikhara* in Islam that is used both by Sufis and ordinary pilgrims, which entailed dream incubation, sleeping at tombs, and performing the aforementioned cycle of special prayers. Also, Shaw (1992: 47) refers to the Temne people of northeastern Sierra Leone's use of *Istikhara* (called the *an-Listikhaar*). There an Islamic dream diviner

constructs an Islamic amulet or simply writes a passage from the Qur'an together with the client's name on a piece of paper, and prays to Allah for the solution to the client's problem before going to sleep with his head resting on the written sheet. The answer is revealed in the diviner's dreams.

In his study of the Tukolor weavers in Senegal and their reported inspiration through dreams in their craftwork, Dilley (1992) also describes the *Istikhara* practice (here called *Listikhaar*). The learned Islamic clerics are called *marabouts.* Dilley describes this practice thus:

A person concerned over a family or personal matter might consult a marabout who practices *Listikhaar.* The client reveals his problem to him and requests that it be addressed to Allah through his intermediary, the marabout. The marabout then uses specified procedures to evoke dreams during a night retreat after the consultation with his client. He first prepares himself by performing ritual ablutions, offering up prayers and reciting his client's request that evening before he finally falls asleep. During the night it is said that a dream which contains guidance over the client's problem comes to the marabout, making it known whether his prayers have been granted or not. (1992: 74–75)

Aydar describes the essence of *Istikhara:*

In such cases [where a Muslim is unsure as to the correct action to take] people frequently ask God to send them a sign concerning the outcome. Then they pray and go to sleep. If they see the colours white or green in their dream, or important religious personages, or envision peace and tranquillity, or pleasant, beneficial or beautiful things, then they decide that the waking life action will be beneficial and they undertake it with an easy heart. If they see the colours black, yellow or red, or an unpleasant type of person, or things that make them uneasy or which are ugly, then they decide that this action is not beneficial and they forgo performing it. (2009: 123)

Aydar (2009: 126) reports that in several hadiths, including Bukhari (for a fuller list see Aydin 2009: 134), it is said that the Prophet Muhammed taught his companions the *Istikhara* prayer and recommended it to them. The Bukhari reference (vol. 8, book 75, no. 391), according to Aydar (2009: 126), is based upon the hadith of Jabir b. Abdillah that refers to the Prophet's teaching of *Istikhara* to his companions. Aydar is clear though that this original definition and recommendation by the Prophet to undertake *Istikhara* does not include dreams, rather the two additional nighttime prayers and then the following supplication:

My God, I entreat you to show me through knowledge that which is blessed for me. I entreat you to give me strength; your strength is enough for everything. I entreat You for the grace and favor of showing me which way is the blessed way; you are all omnipotent, I am powerless; you are omniscient, I am ignorant. You know all the secrets of the unknown. My God, if the result of [the task is here stated] is of those that are beneficial for my religion, my life and my afterlife then make it easy for me and destine it. My God, if the result of [the task here stated] is of those that are harmful for my religion, life and afterlife, then make me turn away from it. Wherever it may be, predestine for me that which is beneficial. Then make me satisfied with the benefit.

Aydar further reports that given the Prophet's recommendation to undertake *Istikhara,* then it is a Sunnah action (Prophetic example) to be undertaken before embarking on any enterprise (2009: 192). Interestingly, Aydar reports that in 1991 he was considering marriage to a particular young woman. The family asked their shaykh to perform *Istikhara* for them, and on the basis of that *Istikhara,* refused his marriage request! Aydar then describes the psychological benefits of performing *Istikhara:* in following the advice of an *Istikhara* experience, the person gains confidence in their choice of action, and (as we know through the idea of the

self-fulfilling prophecy) a positive approach to any endeavor may benefi-
cially effect the outcome. Finally, having confirmed the very widespread
use of *Istikhara* across Islamic countries, Aydar writes that the dream version of *Istikhara* is not specifically sanctioned in "true religious sources,"
by which I take him to mean the Qur'an and the strongest hadiths, such
as Bukhari and Muslim. Yet, according to Aydar (2009: 133), the dream
version of *Istikhara* is the result of "additional beliefs and cultural practices incorporated into its practice."

As we have seen above, *Istikhara* involves reciting special ritual prayers
before going to bed and meditation upon life choices before sleeping.
One Pakistani woman in the United Kingdom did *Istikhara* about her
daughter's future marriage and dreamed of a good-looking bowl of dates,
which, however, did not taste very nice. She reported how this imagery
anticipated the outcome of the marriage. A Pakistani female student in
her twenties studying in the United Kingdom told me how she did *Istikhara* to finally make a marriage choice. Her parents were opposed to the
marriage, but she had known him for five years and was keen to continue
the relationship. Her two friends and her mother also did *Istikhara,* as did
a male family friend in the United States. The student dreamed of losing
control of her car and crashing into the side of the mountain on the way
to a hill station in bad weather. This nightmare experience and the other
negative dreams and feelings of her friends and family convinced her that
she shouldn't marry this man. Likewise, regarding her brother's marriage,
her grandmother did *Istikhara* and dreamed of her brother and his potential bride in a field with the woman wearing a green bridal scarf. This
dream image was seen as a good sign, and the marriage went ahead.

The following example, from my study, is of a daughter (grand-
daughter of an ex-leader of an Islamic country) talking of her father's use
of *Istikhara* concerning a business deal, when making a big investment
with rather unknown people. After doing *Istikhara,* he dreamed of

> a large white cake that was cut into pieces: as white is a good color and had
> a happy feeling, he went ahead with the investment. Halfway through the
> investment, people turned out to be too clever; he had invested a lot of
> money and they were wondering if it had been a good investment. When
> the money was returned, it was much more than was expected; there was a
> rocky period, but it came out well eventually.

One of my main informants in Pakistan, Rahimullah Yusufzai, was
asked to perform *Istikhara* before he finally decided whether to accept a
cabinet job in the newly formed government of the North West Frontier
Province in Pakistan. He did *Istikhara* and then finally refused the post
(see interview with him in chapter 6).

Another example is of a young woman's mother who did *Istikhara* about a marriage proposal, which is a common practice among Muslims in Pakistan and also in the United Kingdom among Pakistani Muslims:

> My mother did Istikhara for her cousin; there was a proposal and she wanted to see: in her dream she saw a festive occasion and her daughter is standing in front of a pot of milk and you know, white is good; but my cousin was actually pouring this red liquid juice into it so there was a catch in it; eventually the whole pot turned; the marriage didn't happen and later they found out that he didn't come from such a good or nice family. Allen also reports that salat al Istikhara (prayer of proper guidance) is commonplace amongst Palestinian refugees in Shatil refugee camps (Edgar 2006: 28).

*Istikhara* may be perceived as particularly efficacious if the dream imagery seems to actually show a vision of the future; such a case was reported on the BBC 4 radio program *Beyond Belief* on 23 March 2009 in which a Muslim woman in her early thirties reported that she had done *Istikhara* after two previous marriages had not worked out and she was dating a man with whom she did not have a first language in common. She wanted to marry again, but was very worried about it not working once more. She did *Istikhara* for several nights about possibly marrying this man and had three significant dreams. In the first dream she actually "saw" herself getting married to this man and receiving a gift of salt and pepper pots that were shaped like inverted commas and fitted very well together. The second dream was in her kitchen, washing up, and her husband came and gave her a hug. After this dream she felt very reassured, as the dream took place in her kitchen. The third dream "showed" the couple in a flat, getting ready for Friday prayer with two children, a girl with plaited hair and a boy. She decided to get married after this succession of positive dreams and said that over the last ten years, the marriage had improved every day. They now had three children, and the *Istikhara* dreams had helped her make the "leap of faith" into marriage with confidence. She had not properly been able to get to know him because of language issues, but after the *Istikhara* dreams, she felt she had to marry him.

Such a narrative of marital success after very clearly optimistic dreams of their future life together is impressive and difficult to simply rationalize as being solely the product of an optimistic personality and very anxious previous marital reality. Clearly, this woman had a vested interest in a successful outcome to her search for a compatible husband. Hence, these significant dreams might be seen as either a form of unconscious wish fulfillment or the vagaries of imaginative chance. However, we also see from her report that future events and prior dreamed realities appear to have a congruence. Therefore, the dream might have inspired her to make a very positive future marriage situation.

## Case Study from Sarajevo, Bosnia[1]

In this case study I describe *Istikhara* as practiced by a seventy-year-old woman, living in Sarajevo in 2009, who was "called" to practice *Istikhara* at the age of fifty-three through dream messages that she received from a young and handsome man of approximately twenty-five years old. This case study emerged out of an extended case study conducted during field-work and arose via serendipity and snowballing techniques. Bringa (1995: 215) briefly refers to this traditional healing and divinatory practice.

Sadeta was dressed in slightly shabby, modest blouse and skirt. She was a friend of the landlord we were staying with, and he contacted her after I gave a short introduction about Islam and dreaming on Bosnian Federation morning television. Sadeta was very friendly, with a smiling, happy face and very good eye contact. She seemed a happy and very gen-uine person, did not ask for money although I later pressed her to take a small amount to cover her bus fare in Sarajevo. She said she did *Istikhara* without charging money but accepted gifts of money. An imam who had told her she had a gift from Allah told her to do *Istikhara* for others and gave her two books to work with: a guide to Qur'anic healing and one for *Istikhara* practice.

In dreams Sadeta had been called, arguably similarly to shamanic dream calling examples, to be a Qur'anic and *Istikhara* dream healer. She said:

> I dreamed, dreamed a lot and I didn't know the meaning "why" I had been dreaming. Therefore I went to visit one well-educated imam whom I told about my dreams.

Sadeta practiced two types of Islamic healing, saying specific prayers from the Qur'an for conditions such as exam nerves, as the interview took place during the exam season:

> It depends, case from case, as to what is needed. This doesn't mean a medi-cal curing but curing with the Qur'an. In this book [giving specific guidance concerning reading specific Qur'anic verses for specific medical conditions] I usually find what is needed and then I take the Qur'an and pray with the Qur'an. Look at this book, you can see which prayers are appropriate for particular illnesses. For example, nowadays I am very busy because many young people are preparing for their exams, and they might be very nervous and lacking in confidence. But that's [Qur'anic healing] something when you can't drink any pill to calm you, otherwise you would be sleepy and so on. Ehh, and now, I do pray for them to lose their nervousness, to liberate themselves, and success, to pass the exams. However, it can't help every-body, only for those who believe that I have such a capacity to help. Look at the books, they are small; I find later in Qur'an "the number" referred to in the book and "how many times" it is necessary to pray the particular prayer. Afterwards I'll take the Qur'an and do the prayer.

Belief in the efficacy of the healer, Sadeta, and the Islamic faith are both apparently indispensable requirements for successful healing to take place. The healing is done from Allah, and Sadeta is a vehicle for this form of divine grace.

She prayed for her clients on certain days and times of her own choosing:

> I do it alone. And why? Because when you pray to Allah, I could pray all day but God couldn't receive my prayers. Therefore, I ask God, between Akšam and Jacija. Akšam [fourth daily prayer] is now about 8:30 PM and Jacija [fifth daily prayer] about 10:30 PM, and between the two prayers I do remember the complete name of the one I am praying for and then the particular prayer. And again the following morning when I do pray Sabah [first morning prayer]; I do it again because I don't know whether God wants to receive my prayers or not. It isn't like doing shopping when you take a loaf of bread and the work is done. Therefore I usually repeat everything two or three times to make sure that God will help, but I can't guarantee 100 percent success. But I have success, thanks to Allah. I do not advertise myself anywhere, neither in newspapers nor on radio as many others do. Nothing like this. People just come and I am glad that God helps and still I have a lot of work to do.

Sadeta also does *Istikhara* using another little book given her by the imam. Sadeta describes doing *Istikhara:*

> Ehh, to pray *Istikhara*, I have another book, look. Do you know how to pray *Istikhara*? You have to wake up during the night, about 1:00 AM and you pray a "nonobligatory" prayer, nonobligatory because we [Muslims] have to pray five times a day, but you pray *Istikhara*. When I do pray the prayer, I remember the person I am praying for and subsequently I go to sleep. Moreover, I do remember the prayer and the person I prayed for again while I am already lying in my bed. And then I do dream, but the dream has to be interpreted later on.

Sadeta usually dreams after undertaking her prayer practice:

> Yes, I usually have a dream. It might happen that I don't have one, but it's rare. Sometimes, the meaning of a dream is rather unclear and has to be interpreted. For example, "a house": the nice house with flowers around might symbolize organizing the *mevlud* [special prayer honoring the birth of the Prophet Muhammed or for a special celebratory occasion] prayer at home; for somebody without success or with problems, so the message of the dream might be for example to slaughter *kurban* [sacrifical ram/sheep] and to give food to people. Or sometimes I do dream and the interpretation is that I have to pray the sura "Yusuf," ehh, Yusuf suffered a lot in his life—so if someone suffers like Yusuf than I do pray the sura "Yusuf," but there is written [in the book] how many times I have to pray the sura.

Sadeta gives examples of her *Istikhara* practice:

Ehh, one young woman asked me for Istikhara, she gave me her name and surname. I dreamed about a house (she didn't tell me where she lives), I came [in the dream] in front of a house, I see a house with two entrances. When I've entered the house I see a small, wild garden and there were lambs and sheep. While I was in the garden I heard a voice saying: "I am interested in the young woman, I want to marry her, she will have much happiness in her life." When I told her about the dream, she said that her boyfriend has the same house. So, it means their fate is to stay together. Moreover, sheep and lambs are usually slaughtered during such an occasion like a marriage; and also wool makes life easy so everything was beautiful in the dream.

Sometimes the interpretation of a dream might be sorcery. One woman had a flat in Sarajevo and she bought a door, but she couldn't place it properly; it was impossible. Therefore, I did pray Istikhara for her; I dreamed. It's very bad when you dream like this, that in front of the door someone hooked an ox. And now, I see an ox clearly, I see his meat is rotting, it isn't good. So, when I dreamed about the rotting ox, the dream itself was terrible, I told her—you have to dig up the threshold and the doorframe, there has to be *sihir* [sorcery]. Moreover, I had to pray various prayers against the evil powers for her to protect herself. I got a special prayer from one *hafiz* [educated Muslim who knows the Qur'an by heart] and it needs to be prayed thirty-seven times. When the woman had dug up the threshold around the door, she found everything that you can imagine [sorcery items].

Sadeta started to dream in 1990, her dream guide being a young, handsome man dressed in white. She does not know him but thinks he may be a former, now deceased, *shahida* (martyr):

I started to dream in 1990 in the flat that I now live in. I have lived in about five flats during my life, before, during and after the war; in one flat I lived for more than eighteen years, but I do *Istikhara* dreaming only in this one flat. No one else has dreamt *Istikhara* in the flat.

I've dreamed about a young man aged twenty-five to thirty, very nice, in a white shirt, and he tells me what I have to do, to help people, to heal people. And this has been since the very beginning. What is interesting is that I do dream only in the kitchen, not in other rooms. It's unbelievable but during the war, everything was damaged roundabout, except for my flat where even the windows stayed untouched. I couldn't believe it. What is there, in the flat, I don't know. I didn't pray *Istikhara* before; it happened when I told other people about my dreams. They explained to me that I could have the capacity for dreaming *Istikhara* and healing.

Sadeta continues talking about her dream guide and the beginnings of her *Istikhara* practice:

I call him *momak* [young man] because he looks like that. When I've asked other people and described him, I was told that it means something good. According to some interpretations, he might be a martyr who had died there, and look what happened when I had moved to the flat?

People who came back from Hajj usually brought yellow *abaniya* [scarf] with them, and I dreamed about the young man who told me that I have to put on *abaniya*, to veil myself and go to the mosque to pray. After a discussion with my husband, I didn't pay attention to the dream. However, I dreamed the same dream again and again, the young man didn't calm me down until I followed him and the dream message about wearing the scarf. Therefore I asked for an *abaniya* from one old *hajji* [one who has preformed the Hajj pilgrimage to Mecca]. He couldn't give it to me because when a *hajji* dies then he is covered by his/her *abaniya*. But he lent it to me. Later on, one woman when she heard about my dreams decided to give such a scarf to me. Yet another woman gave one to me. Unfortunately, I left the *abaniya* in the flat when the war started, and when I returned to the flat after the war, I couldn't find them. Anyway, since I had the first *abaniya* and went to the mosque to pray, I haven't had the dream any more.

And when I pray *Istikhara* I do usually dream about the young man who is telling me what should I do.

Sadeta is confident about her success with her *Istikhara* practice but admits to the occasional failure:

Sometimes I dream about a good marriage, and later people divorce. It's possible, of course. I, for example, dreamed about *rozmarin* [flower usually used for wedding flowers], and the woman I had dreamed for later divorced her husband. But in most cases, I am successful.

What happened to me, just one example. I dreamed for one woman, she met a man who was a widower and the woman wanted to marry him. So she told me "Sadeta, please, pray *Istikhara* for me," as to whether she could marry the man or not; whether she would be happy with the man or not. So I was dreaming that I entered into a house, or into a flat because the man lives in the flat. And in the flat I see three flowers, and now I was dreaming about the widower's dead wife and she was telling me, "I do not have anything about [against] the woman nor about the marriage but please"—she was showing me, holding in her hands the three flowers—"make sure that she will look after the flowers," and the flowers were very beautiful in my dream. I woke up, and told the dream to the woman; she had never entered the widower's flat before so she asked him about the flowers in his flat. He asked her to come to his flat to see that he had the flowers in the flat. She found the same flowers I dreamed about in my dream. They got married and have stayed happily together. So I mean, it might happen that I do make mistakes but also … !

Sadeta was asked how common the practice of *Istikhara* is in Sarajevo and when she does her practice:

It's rare, only a few people. There aren't many people. I pray *Istikhara* on Friday and Monday. Only these two nights and that is because, well, Friday is a given in Islam—it's an important day for Muslims so people usually ask for me to do *Istikhara* for them on a Friday, but also I do *yasine,* praying for the dead. And I do also pray *Istikhara* on Monday, which is a less-important day. I chose Monday because my father was an imam and I know that these two days are better than the other days in a week. Another reason why I do *Istikhara* only twice a week is that you have to wake up, and you can't be tired to do *Istikhara* otherwise you wouldn't probably have any dream, so I usually have to take a rest the day before to be fresh and ready.

### Sorcery and the fight against it is part of her practice:

It's spread now, a lot of people do it to other people. Jinns [often negative spirits in the Islamic cosmology] attack but not without reason. But people do *sihiri* [sorcery], make *sihiri*. Especially since the end of the war there has been a lot of *sihiri*, because of envy among people; a man attacks a woman, people attack the harmony and the well-being of other households. I don't know who does it, but there is a lot of *sihiri*. Maybe you won't believe it, but many women come to me, and they do often divorce.

This *Istikhara* was a good one. She had been engaged with a man for seven years. The man had wanted to marry her, but she didn't want to yet. Later on she had wanted to marry him, but he didn't want that. So her mother came to ask me for *Istikhara;* seven years they were engaged and everything I had dreamed about happened. I dreamed that she wouldn't marry him, but she will meet another man very soon and she will marry him and they will be happy. You can believe it or not. The following day I told the dream to her mother, and she said, "I can't tell her the dream, she is engaged for seven years and she really loves the man; please do pray *Istikhara* once more." And you can believe it or not, but the following dream was the same, a hundred per cent. Two months later, she met another man and she got married to him. They have a beautiful three-story house and two beautiful children. It couldn't be better. That's the complete truth.

Sadeta says she does not use the Qur'an to interpret dreams. Rather, she interprets them intuitively or sometimes asks a friend:

No, in most cases I understand my dreams and don't need it. But if I am not sure, I usually call to one woman to help me translate a dream; she doesn't do it for everybody, but she likes me and we help each other. I know for example that lambs and sheep in a dream means "goodness," but neither does the woman use the Qur'an, she just has the knowledge in her head.

Once I prayed *Istikhara* for a woman and I wasn't sure about the interpretation, so I asked my friend and she told me that I have to go to the woman's cottage and to pray at three places there a prayer and I did it. But usually I pray over water. I take a bottle of water, names and surnames of the respective people and pray over the water. Then you can wash yourself with the water, drink the water. I take the prayers from the Qur'an and pray.

### Finally, Sadeta describes the kinds of people she helps:

Educated, doctors, people from television, pop singers, more women than men.

## Discussion

Overall, Sadeta presented as a sincere and committed *Istikhara* healer in the Islamic tradition. Her practice was arguably simple, intuitive, and without recourse to Islamic dream interpretation books such as the ubiquitous (in Islamic countries and communities) Ibn Sirin volume for interpreting dream symbols. She did not refer to the Qur'an, and many if not most of the dream messages were from her perceived dream guide, the handsome young man. Auditory dream messages were commonplace, but sometimes human and nature symbols were interpreted as they might be symbolically experienced in reality, such as flowers, sheep, and houses: for example, sheep and lambs were a good sign of impending marriage, as such animals were slaughtered on such occasions. Sadeta was called to practice *Istikhara* through dreams. She could only do her practice in this one flat and led by one dream guide: a case of a perceived localized spirit of place perhaps! She presented her practice as generally successful but with occasional negative outcomes, such as divorce. Her practice was stressful as her experienced and interpreted dream messages could contradict the supplicants' conscious wishes—for instance, when she did *Istikhara* for a young female relative about a possible marriage but only dreamed of a successful university education for her (which later turned out to be the case in reality). Her practice of *Istikhara* generally seemed to be about marriage choice, a way to discern beneficial and long-lasting futures involving many unpredictable future events and possibilities. Her practice involved ritual times and place without wall hangings, special prayers, and with high levels of belief, commitment, and attention. She mainly claims to do *Istikhara* for educated and female clients, and compared herself favorably with unskilled *Istikhara* practitioners who advertised in local magazines such as *Aura*. She herself, her clients, and some imams saw her skill as an *Istikhara* practitioner as a gift from God/Allah. Her clients also experienced her practice as helpful in dealing with the upsurge of sorcery cases in Bosnia since the 1992–1995 war.

## Conclusion

While previously *Istikhara* practitioners I have encountered in the United Kingdom, Turkey, and Pakistan have only done *Istikhara* for themselves or their immediate family, Sadeta's example demonstrates that this practice is a kind of Islamic folk healing. Moreover, the prevalence of advertisements for *Istikhara* in popular magazines also shows that it is a popular form of indigenous, nonbiomedical, Islamic form of spiritual mental health healing or, at least, personal life choice guidance. The folk-healing practice of *Istikhara* also includes countering perceived sorcery and reestablishing personal well-being in a dangerous world in which the future is known only to Allah/God. *Istikhara* is the only sanctioned form of divination in Islam and is derived from a metaphysical and embodied epistemology of the human self constituted in part through the revelatory potential of the unconscious as known through night dreams. There are comparisons to be made with other forms of traditional folk and spirit-based healing traditions.

Overall, *Istikhara* in both its practice of daytime guidance and night dream interpretation appears to be a ubiquitous practice across many Islamic lands. However, there is almost a complete absence of scholarly analysis of this practice, and therefore apart from recommending further in-depth qualitative studies, it is impossible to be certain about how widespread, for example, this practice is currently among Islamic communities in Britain. From my interviewing of middle-class women in Pakistan, however, I would think that a study of marriage choice in contemporary Pakistan would be deficient without incorporating the study of associated *Istikhara* practices.

## Notes

1. I made the case study in Sarajevo with David Henig, whom I greatly thank.

&#x1F660;&#x2022; &#x1F660;&#x2022; &#x1F660;&#x2022;

CHAPTER 4

# Sufism and Dreaming

There is a long tradition in Sufism, the mystical way of Islam, of the inner guide, Friend of God, or shaykh who advises the seeker of his/her path of return to God. Sufi shaykhs are typically guided by true dreams (*al-ruya*). This guide can be found in the outer world and/or in the world of dreams. Sometimes the seeker will dream of their mystical Friend many years before actually meeting him, and then may carry on receiving guidance dreams. In Shia Islam, the inner guide is often one of the Twelve Imams, eleven of whom died and the twelfth, who disappeared, is Muhammed Al-Madhi, the hidden imam whose return "will announce the end of the cycle of our aion" (Corbin 1966: 385–87). Corbin describes such an inner guide as "the Gabriel of his being" (1966: 387), after the angel Gabriel who guided the Prophet Muhammed.

Sedgwick (2000: 9–10) defines Sufism as submission (*Islam* meaning "surrender") to Allah and his instructions, and "preparation for the Final Day." Specifically, Sufis attempt to control the *nafs* or Ego in order to open the heart to God. Stepping away from materialism allows the spiritual higher Self to emerge. There are at least forty different orders or *tariquas* of Sufism (see Trimingham 1971). Sedgwick (2000: 30) writes that "as recently as the nineteenth century, shaykhs have received the command to start a new order from the Prophet in a dream, which results in a relatively short documented lineage transmission (*silsila*)." Sedgwick (2000: 68) presents an example of how lineage transmission is accounted for by a dream. Muhammad ibn al-Sanusi (1787–1859) took over as shaykh of the Ahmadiyya Sufi order from its founder Ahmad ibn Idris (1760–1837) following a self-reported dream and went onto become a leading shaykh in parts of the Middle East and North Africa. In his study of Sufi orders, Trimingham (1971: 188) writes of the overwhelming and often decisive role of dreaming in Sufism:

> The importance of dreams and visions in the whole scheme of the Sufi path can hardly be overstressed; the literature of Sufism and the hagiographa in particular are full of them, and their significance in the life of individuals and

society. Ibn al-Arabi's *Al-Futuhat al-Makkiya* derives directly from such an experience and he shows how the decisive stages of his life were marked by dreams.

Al-Ghazali is one of the most prominent Islamic Sufi-oriented philosophers, who wrote about the differing kinds of knowledge experienced through the senses, the intellect, and through night dreams. Like Sviri (1997), al-Ghazali sees dreams as "tastes" (Ormsby 2008: 146) of the divine. Ormsby states that night dreams are the "poor man's prophecy" (2008: 142). The spiritual evolutionary aim for humankind is to develop the "inner eye" with which to "see" the invisible, and the night dream is a core potentiality for that evolution. Learning to see with the "heart" is the crucial aspect of this human journey to continual awareness of the divine. Perhaps the inner eye can "see" through the subtle "heart" center.

Ormsby translates from al-Ghazali's classic work, *Munqidh:*

> Just as the intellect is one of the human levels in which there exists an eye by which one sees types of intelligible things while the senses remain distant, so too is prophecy a term for a level in which there exists an eye possessed of a light in whose luminance the hidden is made visible together with other things unperceived by the intellect. (2008: 146)

For al-Ghazali, the human intellect is a guide to the potentially transcendental realm of sleep and dreaming (Ormsby 2008: 151). Moreover, he relies on dreams and visions of his own and trusted friends to make core decisions about his life course (Ormsby 2008: 147). Indeed, as Nile Green writes:

> To this day the interpretation of dreams forms one of the most important services expected from Sufi masters in many parts of the Muslim world, forming a style of Islamic psychoanalysis. Sufi masters regularly interrogate their disciples concerning their dream lives in *khanaq* as in Iran no less than Pakistan and Morocco. (2003: 297)

In my aforementioned fieldwork, I found similar views about the importance of dreams to the spiritual wayfarer expressed by various Muslims, especially Sufis. The heart, seen as a spiritual facility, is veiled from awareness and potential union with the divine by forty thousand veils, and the ideal Sufi shaykh is said to be the one who has developed, or been graced, to have a continual heart connection to Allah. Certainly, the followers of the Naqshbandi shaykh Nazim considered him in this way. A retired Pakistani nuclear physicist in Islamabad who ran an Islamic educational center described it to me as a matter of "tuning the heart" into the divine airwaves.

Sufism has become a part of the spiritual complexity of North America and Europe (Westerlund 2004). However, an order like the Bektashi has a long history in the Balkans (McElwain 2004: 95–108). It is not the intention of this book to specifically study and present an account of Sufism but rather to note the particular importance of night dream transmission and interpretation in many Sufi orders. Indeed, there is one contemporary Sufi center, near San Francisco, California, the Golden Sufi order, where a strong integration of Jungian dreamwork practice and Sufi heart meditation practices took place. There is also a Golden Sufi center in the United Kingdom. The US center was founded by Irina Tweedie, and her work has been continued above all by Llewellyn Vaughan-Lee (1998). Such centers espouse a form of Naqshbandi Sufism in which classical Islamic rituals are barely, if at all, present. The focus is on meditation, the silent *zikr* or *dhikr,* the inner repetition of the names of God/Allah, and on Jungian dreamwork. In such Western Sufi centers, Sufism is considered as an independent form of spiritual practice in which believers from all religions can participate. Indeed, I have heard Vaughan-Lee say that Sufism predates Islam. As Westerlund argues, "In studies of Sufism in a Western setting it is particularly important to differentiate between Islam-orientated and more universalistically focused forms of Sufism" (2004: 17). Westerlund argues that such forms of Euro-Sufism are characterized by low degrees of institutionalization and political focus and high degrees of individualism: an attractive mix in the "New Age" spiritual and religious supermarket.

The Sufi tradition understands true dreams as inner "tastes" (Sviri: 1997) of the divine. As in Jungian psychology, the dream is the potential connection between the unconscious and the conscious mind. So, in Sufism the imagination and especially the true dream is the bridge between the sensible world and the archetypal intelligible world. Sufism as the mystical path of Islam is replete with dream narratives. Spiritual growth is offered to the dreamer as he or she integrates such "big" dreams into their journey towards their higher self. Sviri recounts the exceptional narrative of at-Tirmidhi, a ninth-century seeker, whose wife's dreams are part of his personal odyssey. Sviri records several dreams of this husband and wife team. Here, I present the first two dreams to give a flavor of the role of dreams in one of the most famous Sufi's life:

> The love of solitude came into my heart. I would go out into the wilderness and wander in the ruins and graveyards around my town. This was my practice, and I kept it tirelessly. I was looking for true companions who would support me in this, but I found none. So I took refuge in ruins and in solitary places. One day, whilst in this state, I saw, as if in a dream, the Messenger of God, peace be upon him. He entered the Friday mosque of our town and I followed him closely step by step. He walked until he entered the *maqsura* (the section reserved for the dignitaries) and I followed, almost

cleaving to his back, stepping upon his very footsteps. ... Then he climbed up a pulpit, and so did I. Each step that he climbed, I climbed behind him. When he reached the uppermost step he sat down and I sat at his feet, on the step beneath him, my right side facing his face, my face facing the gates which lead to the market, and my left facing the people (in the mosque). I woke up in this position. (1997: 62–63)

This narrative can be read as reporting a day dream or vision. Hence, one of the issues in writing about specifically night dreams in Islam is that *al-ruya,* "true dream," in Arabic can refer to either a day vision or night dream. As the figure of the Prophet Muhammed is seen and followed in this dream, within the Islamic teaching this is seen as a true dream and is regarded as auspicious and a sign of spiritual progress, reflected in at-Tirmidhi's "physical" closeness to the Prophet.

There is no interpretation of this dream as the dreamer considers that the dream speaks for itself. In this second dream, at-Tirmidhi is overcome by a deep tiredness and then "puts his head on a prayer rug."

> I saw a huge and empty space, a wilderness unfamiliar to me. I saw a huge assembly with an embellished seat and a pitched canopy the clothing and covering of which I cannot describe. And as it was conveyed to me: "You are taken to your Lord." I entered through the veils and saw neither a person nor a form. But as I entered through the veils an (overwhelming) awe descended upon my heart. And in my dream I knew with certainty (*ayqantu*) that I was standing in front of Him (*bayna yadayhi*). After a while I found myself outside the veils. I stood by the opening of the (outer?) veil exclaiming: "He has forgiven me!" And I saw that my breath relaxed of the fear. (1997: 63–64)

Such a dream narrative describes the mystical experience of a perceived and apparent encounter with a God image in the dream state. In a later dream, at-Tirmidhi is given a divine mandate by Jesus and Muhammed Ahmad to be a "peg" in this world. In Sufism, there is thought to be an inner hierarchy of enlightened humans who sustain this world. The "pole" (*qutb*) is at the apex of this hierarchy while the pegs are a step below, responsible for areas of this world.

While most Sufis have teachers in this world, a minority believe themselves to be guided by teachers from within, who are sometimes deceased,. One such notable Sufi was Abd al-Ghani al-Nabulusi, 1641–1731, who believed himself guided through the figure of Ibn Arabi in his dreams. Sirriyeh reports that these experiences continued even until al-Nabulusi was eighty years old, when he reported experiencing a dream in which Ibn Arabi was eating breakfast with him near the Umayyad Mosque in Damascus (2005: 18). Al-Nabulusi wrote one of the most important of Islamic dream dictionaries, *Scented Sleep through the Interpretation of Dreams* (Taatirul Anam Fi Taabiril Manam). Lamoreaux, for instance, describes this dictionary as "one of the truly classic dream manuals" (2002: 103). However, Sirriyeh (2005: 71–72) evaluates it as unoriginal, except in its encyclopedic organization. Previously, Islamic dream dictionaries had been hierarchically organized with Allah, prophets, angels, etc. However, in Islamic countries, al-Nabulusi's dream encyclopedia still is a popular dream interpretation book. Overall, Sirriyeh notes that al-Nabulusi had the conviction that "the two worlds are one" and that which was "accomplished in the world of dream is as valid as, or may actually be more valid than, the actions of waking life" (Sirriyeh 2005: 57). Nile Green confirms this tradition:

> Sufis claimed to have been initiated into the mystical path not through the more usual and mundane mode of clasping the hand of a living master but through the means of a visionary initiatory encounter. Usually this visionary initiation would be with the enigmatic green-man of Islam, al Kidhr, or else with the Prophet himself. Two no lesser figures than Ibn Arabi and the great Indian Naqshbandi sufi Ahmad Sirhindi (d. 1624 AD) claimed initiations of this kind. (2003: 300)

Poets in Islam also seem to have a dream inspiration tradition. Mittermaier (2007) studied a contemporary Sufi-oriented group in Cairo led by their shaykh Salah al-Din al-Qousy, who kept a group book of dreams, visions, and poems. The shaykh's poems were inspired through his night dreams. Group members' visions/dreams were seen to confirm their shaykh's holy inspiration. Mittermaier (2007) writes of the powerful tradition and record of Muslim, and particularly Sufi, poets as having been inspired by dreams about their poetic composition, publication, and successful outcome. She quotes Kinberg (1994: 133) concerning Ibn Abi al-Dunya's ninth-century poetry, "poetry that has been transmitted in sleep and then was memorised."

Ewing (2006: 144) reports a similar tale of esoteric initiation and guidance of a Sufi shaykh. In her study of Pakistani Sufi shaykhs or *Pirs,* her main informant was Sufi Ghulam Rasul (Sahib). She came to realize that his initiation and his succession to the Khilafat (leadership of a Naqshbandi Sufi order) had all been experienced in night dreams. Sufi Sahib had only met his initiating shaykh, Mian Sher Muhammad, once when he was ten years old. Indeed, Ewing writes that "Sufi Sahib received some of his instructions while praying and sleeping at his (Mian Sher Muhammad) shrine" (Ewing 2006: 144). Interestingly, Ewing reports that Sufi Sahib promises her that he will come to her in a dream:

> But Sufi Sahid did as he had promised. At the time, I was living with Yasmin's family. That night I awoke in the middle of the night, so startled from

a dream that I sat upright. My awakening woke Yasmin, who was sleeping on a cot next to mine. I told her the dream, in which I had seen a white horse approach me. In the dream I had the clear sensation of something touching my thumb, which startled me awake. Yasmin declared that it had been the saint, just as he had promised. I marveled aloud at the power of suggestion, thereby placing the phenomenon immediately within a psychological interpretive scheme (i.e., that dreams come only from the dreamer's internal states) but was haunted by the odd sensation of the touch. A feeling of what Freud called the "uncanny" (Freud 1955b) washed over me. (Ewing 2006: 160)

Ewing writes at length about this experience and how it affected her (1994). She was particularly disoriented by the reactions of other people, including a Pakistani psychiatrist colleague, who took her dream report immensely seriously. This is reminiscent of Steve Lyon's experience in the introductory essay: he was also very surprised by how seriously his Pakistani friends took his night dream, in which he memorized and knew the Qur'an. This night dream experience of Ewing led her to question the anthropological tradition of observational skepticism with regard to data collection in the field. Based on this dream experience, she began to value the possibility that aspects of her informants' worldview could coexist with rigorous anthropological enquiry.

Sufis, particularly, seemed to inhabit an alternative mystical universe, coexisting with our understanding of this reality, in which very significant and often precognitive dream experiences of and by shaykhs/*pirs* and their followers were commonplace. Pnina Werbner, who has extensively studied Sufi groups in the United Kingdom and Pakistan, gives an example of a friend, crucially interpreting a dream in Pakistan, which leads to a Sufi conversion experience:

The story one *murid* [follower of a Sufi shaykh] whom I encountered hard at work with a team of builders building new modern flush toilets for the women's quarters, exemplifies this process [the liberating experience of a shaykh's guidance]. Mr Saghir had had a dream (*khuab*) in which he was building a stone wall in a place surrounded by hills, with a very beautiful mosque and garden. A *shaikh* came by while he was working and praised him. He did not know where the place was or who the *shaikh* was. He recounted the dream to his friend and the friend, already a *murid,* suggested that the person in the dream might be Zindapir [a major, now deceased Naqshbandi shaykh], the *shaikh* Ghamkol. So, the disciple told me, he came to Ghamkol Sharif and met the *shaikh,* and the first thing the *shaikh* asked him to do was to start building a wall. He realised then that this was the *shaikh* of his dream. So he became a *murid* and his whole village, located about thirty kilometres south of 'Pindi, all became *murids,* 500 strong. He was the first *murid* in his family (Werbner 2003: 154).

In the Summer of 2007, I met a Sufi at the International Association for the Study of Dreams Conference at Sonoma State University in California. I ate with his family, and he later sent me his story of his becoming a Sufi partly through synchronicitous dreams:

> In February of 1984, I attended a lecture series by Pir ——, head of a Californian Sufi order. I was particularly interested in his first lecture on the topic of dreams. ... That night I dreamed that I decided to be initiated by Pir ——. In the dream he explains to me the importance of what I am doing and the danger of breaking my vow to God and the spiritual path. Pir —— reads this to me from a text. We are outside in nature and there are two initiations. In the first he begins by saying he is pleased that I have made this decision. There are two women present and I'm told they are "recorders." It is an intermediary step I am taking because these women, Pir —— explains, are like "rivers of the unconscious" and I can still back out if I want to. The unconscious is the witness and I become aware of a vast underground river beneath where we are standing. My friend N., who introduced me to the Sufi community and who has been mentoring me in various practices, is standing to my right and is watching the proceedings with some dismay. He calls one of the women "Samya" and she replies "Why? I am not Samya." He says, "*Samya* means flowing, like a river." She then calls him "Samya" and says it means "donkey head, because you are stubborn." Pir —— then talks about a special sort of person—a Capricorn with certain other attributes. He says they are gifted because they are able to actualize certain spiritual values. He then gives me the second initiation. I forget what I am supposed to say and start to feel silly doing all of this. It's against my own religion to join things, and I feel as if I am giving up part of my basic freedom. On the one hand, it feels like I'm not giving up part of my basic freedom. On the other hand, it feels like I'm not giving anything up but rather acknowledging what is already true.
>
> In a later dream Pir —— reappears, stressing to me the importance of not delaying with the initiation. He is on his way to the Middle East and implores me to act. The following night I attended the second lecture by Pir ——. In part of his talk he described the lineage of teachers of the Chisti order, of which he is a part. He told of several instances in which the *pirs* of the order had been first initiated in dreams that had led them to their *murshids* [teachers]. He related a story of one of the predecessors in the Chisti order lineage who was actively seeking initiation from a well-regarded Sufi master who had many initiates. This teacher lived in a large house, and on several occasions as this seeker left the house, he passed a beggar on the doorstep dressed in rags. He had several dreams in which the beggar repeated to him, "I am your initiator." Then one day, as he was leaving the home of his prospective master, the beggar said, "I am your initiator. Don't you recall your dream last night?" At this point the beggar revealed himself to be the true spiritual master who had disguised himself as a beggar, and recognized that the dream had pointed him in this direction; he immediately took initiation.

In another instance of dreams preceding initiation, Pir —— recounted the story of his father, whose dreams and meditative visions led him to his *murshid*.

I was overwhelmed by the synchronicity of my dream and these stories, of which I had not been previously aware. After the lecture, I took initiation from Pir ——, telling him about my dreams and sharing my apprehensions of losing my freedom. He reassured me and asked if it would be alright for a (national) film crew to "record" the initiation, for a television special. It seemed like another confirmation of my dream in which there were "recorders," witnesses representing the "river of the unconscious." In another confirmation, I learned that Pir ——'s next stop was a trip to the Middle East, just as he had told me about in the previous night's dream.

In this statement, we again see the critical role of dreams in the Sufi conversion process, especially when the core manifest content is so apparently clear. Dreaming of your teacher (*murshid*) directly is an important trope in many Sufi orders. Some of the stories seem to have a magical flavor to them, like the aforementioned Chisti "beggar" (*murshid*), who apparently has knowledge of the seeker's previous night's dream. There are very few recorded examples of even a prophet's knowledge of another person's unrevealed dreams. However, Daniel has this knowledge in the Hebrew Bible twice in relation to Nebuchadnezzar (Daniel 2:16–19, 26–45). Of course, such dream contents can be explained psychologically in terms of the man's susceptibility to dream of his future teacher recommending initiation, following Pir —— 's telling him about conversion dreams in Sufism and his clear, keen interest in finding a Sufi teacher. Once he has decided to convert to Sufism, despite some degree of fear and ambivalence about conversion also present in the dream content, he interprets other parts of the dream as confirmatory symbols. For example, he reads the "recorders" to imply the film crew. Also, he reads the fact that the *pir* is in fact, as well as in the dream content, traveling soon to the Middle East, as another confirmatory fact. He presumably thought he otherwise was not mentally aware of his *pir*'s forthcoming trip.

## Ethnographic Study of Dreaming in a UK Sufi Center

I visited a Sufi center in a major English city many times between 2002 and 2004. I visited usually on the Sunday evening for a *zikr*, which is a ceremony in which the many names and attributes of Allah are recited. After the ceremony, a vegetarian meal is shared and after some time for discussion, people headed home. Sometimes, I also visited the Thursday evening *zikr* in the shaykh's home, which was more informal. Both ceremonies lasted for about two hours. The main Sunday evening *zikr* was held in a slightly run down ex-church fairly near the center of the city. The shaykh's home was near the Sufi center in the church. Normally no one lived in the church. My visits were limited to attending and participating in the zikr ceremonies, as well as interviewing the shaykh concerning his dreams. I had originally met the shaykh in the wake of 9/11 at a seminar at Newcastle.

## The Sunday Evening *Zikr*

Approximately twenty to thirty-five people attended the *zikr* on an average evening. The *zikr* is the hallmark of most Sufi groups. The *zikr* is usually a forty-minute song or chant in Arabic, praising the glorious attributes and names of Allah. The meetings of this group were open to anyone interested. Perhaps half of the members were of Pakistani origin, either British born or immigrants, typically from Pakistani Kashmir. The rest were British converts. Women, and sometimes children, mostly sat behind a three-foot-high screen in the hall. The evening began at about 7 PM. Male members would come in and typically shake hands with all the other males and usually also cross their right hand over their heart as they did so. Males did not physically greet females unless they were family members. There was a core membership that attended. After a period of informal discussion, there was the usual Muslim prayer time, led by one of the core members, often the shaykh. The shaykh was dressed in very colorful robes with a pointed green turban on his head. For the *zikr* the men sat in a large circle around the edge of a large carpet. Many candles burned close to where the shaykh sat. I was given an English translation of the Arabic chant. I experienced the singing as powerful and meditative, sonorous and beautiful at the same time. At the end all the men again shook hands with each other, putting their right hand over their heart as a gesture of sincerity.

Then informal conversations ensued, and occasionally a member had some kind of private consultation with the shaykh. After a few minutes, the meal was served, often with children handing food around. A little while after the meal, people slowly left, collecting their shoes at the entrance to the building. The Sunday evening *zikr* in the shaykh's home was similar in structure and content, but fewer people typically attended.

Members knew I was studying the role of dreams in Islam. Later on I shared copies of what I had written with them. Several told me about dreams they had had, particularly of their Shaykh Nazim, who then was eighty-four years old and mostly lived in Northern Cyprus. The view of dreams held by members was consistent with the general Islamic perspective on dreaming. Significantly, in the Naqshbandi Sufi group, at least some of the members considered dreams of their Shaykh Nazim to be true dreams from Allah. One person spoke of his precognitive dream of his trip to Damascus and of how his shaykh had advised him in a dream to pray daily.

There can even be spiritual competition shown in dream reports. A member of a different Sufi order spoke of a dream in which his own shaykh had remonstrated with him for getting advice on the wisdom of his second marriage from yet another shaykh rather than from him—even though this shaykh was dead. Apparently, the dead shaykh was not complaining, but pointing out that formalities had not been observed. Therefore this dream message balanced out the lack of spiritual manners. The Sufi wrote about the background to his dream and the dream itself:

> I joined a Sufi order—a branch of the Qadari Tariquat—just before my nineteenth birthday. Subsequently, the shaykh of this order died and was not replaced. After this I wanted advice on my marriage to my present wife and went to another shaykh from another order. This shaykh told us to marry quickly, and we did within the week. On my wedding night I had this dream: my shaykh who had died appeared looking slightly annoyed, then the second shaykh appeared. My shaykh said, "The advice that man gave you was correct, but you should have come to me for that advice." The backcloth of this dream was an airport, we were standing at a sort of crossroads of runways. I understood in the dream that both shaykhs had flown in for the meeting. I also understood that the error I had made in not seeking my shaykh's advice/permission had been corrected. (personal communication, March 28, 2003)

This second shaykh was Shaykh Nazim. Here, we see another example of a Sufi dreamer interpreting his own dream quite literally. Often the dream messages seemed to be relatively clear and explicit, as they for instance conveyed key advice about marriages and careers.

I tended to talk about dreams where possible after or sometimes before the *zikr*. Perhaps 60 percent of members were male. I spoke almost exclusively with male members. The female members of the community seemed to mostly interact among themselves. I did, however, talk a lot with the Russian Sufi wife of one of the male Sufis and visited them both in their home. She told me of her precognitive dream of meeting her future husband in Istanbul.

The shaykh was very oriented to dreams and told me that, as a complimentary therapist, he used his dreams as part of his diagnosis and treatment for his clients, some of whom were also Sufi members. He had complete faith in the power of his dreams on occasions, and believed himself to be in touch with Shaykh Nazim through night dreams.

## Shaykh Nazim in Northern Cyprus

These reports of true dreams of Shaykh Nazim aroused my curiosity, and in April 2005 I spent three days at his house in Lefte, Northern Cyprus. About two hundred people, among whom followers from the United States, the United Kingdom, Eastern Europe, and Africa were present. Shaykh Nazim was much loved, and whenever he appeared for one of the five daily prayers, some of his followers would be waiting to bow and just touch him so as to receive his blessing (*Baraka*). He was believed to be in constant contact with Allah, and probably has thousands, even tens of thousands, of followers worldwide, including, I was told by his followers, powerful politicians from the East and Western celebrity musicians.

Most of his male followers who were staying there slept in a large hall, which was also used for prayers. The women stayed in the female quarters, which I did not visit. Many of the men were dressed in Sufi costume, bright clothes and green turban headdresses. There were stalls outside selling Shaykh Nazim pictures, prayer beads, and other religious accessories. There were a couple of Sufi-owned shops in the small village, including a café. The focus of the day was on the five prayer times (*Adhan*) and some evenings there was a *zikr,* which was not so different from the one in the English city. However, the atmosphere was more intense, and some people danced in a whirling fashion. At the end, the men walked around in a circle shaking hands with everyone else, making the same gesture of the right hand on their hearts.

Relaxation time was spent in the small garden, and there was a communal feeding arrangement; oranges were plentiful. Access to the shaykh was tightly controlled, due to the numbers of people who wanted to consult with him. The shaykh was committed to see each of his followers. I myself eventually saw him after waiting three days, and even then only had access as a companion of the English shaykh. Hence, I asked him about the reports that he had sent dreams to his followers. He said, "Yes, sometimes I send my power in dreams, when necessary." I asked how he did this, and he said, "First you must take a step, even a half step, away from the material world, and we Sufis have ways to do this"; enigmatic, as one would no doubt expect. On my leaving, Shaykh Nazim gave me a bag of oranges from his garden.

While in the Lefte community, I spoke about dreams with several of his followers, again confirming the extraordinary significance of dreams for this group of people.

ஃ ஃ ஃ

# CHAPTER 5

# Militant Jihadist Dreaming in the Middle East and the United Kingdom

## The Patterns and Threads Running through Jihadist Dream Interpretation

In the prophetic Islamic tradition, militant Islamic jihadists also seem to relate to their night dreams. Certain patterns inform jihadist dream interpretive narratives: First, jihadists are reported to receive divine inspiration, guidance, and divinatory "news" of future events in this world and the world hereafter. Second, dream narratives in part legitimate jihadist actions for the dreamers themselves, for their followers, and for the Islamic nation, the *Ummah*. Third, dream visions connect the dreamers with the past (mythical) reality of the Prophet Muhammed and his companions, the Golden Age of Islam. Also, dreams actually introduce this glorious past into the present. Hence, the visionary and revelatory world of Islam is reborn today, as dreamers base their inspired jihad upon the "glad tiding" that Muhammed said would come through true dreams. Fourth, there is often a marked reliance on the manifest content of the dream symbolism. Sacred figures from the visionary history of Islam (particularly the Prophet and his companions, Hasan and Hussein) communicate, usually through the spoken word, directly to the dreamer as in a revelation, announcing and instructing the dreamer. Dreams of heavenly spaces and the glorious reception of the martyrs are reported. Dead friends appear with metaphysical information.

As in all dream cultures, jihadists both dream and interpret their dreams within their own culturally specific world view, in this case that of Islam, according to which this material world is not our final destination but rather a series of lessons and tests and a preparation for the hereafter and the time of judgment at death. The more real world of the hereafter does, however, occasionally intersect with this material world through night dreams, and more rarely through waking visions. Such hyperlucid experiences can define actions and events in this world. This interrelationship between dreams and actual events positions dreaming as potentially related to the future rather than—as is the case in most Western psychoanalytic theories of dreaming, such as that of Freud—to the past (see Basso 1987). Unlike in the West, in Islam dreams and future events in this world can be clearly related. The Joseph sura in the Qur'an (12.6) makes this especially clear as Joseph, through his interpretation of the dream of seven fat and thin cows of the Egyptian pharaoh, enables the pharaoh to plan ahead for a succession of bad harvests. This is the first reported climate change warning dream. Specifically, through the prophetic example of Muhammed, dreams can be related to success in warfare. Muhammed dreams before the battle of Badr that the enemy forces are smaller than they actually are, so giving him and his army confidence in victory (Qur'an 8.43).

## The Dreams of Al-Qaeda Members

There are many reports of the power and significance of true dreams on many of the best known jihadist commanders and followers. These accounts come from secondary sources such as websites and newspaper reports. Overall, I suggest that—whatever veracity issues there may be concerning particular individual dream narratives—there are definitely thematic patterns in these dream narratives and in their legitimacy claims, which are fully consistent with Islamic night dream teachings and practices.

### Osama bin Laden

Osama bin Laden, leader of al-Qaeda, does seem to relate to night dreams. Reeve writes in *Ecologist* magazine that "even when Al-Qaeda was based in Sudan … [it] … had a cleric specialising in interpreting dreams" (Reeve 2001). Following the 9/11 attack in New York, many newspapers (Lines 2001) reported a transcript of a video in which bin Laden refers to the anticipatory dreams of some of his followers. While these followers apparently did not know of the planned attacks, bin Laden is concerned with the fact that "the secret [of the attacks] would be revealed if everyone starts seeing it in their dreams." Early in the video bin Laden says:

> Abu'l-Hassan al-Masri told me a year ago: "I saw in a dream, we were playing a soccer game against the Americans. When our team showed up in the field, they were all pilots!" He [Al-Masri] didn't know anything about the

operation until he heard it on the radio. He said the game went on and we defeated them. That was a good omen for us.

The use of the term *omen* indicates a belief that dreams are a potential source of divination, especially for pious and spiritually oriented Muslims. Moreover, while the military contest is disguised as a soccer match, the victory over the Americans by the jihadist "pilots" is made manifest in the dream symbolism. Future victory is clearly symbolized.

Yosri Fouda was the *Al-Jazeera* journalist who in 2002 in Karachi, Pakistan, interviewed two of the al-Qaeda planners of the 9/11 attacks, Ramzi bin al-Shibh and Khalid Sheikh Muhammad. He wrote about the role of dreaming for the 9/11 attackers:

> Dreams and visions and their interpretations are also an integral part of these spiritual beliefs. They mean that the Mujahideen are close to the Prophet, for whatever the Prophet dreams will come true. In a videotape recorded shortly after 11 September, al-Qaeda spokesman Sulaiman Abu Ghaith is seen and heard speaking in the company of bin Laden, who was playing host to a visitor from Mecca: "I saw in my dreams that I was sitting in a room with the Sheikh [Bin Laden], and all of a sudden there was breaking news on TV. It showed an Egyptian family going about its business and a rotating strap that said: 'In revenge for the sons of Al-Aqsa [that is, the Palestinians], Osama bin Laden executes strikes against the Americans.'" That was before the event.

> Bin Laden then interprets: "The Egyptian family symbolises Muhammed Atta, may Allah have mercy on his soul. He was in charge of the group." Muhammed Atta was the Egyptian leader of the 9/11 attacks.

> Ramzi bin al-Shibh would later tell Fouda long stories about the many dreams and visions of the "brothers" in the run-up to 11 September. He would speak of the Prophet and his close companions as if he had actually met them. ... Atta ... also told Ramzi a little anecdote about "brother" Marwan (al-Shehdi) [one of the 9/11 attackers] that he knew would please him. "Muhammed (Atta) told me that Marwan had a beautiful dream that he was [physically] flying high in the sky surrounded by green birds not from our world, and that he was crashing into things, and that he felt so happy."

> "What things?" Fouda asked.

> "Just things," answered Ramzi.

> Green birds are often given significance in these dreams.

While Ramzi is shy about explaining this dream, it would be likely that the "green birds not from our world" would be interpreted as a heavenly symbol: green is a spiritual color in Islam, and flying birds are a common symbol of heaven. Marwan reporting that he was flying high in a symbolically constituted heavenly realm, and also crashing into things could easily be interpreted as another "good" omen for the 9/11 jihadists. The rotating strap may refer to a continuous news feed. The message is clear though: that the basic political cause fueling the jihad is the continual oppression of the Palestinian people by Israel, the United States, and its allies. Revenge is indeed in the air, and success against the Americans is foretold through the medium of television, a medium that later so graphically presented the 9/11 attack.

By defining the meaning of the dream in relating the Egyptian family image to the person of Atta, bin Laden is taking on the part of the traditional spiritually authoritative role of a shaykh, a spiritual master, as an interpreter of dreams. Bin al-Shibh speaks of the Prophet and his companions as if he had actually met them in his visions and dreams, thereby showing his apparent familiarity with and connection to the first days of Islam. His mindset is tuned into an eternally enduring hyper-reality, in which linear temporality is confounded and the glorious Islamist past is evoked in an ongoing intimacy and immediacy. The days of revelation are indeed present today.

Robert Fisk, the Middle Eastern correspondent for the *Independent,* reports (2005: 34) that during one of his three meetings with bin Laden, the al-Qaeda leader said: "Mr Robert ... one of our brothers had a dream. He dreamt that you came to us one day on a horse, that you had a beard and that you were a spiritual person. You wore a robe like us. This means you are a true Muslim." This terrified Fisk, who feared he is meant to "accept this 'dream' as a prophecy and a divine instruction. Fisk says "I am not a Muslim, I am a journalist." Osama replies, "If you tell the truth, that means you are a good Muslim." The moment passes.

One view of this dialogue could be that bin Laden is using the dream trope as a way of challenging Fisk, or as a device to influence his followers. However, since it is considered wrong to lie about a dream in the Islamic tradition, it is more likely that this provides further evidence of bin Laden's consideration that dreams are a potentially divinatory form of communication. The beard is a sign of a devout Muslim, and in Islamic dream dictionaries, the horse is traditionally interpreted as symbolizing a "person's status, rank, honor, dignity, power and glory" (Ibn Sirin 2000a: 99). Again, we see bin Laden acting as a spiritual master, defining the meaning of this dream, and reframing Fisk's reply to confirm his interpretation of the dream. Bin Laden utilizes his companion's dream as a source of spiritual certainty in the prophetic tradition.

### Zacarias Moussaoui

Zacarias Moussaoui has often been described as the twentieth member of the 9/11 New York attacks. He is a French citizen of Moroccan origins. Moussaoui was an al-Qaeda member who had given allegiance to his shaykh, Osama bin Laden, and had attended flight training school in the United States before 9/11. He was tried in the United States in 2006, and was found guilty of conspiring to kill US citizens in the 9/11 New York attack. Even though the death sentence was considered as a verdict, he currently serves a life sentence in the United States. Moussaoui's reported night dream of flying a plane into a tall building was a significant issue in his trial. The trial debated whether such a dream was evidence of schizophrenia or rather an aspect of Moussaoui's fundamentalist Islamic belief. Prosecutors argued that "Mousaoui's fervent belief in his dream is consistent with religious beliefs of Muslims—especially fundamentalist Muslims—and is no more crazy than Christians believing in the resurrection" (*USA Today* 2006).

In his trial, Moussaoui's night dreams appear to have led him to make his mind up to become a *shahid,* a martyr. Donahue, in her book about Moussaoui's life and trial, quotes from the trial transcript in which Moussaoui says:

> Basically, I had, I had a dream, and I had more later, but I had a dream, and I went to see Sheikh Usama Bin Laden, and I told him about my dream. He told me, "Good." Maybe, I don't know, a few days later, I have another dream. So I went again, I saw him, and I told him about this. This was after I had declined, I was asked before. Then I had this dream. Then maybe a week, a short time, Sheikh Abu Hafs [Muhammed Atef] came to the guesthouse and asked me again if I wanted to be part of the suicide operation, me and Richard Reid, and this time I said yes. (2007: 80–81)

Later on the same day of the trial, Donahue recounts Moussaoui seeing a map with the target of the White House on it in one of his dreams:

> He went on to describe his reason for wanting to fly a 747:
>
> … but if want to say the original reason, okay, what I believe, okay, it is I thought I had a dream where I was into the runway of an airport and I actually took a map out, okay, and I open it and it was the White House with a circle with a cross, like when you do when you do target.
>
> And next to me, okay, in front of there was the four brother, I couldn't recognize. And next to me there was a 747, the very distinct, you know, like the cockpit, was very distant (tr. March 27, 2006, page 2402, lines 18–250).

Later still the same day, Donahue reports how Moussaoui understood dream interpretation in Islam, which was congruent with Islam's traditional teaching on dream interpretation. Moussaoui says,

> So I refer to sheikh Usama Bin laden and some other sheikh there to explain to me the reality, but the dream about the White House, it was very clear to me (tr. March 27, 2006, page 2403, line 24). (2007: 80–81)

In these trial transcripts we see how Moussaoui experienced night dreams as decisive in his motivation to become a martyr. Moreover, he reports an accurate dream of an intended target, the White House.

From the same Associated Press source (Newsmax.com 2006):

> In his sleep, Zacarias Moussaoui dreamed about piloting a plane and crashing it into the White House. The dream was important enough that he told his supreme commander, Osama bin Laden, all about it. That dream has taken on a significant role in Moussaoui's death-penalty trial. Prosecutors say Moussaoui took flight training to try to make his dream of piloting an aircraft in a terrorist attack become reality. The defense argues it was the fanciful musings of a deranged mind. An Islamic radical testified Wednesday that Moussaoui told him about the dream during a visit Moussaoui made to Malaysia in 2000. The radical, a top official in an al-Qaida affiliate group called Jemaah Islamiyah, also said during a November 2002 deposition that was played Wednesday for the jury at Moussaoui's death-penalty trial that Moussaoui said he had shared his dream with bin Laden. Moussaoui does not dispute the dream. When Moussaoui pleaded guilty in April to conspiring with al-Qaida to hijack aircraft and other crimes, he said bin Laden told him, "Remember your dream."

Also, from a CNN trial transcript (Hirschkorn 2006), Moussaoui recounts a dream in which President Bush will release him. Again, these dream reports are viewed by the prosecution lawyer as part of his fundamentalist Islamic beliefs. What defense experts view as delusions, he said, are beliefs based on Moussaoui's religious faith:

> "I don't find anything bizarre about what Mr. Moussaoui is saying, because he backs it up with the Qur'an," Dr. Patterson told the jury. He said Moussaoui's belief that his own attorneys were out to kill him was partly rooted in strategic differences. He did not want them to portray him as mentally ill. The doctor disagreed with the defense that Moussaoui's persistent dream that President Bush will free him before he leaves office is irrational. "He is basing his belief on his faith, and I don't believe, as a psychiatrist, I can declare his faith is delusional," Dr. Patterson said. Dr. Patterson said the idea raised by Moussaoui that he could be freed as part of a prisoner exchange with al Qaeda "was not beyond the realm of possibility."

In these dialogues we see bin Laden as a dream-interpreting shaykh, the sieving of dream material to determine any possible spiritual truth, and a key debate as to the nature of the true dream tradition in Islam.

## Richard Reid

Richard Reid is the British al-Qaeda sympathizer sentenced to life imprisonment for attempting to blow up an American Airlines airplane flying from France to the United States in December 2001. He was found to be carrying explosives in his shoes. He is reported as divining special meaning about his role as an Islamic militant from his dreams, which he refers to in one of his final three e-mails (London *Times* 2003). I have been unable to obtain a copy of these e-mails, but the dream is referred to in Moussaoui's 2006 trial. According to the transcript:

> In the dream, Reid was waiting for a ride, but when the ride (a pick-up truck) came, it was full and Reid could not go. He was upset and had to go later in a smaller car. Reid explained the meaning of the dream as follows: "I now believe that the pickup that came first was 9/11 as it's true that I was upset at not being sent." (Hirschkorn 2006)

There is little evidence how Reid interpreted this dream. However, this narrative demonstrates his perception of its veracity and potential guidance. Reid interprets and translates the symbolism of the pickup truck into that of the airplane; both are forms of group conveyance. The fact that he is upset in the dream relates to his real-world loss of the 9/11 attack opportunity.

## Abu Mussab al-Zarqawi and Other Iraqi Martyrs

Abu Mussab al-Zarqawi was the Jordanian leader of al-Qaeda in Iraq until his death in June 2006. One of his Jordanian jail mates reports on a website (News24.com 2006) that he converted to radical Islam partly through his sister's dream of a sword with the word "jihad" written on the one side and the Qur'anic verse: "God will never abandon you and will never forget you" (this probably is an inaccurate reference to sura 47, v. 38.4) on the other. The sacred communication is manifest: divine instructions are perceived as having been received. Jihad is authorized and a spiritual promise made. Unfortunately, no more details of his dreams are known.

Another website (Global Terrorist Alert 2006) carries Islamic martyrs' biographies. The following extracts concerning two Saudi Arabian martyrs refer to dream narratives as significant. The first is that of Abu Bakr al-Qasimi, from the city of Al-Haboob in the Qassem region, who was killed in Iraq. His dream refers to the idea that holy warriors will be welcomed and attended in heaven by beautiful maidens:

> Abu Bakr would stay up at night for prayer. ... the martyr, may God have mercy on his soul, saw the beautiful black-eyed women in paradise [in dreams] more than once [in fact, three times], and he became increasingly passionate about meeting blessed God. (Global Terrorist Alert 2006)

The dream imagery is understood as referring to an actual paradisiacal "other" world. Apparently Abu Bakr is increasingly drawn to this envisioned world and its consummate promise. The Islamic houri narrative (the tradition of the seventy-two black-eyed virgins that await in paradise for the martyr who dies in the cause and name of Allah) is one that possesses considerable influence among many Muslims and is obviously open to Western psychoanalytical analysis for a differential analysis of psychological causation. Bonney recently analyzed the meaning of jihad and its use in Islamic history. He argues that the houri tradition holds little, if any, theological veracity. Rather, it is an "isolated hadith" (2004: 41) and it is not found in the strongest hadiths, such as that of Bukhari or Muslim; neither is this idea present in the Qur'an. Nonetheless, it is an idea apparently regularly propagated by militant jihadist recruiters in regions where poverty makes it extremely difficult for young Arabic men to afford to marry. Moreover, while the Qur'an does not appear to promise the holy martyrs such a number of houris, it does describe the presence of beautiful retiring and virginal maidens, as in:

> And they who were foremost on earth—the foremost still.
>
> These are they who shall be brought nigh to God,
>
> In gardens of delight;
>
> A crowd of the former
>
> And few of the latter generations;
>
> On inwrought couches
>
> Reclining on them face to face:
>
> Aye—blooming youths go round about to them
>
> With goblets and ewers and a cup of flowing wine;
>
> Their brows ache not from it, nor fails the senses:
>
> And with such fruits, as shall please them best,
>
> And with the flesh of such birds, as they shall long for:
>
> And theirs shall be the Houris, with large dark eyes, like pearls hidden in their shells,
>
> In recompense of their labours past.
>
> (Qur'an 1977: sura 56)

The second biography is that of Abu Uthman al-Yamani, from Yemen, who appeared, following his martyrdom in Iraq, in one of the dreams of Ab'ul-Harith al-Dusari:

> One of Abu Uthman's brothers saw him in his dream. He dreamt that someone called out to him and told him that Abu Uthman had managed to secure a place in one of the best gardens of paradise—a dream that I interpret as a sign that he indeed became a martyr, though only God knows. One of his brothers from the peninsula of blessed Muhammad [Saudi Arabia] made him swear that he would appear in his dreams if God allowed him to join the

ranks of martyrs. And, indeed, this is exactly what happened, and Abu Uthman appeared in his dreams urging him to come and join him in paradise. Farewell, Abu Uthman, and may God have mercy upon your soul. (Global Terrorist Alert 2006)

The interpretation is explicit to the dreamer, a sign to be read just as it is, a message from another more and differently real world. The dream communication beckons the dreamer to follow him to paradise. There is no phantasmagoric or surreal incomprehensibility to unravel. The dream is its own interpretation, as Jung wrote quoting the Jewish Talmud (Jung 1964: 90).

## The Dreams of Other Jihadists

The significant pattern and use of night dreams and their interpretations that have been noted above in the cases of members of al-Qaeda are repeated with other jihadists.

### Pakistani Relations

Dreaming also plays a role in the process of becoming a jihadist in the Pakistani-based movement against the Indian occupation of a large part of Kashmir. Before a young man can go on a martyrdom operation in India-held Kashmir, he has to obtain parental permission, which may ultimately be given by a mother or maternal uncle following a dream:

In many cases, a few days before the boy "drinks the cup of martyrdom" [*jam-e shahadat nush karna*] mothers and often maternal uncles see him in Paradise, wearing beautiful white clothes, smiling, surrounded by trees and flowers and drinking milk.

Here, paradisiacal imagery from the Qur'an justifies martyrdom. The mythical world of Islam is seen, recognized, and made present (Zahab 2008: 133–60).

Such dreams also occur among radical Muslims in Europe, as in the case of Amir Cheema (BBC news). Amir was a twenty-eight-year-old Pakistani textile-engineering student, who died in 2006 in a German prison while awaiting trial for entering the offices of the German newspaper *Die Welt* with a large knife, intending to kill the editor for reprinting the Danish cartoons of the Prophet Muhammed. Later fifty thousand people attended his funeral in Pakistan. Cheema's father published the following dream narrative in the Urdu press, and this dream report was then reprinted in English in the weekly *Friday Times* in Pakistan:

Fountains of light (noor) had burst forth in all directions as the sacred gathering became visible. It was announced that the companions (of the Prophet) had arrived. Then it was declared that the Prophet PBUH himself was seated in the vicinity but his face could not be seen. Then the voice of the Prophet PBUH was heard saying Amir Cheema is coming! (Amir aa raha hai). The companions stood up in respect and started looking in one direction. Then the voice of the Prophet PBUH said: "Hasan and Husain, look who I am sending to you, look after him ("Amir Cheema in Heaven," in "Nuggets from the Urdu Press," *Friday Times,* 30 June–6 July 2006).

Hasan and Hussein were the sons of Ali and Fatima, and so the grandsons of the Prophet Muhammed. The dream announces the elevated spiritual status of Amir Cheema through the word of the Prophet Muhammed, attended by his companions. We again find the themes of sacred light, and of the clear communication of the spiritually elevated status of the martyr.

## Guantanamo Bay

Many of the detainees at Guantanamo Bay were from Pakistan. In May 2005, a Pakistani newspaper published the following dream narrative:

A Guantanamo ex-prisoner named Qari Badruzzaman Badr said in an interview that at Guantanamo many Arabs had dreams in which the Holy Prophet (PBUH) personally gave them news of their freedom and called them the People of Badr. The Prophet said that Christ will soon arrive. One Arab saw Jesus who took his hand and told him that Christians were now misled. Later the other prisoners could smell the sweet smell of Jesus from his hand. His hand was rubbed on all the prisoners. (Ahmed, "TV review," *Daily Times* (Pakistan), 23 May 2005).

Again, the dream message is explicit. It is Jesus, a major prophet in Islam, who informs them that the Christian nation, the Crusaders that imprison them, are misled. What a transcendence of their oppression this dream message must have seemed. It is immediately communicated, not only by word of mouth, but also by touch, presumably to transfer the blessing (*baraka*) from the dream.

Hence, ex-Guantanamo Bay residents are likely to be a fruitful source of information on significant and even "true" dreams. Jaram al-Harith is a UK citizen, a convert to Islam, who testified that he is not involved with al-Qaeda, but accidentally got caught up in Afghanistan and taken to Guantanamo Bay. The UK *Mirror* newspaper reported his apparently accurate and anticipatory dream:

About a year into my time, I had a dream. A voice said, "You will be here for two years."

In my dream I said, "Two years! You're joking." But when I woke up, I was calmer because at least that meant I would be getting out one day.

I was sent to Guantanamo on February 11, 2002 and left on March 9, 2004, so I was there for just over two years, just like the voice in the dream said. (12 March 2004)

The following quotation is an extract from an interview with Ibrahim Sen, a Turkish national detained in Guantanamo and published in *Vakit,* a German Islamist daily newspaper that is banned in that country due to its anti-Semitism:

*Vakit:* How was the morale among the prisoners?

Sen: Despite all the tortures, morale is alive among the Guantanamo prisoners. Sacred dreams help with this. ... One day an Afghani brother called to a Kuwaiti sage and told him that he had dreamed that the Prophet [Muhammed] had spoken to him and said that Allah had not forgotten them and that the angels were watching them—and that a good surprise was awaiting them. (10–11 April 2006)

In such almost hopeless situations, without any foreseeable prospect of a fair trial or release, such dreams must have a very powerful emotional effect on their recipients.

Moazzam Begg was one of the nine UK citizens detained at Guantanamo Bay. He was released with three others in January 2005 and subsequently coauthored a book with Victoria Brittain about his experiences as an inmate at Guantanamo Bay. Begg, a devout Muslim, is by his account not a member of either the Taliban or al-Qaeda, but accidentally got caught up in the events in Afghanistan. In the main text of his book, he barely refers to dreams, but in the prologue he writes about the precognitive dream he had years before his time in Guanatanamo Bay:

The concertina wire is ingrained deepest in my memory. As we strolled meaninglessly around the enclosure, cameras surmounted with machine guns, and guards in military uniform followed our every move. The situation was hopeless—without a foreseeable end. The dismal monotony of daily existence was becoming unbearable. The uncertainty of the future compounded the atmosphere of apprehension and fear.

I whispered to a fellow detainee, "How much more of this can we take? It's becoming impossible. If we don't make a stand now we'll lose our self-respect, in addition to our freedom." My companion sedately replied, "Patience, my brother, we must have patience."

And then it began. The firing was indiscriminate; rounds whistled overhead, the bodies fell around me. Turning back towards my confidant I began to spurt out muffled words about running, but he was already on the ground like the others, dead. Everyone was getting shot—except me. I felt unable to do a thing, but then I did. I called the Adhan as loud as possible, for the world to hear. It did hear—eventually.

I had known all along that my wife was expecting a baby, and I still had some hope of being present for its birth. But when I heard someone yell across the wire that the child was about to enter this world—with its father captive amongst coils of razor wire—I knew that even if I survived this massacre, it would be a long while before I was reunited with my family. At this thought I became oblivious of the surrounding carnage. I raised my hands in the traditional Muslim way, towards the sky, and began to weep. Voices in my head whispered to me to seek help from Allah and beseech his mercy. My hands rose, and continued to do so, passing the clouds. And still I wept.

That was how I woke up, next to my wife. She was woken by the sounds of my sobbing and asked me in her gentlest voice why I was so upset. I told her about the nightmare. But it was in 1995. It would be another seven years before I learnt its true meaning. (Begg 2006)

This dream narrative, sited at the beginning of the book, seems to contain a core Islamic narrative of redemption from suffering through prayer, of acute danger and fear and anticipated loss of loved ones, followed by the intervention of a true friend who counsels patience during this trial, leading into a spiritual catharsis and appeal to Allah, which evokes a spiritual transcendence out of this dangerous material world.

## A Dream of a Dead *Mujahid*

Jihadist ideology considers that its fallen holy warriors, shahadha, will go to paradise once they die in this world. Glory awaits them. Abdul Rahman Jabarah's family originally came from Iraq. He was brought up first in Kuwait, and as a teenager lived in Ontario, Canada. He became an al-Qaeda member and part of the cell that bombed Western housing complexes in Riyadh, Saudi Arabia, in 2003. His brother, Muhammed Mansour Jabarah, is in prison in the United States for plotting a terrorist attack against the United States and Israeli embassies in Singapore in 2001. Abdul Rahman Jabarah was killed by Saudi Arabian security forces in that country in July 2003.

Bell sought to explain how a Canadian educated young man became a militant Islamic jihadist. Bell focuses on the story of Muhammed Mansour Jabarah. However, he also writes about his brother, Abdul Rahman Jabarah. His dream narrative Bell recounts as follows:

Those who knew Abdul Rahman and fought Jihad with him penned an overwrought eulogy describing his life and martyrdom. One of them told me about a dream he had about his dead friend.

"We were sitting and Abdul Rahman was in front of us. I asked him: 'Weren't you killed?' and Abdul Rahman answered: 'No, I wasn't killed.'

"Rejoice, for God, may he be glorified and exalted, said in his Qur'an, 'Do not consider those who died for God's sake dead—but alive.'"

Abdul Rahman was "among those whom God used in the Jihad. He was raised on the Jihad and became a martyr on its course," the eulogy said.

"We will never forget you, O guiding martyr. Nor will the families [to] whom you gave their grants. The brothers who lived with you and whom you taught will never forget you. May you receive award and compensation, with God's help."

"Farewell, martyr." (2005: 196)

In many spiritual traditions, such dreams of the departed are considered to be forms of direct communication with the dead, who are alive in the hereafter. Islamic metaphysics asserts the existence of both heaven and hell in the afterlife. Holy martyrs seem to be guaranteed a heavenly time. This belief in an almost guaranteed place in paradise for these *shahadah* is also evident in Fouda's interview with Ramzi Binalshibh. Ramzi tells Fouda:

Muhammed (Atta) used to assure me that we shall meet, God willing, in Paradise, and that our meeting shall be soon. ... I asked him if he were to see the Prophet Muhammed, peace be upon him, and reach the highest place in heaven, he should convey our *salaam* (greetings) to him as well as to Abu bakr, Omar and the rest of the companions, followers and Mujahideen. (2003: 109)

Dreams and visions are to the Islamic militant jihadists a core way of confirming their ideological worldview and their path to becoming a *shahadah*. As to the vexed question whether there can be a clear distinction between the glorious martyrdom of the *shahadah* and the forbidden (*haram*) action of the suicide, there is considerable debate. Bonney quotes Shaykh Yusuf al-Qaradawi, a leader of the Muslim Brotherhood (a large transnational Islamist political party based in Egypt) who vehemently argues against the view that "martyrdom operations" be seen as suicide:

These operations are the supreme form of *jihad* for the sake of Allah, a type of terrorism that is allowed by *Shariah*. ... The term "suicide operations" is an incorrect and misleading term, because these are heroic operations of martyrdom and have nothing to do with suicide. The mentality of those who carry them out has nothing to do with the mentality of someone who commits suicide. ... He who commits suicide kills himself for his own benefit, while he who commits martyrdom sacrifices himself for the sake of his religion and his nation. While someone who commits suicide has lost hope

for himself and with the spirit of Allah, the *mujahid* is full of hope with regard to Allah's spirit and mercy. (2004: 315–16)

The essence of the argument is clearly expressed: the martyr is a Muslim
believer who gives his life for the glory of God/Allah, and not one who
acts for personal ends.

CHAPTER 6

# Dreams of Mullah Omar, Taliban Leader

### Mullah Omar

Mullah Muhammed Omar founded the Taliban movement in Afghanistan and was effectively Afghanistan's ruler from 1996 to 2001 when the regime was ousted by the United States and its allies, following the attack on New York on 9/11. The United States and its allies attacked Afghanistan under the rule of Mullah Omar and the Taliban because it allegedly harbored Osama bin Laden and his al-Qaeda movement. The Taliban regime adopted a form of Sunni Islam that prohibited the education of girls in schools and implemented a strict form of Sha'ria (Islamic law) based on Qur'anic teachings. Stringent dress codes were enforced for women, cinemas and most music were banned, murderers beheaded, adulterers stoned to death, and thieves had their hands amputated. In April 1996, Mullah Omar was given the title of "Commander of the Faithful" by his followers. In October 1997, he subsequently renamed the country the Islamic Emirate of Afghanistan. Mullah Omar is a most reclusive and shy person who gives very few interviews. He is an ethnic Pashtun and is thought to have been born in 1959 in a village near Kandahar.

There were several media and internet references to Mullah Omar and his visionary dreams that I wrote up for my paper in the journal *Dreaming*:

> It has been reported (Judah, 2001, p. 13) that the Taliban leader, Mullah Omar, founded the Taliban movement in Afghanistan, in 1994 following a dream in which "allegedly ... God had commanded him to restore order." Also, I have been told in private correspondence (from Mariam abou Zahab, a French political scientist who has spent many years studying in Pakistan and Afghanistan) that:

> Mollah Omar was allegedly called to action in a visionary dream of a kind similar to those by which Amir Abdul Rahman Khan claimed to have been

inspired. Mollah Omar claims that he saw the Prophet who asked him to take action and save Afghanistan from corruption and foreign powers. This vision gave him a mystical dimension to set him apart from ordinary politicians and was an attempt to give a charismatic basis for his authority. In his autobiography, Abdul Rahman (who reigned over Afghanistan from 1880 to 1901) claims that the Prophet and the Four Companions had appeared to him in a revelation, choosing him as a future Amir. (2004b: 22)

So, Mullah Omar possibly claimed political and spiritual continuity, with him being the contemporary saviour of Afghanistan by asserting a continuity of "anointing" or "calling" dream with Abdul Rahman. There are also other stories of Mullah Omar's prophetic dreams. Again my same informant, Mariam abou Zahab writes:

Mullah Omar's dreams are interpreted by his disciples as signs of God's will. For instance, in 1998 he had a dream that if the Taliban repaired the shrine of the Mujaddidi family in Jalalabad, they would take Mazar-e Sharif (which they had taken before and lost). They did take Mazar-e Sharif in '98. This dream was used to legitimize an action which was considered as contrary to Islam by some of the Taliban and by the Arabs who accused the Taliban of being grave worshippers. (2004b: 22)

Mullah Omar seems to be a prolific dreamer. Mullah Nida Muhammed, uncle to Mullah Omar's wife, says, "Before he attacks some place he dreams, and then in the morning he orders a commander to attack that place" (Arabshahi 1998). The UK *Telegraph* newspaper reported on 20 November 2001 that during the Afghanistan war with America, "the peaceful handover of Kandahar was scuppered at the last minute after the one-eyed leader had a prophetic dream." Mr. Karzai, (leader of Afghanistan) quotes Mullah Omar as saying, "I have had a dream in which I am in charge for as long as I live."

Mullah Omar claims a dreamed spiritual and political lineage with Abdul Rahman. Such an assertion fits well into the Islamic theme of the "dream as political prophecy" (Quinn 1996: 127–47). My informant, Mariam Abou Zahab, told me that it was "common knowledge" in Afghanistan that Mullah Omar had been inspired by a "holy" dream.

As part of my study of contemporary Islamic dreaming, I traveled to Peshawar, Pakistan, where I interviewed Rahimullah Yusufzai during the afternoon of 27 March 2005 at his home. I tape-recorded the interview, and Rahimullah gave me permission to use the content in any way I wished. He knew of my academic interest in dream research and spoke excellent English. He is the BBC correspondent in Peshawar and has frequently written for and contributed to *Time* magazine. He was the first of very few reporters to have met Mullah Omar. According to Yusufzai, he met Omar twelve times and was his main media outlet to the West. Many newspaper, magazine, and internet reports on Mullah Omar are based on references to Yusufzai's interviews ( *Time Asia* 2000).

I am including a large part of the interview I had with Rahimullah, as his descriptions of the importance of dreams to Mullah Omar and his followers are dispersed throughout. I highlight in bold the most significant dream-related sequences.

## Interview with Rahimullah Yusufzai

From the transcript:

*Edgar:* He did come from nowhere?

*Rahimullah:* Oh yes, Mullah Omar was an unknown village man, you can say. I have been to his village, his mosque, his madrasah; it is so basic, mud, and he had a very small room—even standing in that room was difficult, you know, because of the height. I could not enter the room and he used to live there, stay there, and he did not belong to the village. He came from another place, he was living in this place, in fact he was as we say in Pashto a *hamsaya:* you do not have your own room, you are living in someone else's house. He himself told me as I met him a dozen times I think, I was the first reporter to meet him, and he told me, "Look, I am not a mullah; *mullah* means a giver of knowledge and *Taliban* means a seeker of knowledge. I am still a *talib,* a seeker of knowledge, as I have not been able to complete my education because of the Russian occupation; I had to go and fight the Russians." He gave up his madrasah education and he always called himself a *talib* not a mullah; and he would refer every matter to a council of mullahs, who were religious scholars, as he is not a qualified mullah, and [yet] at the same time you know when he was already holding about six or seven provinces. I met him again in Kandahar, which was his seat of power, and I saw an interest to go to his village and for the first time to see his mosque and madrasah; he offered that his driver could take me in his car which was a Land Cruiser and he told all these Taliban leaders, "Look now a journalist like Rahimullah wishes to go and see my village, my home you know, and there was a time when nobody knew me and now I am so famous." I went to his village in his Land Cruiser, and that vehicle looked odd in that village as it was an expensive vehicle; there was a mud house and a very poor locality and this was an expensive car and things were changing you know; he was becoming famous and rich, unlike the past a few years ago when he was a nobody. **So the story I was being told everywhere was because of his courage, because of his very timely decision to fight the Mujahideen that had made him very popular and the Taliban flocked to his ban-**

ner as they thought he has this vision, this dream; he has challenged the Mujahideen and because he has been instructed to fight the Mujahideen they thought he was going to succeed.

*Edgar:* Instructed by God, by Allah, in his dreams?
*Rahimullah:* I didn't ask him who, yes maybe some holy person. Once Mullah Omar narrated a dream of his brother to me as he called me up from Kandahar and asked me if I had been to the White House in Washington and I said yes; [he asked] "Can you tell me about it?" and I said yes and I told him about the White House in Washington. And he said in Pashto "white house," "white palace," [and he said,] "Look, my younger brother had a dream and he was telling me that a white palace somewhere is on fire. I have a belief in dreams and this is what my dreams are saying and if you have been there then this description by my brother means the white palace will catch fire," and this was before 9/11 [Mullah Omar asked about his brother's dream] he would have asked other people, religious scholars. I am convinced that Mullah Omar was not aware of Osama bin Laden's plans to attack 9/11. Osama took them for a ride; they were simple people. Mullah Omar will never give him [Osama] up: "I [Mullah Omar speaking] could not believe that this man sitting on a mountain could have done it; I cannot betray a guest, a Muslim, a Mujahid, someone who was nice to us; who helped us, who gave us his money (rich in my heart: blood thicker than water) a Mujahideen who fought the Russians and who has fallen on bad times and has come to us in need."

*Edgar:* Do you know the dreams?
*Rahimullah:* That was not my specific area. But I can tell you what I know: the genesis of the Taliban Islamic movement was this vision, this night dream that Mullah Omar had; he was one of the thousands of foot soldiers fighting the Soviet occupation.

*Edgar:* He was a nobody?
*Rahimullah:* Yes, he was a nobody, he built up some reputation as a crack marksman as he could hit these Russian tanks with the RPG rockets. His village is just located on the main road to Kandahar and Herat, and they would ambush all these Russian military convoys; he even got himself injured when they ambushed one of these and they fired back and one of the bullets hit the mud wall of the madrasah and it even injured him, his eye, and he lost his eye. **Because the whole project was maybe built on this dream, he had this task or duty to perform and he must lead**

his Taliban, his fighters, and he must restore order and peace and enforce Sha'ria, Islamic law.

*Edgar:* And who appeared in his dreams?
*Rahimullah:* No, I don't know who came in his dream. No, but I was told by so many Taliban leaders, commanders, fighters, look, you know, Mullah Omar is a holy man and he gets instructions in his dream and he follows them up and he is not scared of the Mujahideen or America or any power. Subsequently, you know, whenever there was a big Taliban operation such as in 1997 when the Taliban attacked Mazar-e Sharif and took it with the help of some local commanders—then I was told that that attack was launched after Mullah Omar had a dream. So they had to retreat and next year they came back and took the city for good; 1998 they captured all of the north of Afghanistan and even Bamiyan where they had these statues of Buddha. So you know I kept hearing these stories: no big military operation can happen unless he gets his instructions in his dreams. He was a big believer in dreams; he told me he had been entrusted with a mission, a holy mission, and the mission is to unite Afghan, to save it from divisions and to restore order and enforce Sha'ria law.

*Edgar:* And this was through dreams?
*Rahimullah:* This is what I heard, and because he narrated to me one of his brother's dreams shows he had a great belief in dreams. (His younger brother had a dream [the white palace dream] and Mullah Omar called me up from Kandahar.) I used to phone him sometimes, and I was the only one who had access to him. The BBC is very powerful in Afghanistan; they wanted to have good relations with the BBC and I was the first one to reach Kandahar and report about the emerging Taliban Movement and he was grateful to me; that's why he will call me up. I spoke the same language, Pashto, and I was a Muslim, I was a Pakistani, I was someone he could trust. He called me up and said he knew I had been to the White House, and he called me up and said can you please tell me, my brother has a dream, and he is telling me about a dream about a white palace that is on fire; it didn't happen (I say it is a wish fulfilment).

The Taliban was in power, not Osama—he was beholden to them; he couldn't even hold a press conference without Mullah Omar's permission.

Osama never talked about his dreams, he was a more practical man. Very often in the morning, somebody is narrating his or her dream; it is part of our lives; you don't know how to interpret it;

**some take it seriously, some don't. The fact that Mullah Omar was not captured adds to the mystique.**

Osama is a very shy man, very tall man, but once you get him talking, once he is on his favorite subject—the suffering of Muslims, the unjust American policies, the policies against Palestinians, all that—then he becomes very emotional, very passionate. Mullah Omar is very different, two different characters: Mullah Omar is tongue tied, not a good speaker, not very charismatic, long gaps in speaking; Osama is also not very charismatic. I met him just two times; he comes across as a very nice person, very humble, a lot of humility, soft hands; he doesn't look like a terrorist. He gives you respect, then he talks very softly; you don't start hating him when you meet him, you don't feel this man could be a terrorist, that is the feeling you get. But Mullah Omar is very different; this is a type of man we often meet in our villages, a village mullah, he is just like that.

*Edgar:* Plucked from obscurity!

*Rahimullah:* Oh yes, they were all *talibs.* I tell you one thing why the elite classes, the feudals, the landlords, people who had been to university didn't like the Taliban: because of their very low status in society, they are at the lowest rung of society. I have been to university, I own some land, I own my own house. Taliban normally would not have their own house; they would be the poorest of the poor. There is a very derogatory term we use about Taliban, it is called *chanai.* We don't even call them Taliban, we call them *chanai. Chanai* means you have seen this small bird, it is always on the move, from one tree to another, it doesn't really have a home; *chanai* is that person who goes from door to door, house to house, and asks for food. They do it, literally, the Taliban do this: they don't cook, they don't have money to cook; they at mealtimes go from door to door, they collect bread. *Chanai,* nobody can imagine they can come into power and rule all these rich people, all these people who are feudals, these rich people. The Taliban revolution is something extraordinary, but since they became associated with the al-Qaeda and Osama and there was this 9/11; they were beaten with the same stick but I tell you it is like a true revolution; but it is not a leftist revolution, it is a rightist revolution. If there is a Russian or Chinese revolution, it is hailed because they are poor people, peasants; the same thing happened here: they were homeless, landless, and they took power; but the fact that they were rightists, Muslims, fundamentalists, so nobody gave them that credit as they were poor people who fought rich people and took power; they were ex-Mujahideen. They always fought, but the Taliban always had their distinct presence amongst Mujahideen, they would have their own separate bases. They existed before 9/11. The Taliban were all those guys who were studying in a madrasah, studying religion, very poor. *Taliban* is a common term used for all those students who go to a madrasah. They go to a madrasah because they are very poor, they get free food, free education; they are the poorest of the poor, they are mostly orphans, they are nothing, can't afford conventional school.

*Edgar:* What percentage of population are the Taliban?
*Rahimullah:* Madrasahs were already there but they mushroomed during the war; those countries supporting the Mujahideen, America, etc., they needed all these fighters who were inspired with the spirit of jihad; they wanted tough fighters. Reagan compared them to the Founding Fathers of America; he actually paid tribute to them; they were equal to the Founding Fathers. The seven Mujahideen leaders were invited to the White House by Reagan; they went there with their big turbans and their henna-dyed beards; Reagan paid them glowing tributes, fighting the evil empire. But the term used for them was *Mujahideen holy warriors,* but the Taliban were also there; the Taliban were not organized, Mullah Omar organized them into one movement and the Taliban all joined him, you know; some were defeated but they all joined him.

*Edgar:* Were there other characteristics that distinguished him in any way?
*Rahimullah:* No, he was nothing, I could not find any other attribute; he always avoided interviews! Yes, when I was interviewing him for the first time, he kept me waiting for a week; "Okay [Mullah Omar said], you give me your tape and I will give you my answers." I said, "I need to ask you questions"; he said, "No, give it to an assistant." He was the foreign minister now being held by the Americans; I had to record my questions and give him the tape and what I got in return was a general statement which he made, very inarticulate, and I had to use bits of that. The next time I went there, I said, "I want to record your voice"; he said. "No, just take notes"; the third time I went, I said, "I need your picture"; he said no pictures! So he said he would never give interviews; he never came into public; he went only to Kabul once—in six years of rule, he went to Kabul only once and that was in secret.

*Edgar:* He was completely reclusive?
*Rahimullah:* Yes, yes, he would not even give talks in Friday mosque in Kandahar; he would just sit there in the front row and never make a speech, very shy man also; he had no other characteristics. The only thing going for him was that he organized the Taliban and he scored easy victories; the Mujahideen were at that time becoming very unpopular.

*Edgar:* One of the commanders had abused one of the boys?

*Rahimullah:* That was the thing that spurred the whole thing. There was a checkpoint near Mullah Omar's village; two commanders were manning the checkpoint and stories were circulating in the village that these two commanders were very corrupt morally as well as in other ways. They would stop all these vehicles between Herat and Kandahar and they would take away girls and the boys; the story at that time was that there were two girls taken away from the vehicles and their hair was cut and they were made to wear dresses of boys, made to look as boys, and they were raped all the time. Mullah Omar came to know of it and it was happening just by his village, and he told his thirteen colleagues at the first meeting: "Look, we fought against the Russians and for our homeland and look, this is happening just right in front of our eyes, how can we tolerate this?" You know there was no plan to occupy the land, to rule the country; the plan was just to remove the checkpoint near the village. When he went along to the checkpoint and challenged the Mujahideen, there was a very brief clash and they overpowered everyone and they fled. When they were able to smash the first checkpoint, offers of support came from all these villages: "Please come here and remove this checkpoint, there are Mujahideen here, young men, they take away everything," so they would go there and smash them and so the movement kept growing. There was no plan; it so happened that Kandahar fell almost without a fight. Kandahar, I went to Kandahar when the Mujahideen were in power and Kandahar was being ruled by five different Mujahideen commanders. They had divided the city into five different sectors and practically you need a visa to cross into the different sectors and people were up to their noses, they were fed up. Everyone welcomed the Taliban, they were like angels, so the Mujahideen just fled. It kept happening, it was a series of events, one province after another, and by 1995 they were at the gates of Kabul. That time they couldn't take Kabul but in 1996 they captured Kabul as well; they had easy victories as people were ready for them. My theory is that if the former Communists had emerged at that time, if they had fought the Mujahideen, then people would even have welcomed them; they would have welcomed anyone: the former Communists, Taliban. Afghan people called the Mujahideen (Pashto word) "gunmen"; that was how they were known. These were remarkable events in Afghan; no one thought this would happen. The Mujahideen had this reputation, everyone had helped them with money, guns; they were able to expel the Red Army so no one could believe that these Taliban who had come out of the madrasah, who were landless and shelterless, how could they defeat the Mujahideen. But no one knew about the ground realities: people were fed up with the Mujahideen, they were waiting for someone to kick them out.

The Taliban were also coming from Pakistan too, studying there; in my village fifteen miles from Peshawar there were fifteen Afghans and no Pakistanis. The reason was that all kids from Pakistan could go to school.

**Istikhara** [Islamic dream incubation or heartfelt prayer: see earlier chapter]. I will tell you about the highest ranking civil servant in this government. He is strong believer in *Istikhara*. When General Musharaf captured power and formed the central government and provincial government, they wanted me to join the government, I refused saying I don't believe. Abdullah also asked me and came to me: "This is an offer, why don't you do *Istikhara*? And I will wait for you." He had announced the eight ministers and "We can announce your name tomorrow if you agree." I said, "I don't want to join the cabinet but for your sake I will do *Istikhara*": the first time I had done it. Before sleeping, doing it while awake, pray and focus on question, and I felt I got the answer and I shouldn't do it, and I told Abdullah next day; he said okay, but I was being pressured by the army, so he is a very strong believer in *Istikhara*.

Mullah Omar knew what was coming; he said, "I may be killed, the Taliban may be removed from power but I will not deliver Osama bin Laden; half my country was destroyed by the war. If the remaining half was destroyed protecting bin Laden then so be it; there was no going back." Maybe this was **also a dream;** I don't know. ...

You can't argue with these people. Anyone who sincerely declares jihad, they will never be captured; this is their belief. A strong commitment: they know what will happen, they are doing God's will. A stage comes when you don't care about the consequences. I have seen these Arab fighters, it was amazing, unbelievable: when someone got killed, instead of crying they would celebrate, *MABROOK*! *Mabrook* means "Congratulations, you are a martyr." They would then write letters to those parents of the killed, saying "You are lucky, I am unlucky as I have seen it." They can be very reckless also. I once went to Jalalabad, the front line; the Russians had left and the Mujahideen were fighting the Afghan army, and there were rows and rows of white tents and they were an easy target. I asked them why not use khaki, and he said they are Arabs they want to attract the attention of these planes. Maybe they weren't sleeping there, but this is what I saw.

## Discussion and Contextualization

I have quoted my interview with Yusufzai at length for, as well as containing the core material concerning the role of Mullah Omar's perceived dreaming in the origin and motivation of the Taliban, I think it contains other important contemporary information and views. The Western media almost always write about al-Qaeda and the Taliban in the same breath. In the same way that ex-president George W. Bush succeeded in convincing parts of the United States' population that Iraq and al-Qaeda were related, so are the Taliban and al-Qaeda joined at the hip so to speak by the Western media. Yusufzai was the man outside of Afghanistan who probably knew the reclusive Mullah Omar best before 9/11. He says in my interview that he is convinced that Mullah Omar did not know about the 9/11 attacks, leading up to the occupation of Afghanistan today. Hence, it was the West's interpretation and reaction to the hospitality code preventing Mullah Omar from asking bin Laden to leave Afghanistan after 9/11 that led to war on Afghan soil. Murshed (2006: 294), who was Pakistan's special envoy to Afghanistan from 1996–2001, makes clear that Mullah Omar tried to find a middle way out of his country's post-9/11 dilemma by his requests for evidence of bin Laden's responsibility and involvement; his offer to let a combined selected group of *ulema* from Afghanistan, Saudi Arabia, and a third Islamic country decide what to do; and other efforts. However, the United States and Saudi Arabia refused to consider these proposals.

Another significant difference between the Taliban and al-Qaeda is the former's almost exclusive preoccupation with Afghanistan, while al-Qaeda's focus has always been on international war/jihad against particularly the United States and its core allies. Yusufzai also makes clear that the origin and rapid growth of the Taliban from 1994 was in part due to the prevalent lawless and corrupt situation in Afghanistan after the Soviet Union's withdrawal. Interestingly, Giustozzi (2007: 72) points out the same reemergence of the Taliban, or the neo-Taliban as he names them, from 2002 onwards.

First, contextualizing the history of the Taliban, Murshed confirms the general details of Yusufzai's account of the rise of Mullah Omar: "The Taliban movement was a reaction to the prevailing anarchy after the Soviet withdrawal from Afghanistan and the subsequent misrule of the Rabbani regime." He argues that the Taliban have a long history: "The assumption that they (Taliban) first emerged in the summer of 1994 is erroneous" (2006: 42). Murshed considers the Taliban to be the products of the *madrasahs* or seminaries since the time that Islam came to Afghanistan. These Taliban have always fought the invaders of Afghanistan, e.g., the British twice in the nineteenth century. According to Murshed, the Taliban were the "core of the resistance" to the British. Likewise, the Taliban spearheaded the resistance to the Soviet invasion. Historically they planned to return to their *madrasahs* once the invader was defeated, but in 1994 they "decided to form a government themselves" (2006: 43). Murshed confirms Yusufzai's interview account that the Taliban movement founded by Mullah Omar started in a very small way "to punish a commander who had molested a local family." Hence, it was the "war weariness of the populace that made them welcome any force which could deliver them from the hands of brigands. They hungered for the restoration of peace and the semblance of an honest administration, no matter how harsh its system of justice" (2006: 43).

Yusufzai's first-hand account of the role of Mullah Omar's dreams in the Taliban revolution is not definitely confirmed by other written sources, though Mullah Omar's piety and elusiveness is referred to, as is the very rapid success of the Taliban. Rashid writes on the origin of the Taliban:

> Some Taliban say Mullah Omar was chosen as their leader not for his political or military ability, but for his piety and his unswerving belief in Islam. Others say he was chosen by God. "We selected Mullah Omar to lead this movement. He was the first among equals and we gave him the power to lead us and he has given us the power and authority to deal with peoples' problems," said Mullah Hassan. Mullah Omar himself gave a simple explanation to Pakistani journalist Rahimullah Yusufzai: "We took up arms to achieve the aims of the Afghan *jihad* and save our people from further suffering at the hands of the so-called Mujaheddin. We had complete faith in God Almighty. We never forgot that. He can bless us with victory or plunge us into defeat." (2000: 23)

Rashid acknowledges Rahimullah Yusufzai's contribution (2000: 249, n.6): "This profile of Mullah Omar has been built up over five years after interviews with dozens of Taliban leaders. I am grateful to Rahimullah Yusufzai's articles as he is the only journalist to have interviewed Mullah Omar." Marsden, whose book on the Taliban was published while they were in power, writes: "The Taliban appeared to emerge out of nowhere when they first came to the world's notice in October 1994." Marsden (1998: 44) also confirms Mullah Omar's enigmatic and elusive persona: "He is said to be in his mid-thirties. An aura of mystery surrounds Mullah Omar, because he is rarely seen in public or by visiting dignitaries. He limits his contacts to a few close associates." Rashid (2000: 23) states, "No leader in the world today is surrounded by so much secrecy and mystery as Mullah Muhammed Omar. Aged 39, he has never been photographed or met with Western diplomats and journalists." Yusufzai (Marquand 2001) has also written about Mullah Omar's dreams, for instance:

> Mullah Omar says he formed the Taliban after he was told in a dream that he should save the country. At first the Taliban numbered only 30, but within months it had swelled into a conquering force fanning out of Kandahar to take control of most of Afghanistan.

Murshid writes about the "vision" that inspired Mullah Omar to attack the city of Herat:

> The speed with which the Taliban secured control of Afghanistan convinced them that their success owed itself to divine will. I was told by many of them that after they had taken Kandahar, the natural course for the movement would have been to head north towards Kabul and the Pushtun-dominated eastern provinces but Mullah Omar was said to have had a vision directing him towards Herat. (2006: 277)

Murshid furthermore states that, after the capture of Kabul and two-thirds of Afghanistan, Mullah Omar was convinced that God/Allah was "on his side and that nothing could stop him from the accomplishment of his mission which was to impose the Taliban interpretation of Islam on the long-suffering people of Afghanistan." Murshid was in regular contact with Mullah Omar and describes him as having a "Messiah complex" (2006: 278).

Not everyone I met in Pakistan accepted this view of the importance of Mullah Omar's dreaming: the day after I interviewed Yusufzai, he introduced me to the imam of one of the largest mosques in the province. When I asked him about the possible value of such dream reports of Mullah Omar, the imam said he did not believe the reports. Burke, a UK journalist, explains the Taliban's extraordinary rise to power differently. He writes in his book on al-Qaeda:

> The Taliban themselves, and supporters in Pakistan, say that in the Spring of 1994 a Deobandi mullah in the dirt-poor village of Sinesar to the East of Kandahar became so incensed at the depredations inflicted on local people by the warlords who had carved out fiefdoms there after the end of the war against the Soviets that he gathered a group of men around him to act. Thousands spontaneously joined him in a bid to clean up their neighbourhood, and then their country. Because everyone was sick of violence and chaos, the Taliban had been welcomed everywhere. (2003: 108)

However, Burke admits that this account is contested and "has all the hallmarks of a foundational myth" (2003: 108), arguing that some believe that the extraordinary success of the Taliban and its very rapid rise to power was entirely due to the help of foreign agencies, notably the ISI (the Pakistani Intelligence Service). Certainly, Pakistan was the first state to recognize Afghanistan, only followed by Saudi Arabia and the United Arab Emirates.

Of course, as Rashid (2000), Burke (2003), and Murshed (2006) amply describe, the tortured story of Afghanistan and the Taliban from 1994 to 2002 is situated within a powerful political and military criss-crossing of alliances, betrayals, and warfare between the country's various militarized groupings and ethnicities. Moreover, because of their funding and provision of military equipment and through their backing of opposing groups, the neighboring states, particularly Iran and Pakistan, had enormous influence on internal Afghani affairs. Likewise the United States was a powerful player in this bloodthirsty story, which Rashid, with regard to the regional oil interests, describes as the "New Great Game" (2000: 7), after the nineteenth-century name for the rivalries Britain and Russia fought over, in particular, Afghanistan. However, all informed journalistic and academic analysts confirm the singularly powerful role of Islam and its diverse, often radical, interpretations by the various factions. The Taliban was and still is notorious for its extreme interpretation of Islamic purity for individuals, communities, and the state, particularly with regard to the place and education of women and girls, physical punishment for criminals, the banning of music, and the intolerance of other religions and religious groups such as the Shia arm of Islam. Rashid writes:

> The Taliban were neither radical Islamicists inspired by the Ikhwan [Muslim brotherhood originating in Egypt], nor mystical Sufis, nor traditionalists. They fitted nowhere in the Islamic spectrum of ideas and movements that had emerged in Afghanistan between 1979 and 1984. It could be said that the degeneration and collapse of legitimacy of all three trends (radical Islamicism, Sufism and traditionalism) into a naked rapacious power struggle created the ideological vacuum which the Taliban were to fill. The Taliban represented nobody but themselves and they recognized no Islam except their own. But they did have an ideological base—an extreme form of Deobandism, which was preached by Pakistani Islamic parties in Afghan refugee camps in Pakistan. The Deobandis, a branch of Sunni Hanafi Islam has had a history in Afghanistan, but the Taliban's interpretation of the creed has no parallel anywhere in the Muslim world. ... The Deobandis aimed to train a new generation of learned Muslims who would revive Islamic values based on intellectual learning, spiritual experience, Sharia law and Tariqah or the path. By teaching their students how to interpret Sharia, they aimed to harmonize the classical Sharia texts with current realities. The Deobandis took a restrictive view of the role of women, opposed all forms of hierarchy in the Muslim community and rejected the Shia—but the Taliban were to take these beliefs to an extreme which the original Deobandis would never have recognized. (2000: 87–88)

So, while outer world loyalties, alliances, ethnic and tribal memberships, and funding are extremely important, the inner worlds of perceived identity, belief, radical devotion to Islam, and loyalty to Mullah Omar as a known man of God/Allah—shown by his true dreaming and confirmed by his many military successes—are also significant to our understanding of the remarkable, sudden, and ongoing success of the Taliban. In his study of the rise of militant Islam in central Asia, Rashid demonstrates how these radical Islamist groups depend on a single charismatic leader, an amir, rather than a more demo-cratically constituted organization or parity for governance. They believe that the character, piety, and purity of their leader rather than his political abilities, education, or experience will enable him to lead the new society. (2002: 3)

As Yusufzai told me, Mullah Omar was a very shy, reclusive man with-out discernable charisma, other than his military prowess with a rocket-propelled grenade (RPG), his organizational skills, and his reputation for piety and divine guidance as communicated and discerned though his reported true dreams. Also, Mullah Omar seems to be a serious dreamer within the Islamic dream tradition. As said, he telephoned Yusufzai for help with a dream, which he thought would come true and which he considered to be a divinatory dream concerning the burning of the White House. The case example of Mullah Omar does most probably demon-strate the potential power of the reported dream in a key contemporary political context.

## Conclusions Regarding Jihadists' Dream Reports

For Islamic militant jihadists, dreams and visions are a core way of con-firming and legitimating their ideological worldview and the path to be-coming a *shahid,* a holy martyr. Whatever the veracity of individual dream narratives reported in this study, there is a clear overall pattern of reliance on divinatory dreams for inspiration and guidance, within the Islamic dreaming tradition originated by the Prophet Muhammed. The true dream experience is consistently utilized as a powerful legitimating device within the context of the Islamic theological exegesis of the potential, if very occasional, noumenal power and authority of the night dream. The assertions that jihadists are inspired by night dreams and legitimate their actions partly on the basis of night dreams constitute the first and second analytic threads of my argument.

However, it might be argued that jihadist leaders and their followers adopt such dream narratives for propagandist purposes in the knowledge that faithful Muslims believe in the possibility of such divinely inspired night dreams. While this may be the case in some of my examples, I would contend that the range and number of such reported dream narratives presented in this book strongly militate against such an argument. In-deed, even if it were the case that all my reported jihadist dream narratives are fabricated, the fact that Muslims often believe them and are mobilized to jihad partly on their account, as in the example of Mullah Omar's dream narratives, is of significance.

Social scientists can, through studies of Islamic dreaming, show how particular dream motifs (such as the Prophet and his companions) are part of a shared visionary world that can connect present-day believers with the (mythically) real past, and especially with the imagined early glorious days of Islam, the time of the Prophet himself. Moreover, such true dreams appear to facilitate the reenactment of this past in the present. This merging of (mythical) dreamed reality and mundane reality constitutes the third thread of my argument, and this is shown for instance in the quotation from Fouda (2003: 109) concerning Binalshibh, who "speaks of the Prophet and his close companions as if he had actually met them." The dream world is experienced as more real than this world, and reality becomes more dreamlike, a veil over the sublime glory of hidden paradisiacal worlds. Dreams can be tastes, divinations, of possible welcome futures. Sacred figures are to be emulated and even identified with, and certainly their words are perceived as divine instruction. We see bin Laden clearly interpreting dreams as a spiritual leader.

The fourth thread of my argument is that militant jihadism can be directly authorized by dream content. The classical Freudian distinction between the manifest and latent meanings of a dream is changed. The clearer the manifest communication, the closer to God the dreamer is, as we have seen in many of the dream narratives reported in this article. Mullah Omar is given "instructions" in his dreams as to his military strategy, the US "White House" burns, Bin Laden is said to have "executed" 9/11 to avenge the Palestinians, Moussaoui dreams of flying a plane into a tall building; Abu Cheema is welcomed into paradise and the Prophet is heard speaking clearly; the words of Jesus are heard by a Guantanamo Bay inmate; another is "told" he will be released in two years.

However, not all the dream narratives are understood solely through reliance on their manifest meaning. Reid's interpretation of the "full pickup truck" passing him by as referring to his missing the 9/11 attack is an interpretation from a manifest to a supposed latent meaning, as is bin Laden's claim that it is a good omen to dream his soccer team being dressed as "pilots" and winning against the American team and interpretation of the "Egyptian family going about its business" as a reference to Atta.

These narratives clearly show that jihadists understand their dreams within the context of the Islamic worldview. Dreamed sacred figures, for example, are not unreal projections of the unconscious or deeply encoded manifestations of earlier dysfunctional familial experiences, like they would be in Western interpretations, but figures that inhabit the supernaturally real world of Islam and reassert the eternal truths of the Qur'an and the hadiths.

The relationship between dreams and events is another analytic thread running through the narratives. Mullah Omar is called to save his country and introduce Sha'ria. For a while the Taliban did achieve extraordinary success, which seemed to confirm his dreamed inspiration to his followers. A final thread—that of the prophetic example of Muhammed's advisory dream before the battle of Badr—is again shown in the dream narratives attributed to Mullah Omar.

In conclusion, charismatic leaders like Mullah Omar offer their dreams as a self-justifying and legitimating device, claiming them to be revelations from beyond this world and containing authorization for radical human action in this world.

# CHAPTER 7

# Dream Interpretation Resources (Dictionaries) in Islam

"A general characteristic of the Arabian dream-books is that almost anything can mean everything, a result partly of the compilatory nature of these books and also of the inventiveness of the contributors who exploited the interpretive potential of metonymy, metaphor and paronomasia or false etymology, which are their favourite tools, together, of course, with Quaranic and other allusions" (van Gelder 1999: 509).

In chapter 1 I introduced the significant role of night dreams, *al-ruya,* in the birth and history of Islam. In chapters 5 and 6 I examined how contemporary Islamic militant jihadist groups such as al-Qaeda and the Taliban use them. I have detailed how night dreams were one of the revelatory instruments for the Prophet Muhammed. In the Qur'an there are instances (i.e., Qur'an 8.43; 48.27) of the Prophet experiencing true dreams (from Allah). Also, the Joseph sura (12.6) recounts the famous story of the prophet Joseph and his ability to interpret the dreams of the Egyptian pharoah. Indeed, in many ways the Qur'an and the hadiths are the metaphorical bedrock of dream interpretation practices in Islam today, as well as in past centuries.

In this chapter, I will critically analyze several of the most prominent dream interpretation guides currently used in Islamic cultures. However, first I will refer to some of the core dreams in the Qur'an, as all Islamic dream interpretation books are based on Qur'anic examples and those from the hadiths. Particularly important to Muslims is Abraham's dream in which God/Allah demands that he should sacrifice his son Ishmael. The demand to sacrifice Ishmael can be seen as a key test of Abraham's faith. Once he has submitted to the will of Allah, he is released from this sacrificial necessity (Qur'an 37:102). This story is also contained in the Hebrew Bible (Gen 22:1–24), but the Qur'anic version is much clearer that the instruction to Abraham is given to him in a dream rather than in a vision. Also in the Hebrew Bible it is Abraham's son Isaac, not Ishmael, that he is ordered to sacrifice. This test of Abraham is commemorated in the annual "stoning of the Devil" during the Hajj pilgrimage to Mecca. The Joseph sura in the Qur'an (12.6) tells the same story as in the Hebrew Bible (Gen 37, 41) of Joseph and his famous dreams, including his interpreting the dreams of the Egyptian pharaoh concerning future times of plenty and famine (the seven fat and thin cows dream). In each of the six most reliable (strongest) hadiths, there is an often very similar chapter on dream interpretation (Lamoreaux 2002: 116–17).

## Features of Dream Interpretation

Dream interpretation in Islam, even given the apparently simple classificatory system, is extremely sophisticated. Unlike their Western counterparts, Islamic dream dictionaries may contain many interpretations of the same symbol. For example, if a poor person dreams of honey, it can be a sign of illness as only then will poor people buy honey, whereas for a rich person to dream of honey is a favorable sign.

Dream interpretation focuses first on the manifest or literal meaning of the dream: the dream can be its own interpretation. Also, other realities can be shown in dreams, and commands can be received as how to act in this world. Indeed, along with visions, knowledge of other worlds is only experienced via the portal of night dreams. This way the otherworldly knowledge becomes "known" and affirmed to believers in this world. However, dreams, being keys to the future and human betterment, especially that of the dreamer, are often metaphorical and need interpretation. Often nature imagery—for example, dates, grapes, milk, eggs, and the whole potential abundance of this world's reality—is perceived in dreams. Interestingly, the interpretation of nature imagery seems to generally follow human experience of such realities, for example, fresh grapes dreamed of in the grape season are seen as an excellent sign. Of course, humans do so perceive them also in reality. For example, a young Turkish scholar in 2005 told me he had dreamed of dates the night before he met me. He perceived this as a good augury for our meeting. Indeed our relationship was very positive.

Not only nature symbols are directly translated from experience in this world to understanding and interpretation of dream imagery. A "shirt" and its length is understood from a hadith (Bukhari 1979: 9:113–14, no. 137) in terms of religion as it covers nakedness. This reference presumably takes us back to the Garden of Eden, the story of Adam and Eve and the beginning of humans wearing clothing as a result of the temptation of the serpent. This story also appears in the Qur'an (7:20). The "sword" symbol relates to warfare, casualties, and victory. Of course, in reality the sword is a prominent, warlike weapon that can kill. Likewise silk is regarded as a special, luxuriant fabric and is figured in two of the Prophet Muhammed's reported dreams wrapping up his future wife, Aisha (Bukhari 1979: 9:113–14, no. 137).

While Freud talked of day residues finding their way into dreams, the situation in Islam is almost the opposite. Otherworldly images are understood to occur in our dreams as potentially true signs and symbols. This world is temporal while the Islamic heaven, for example, is transcendentally understood as eternal. Lamoreaux captures this difference between Islamic and Freudian dream interpretation traditions well: "Dream interpretation offered Muslims a royal road that led not inward but outward, providing insight not into the dreamer's psyche but into the hidden affairs of the world. In short, the aim of dream interpretation was not diagnosis, but divination" (2002: 4).

## Range of Sources Studied

In order to understand the complexity of Islamic dream interpretation, I have studied three current versions of Ibn Sirin's famous dream interpretation book (2000a, 2000b, 2000c) and three books of Islamic dream interpretation written by different contemporary authors (al-Jibaly 2006; Fareed 2003; Philips 2001). Also, I have investigated Gouda's compilation and synthesis of three of the early and most famous dream interpretation works (1991). These sources constitute a good range of examples of Islamic dream interpretation. These sources are sufficient to analyze such works as exemplary for the whole range of dream dictionaries, as there is a massive overlap in perspective, style, and content. Also, I take Lamoreaux's *The Early Muslim Tradition of Dream Interpretation* (2002) into account to establish to what extent the early dream interpretation works are different compared to contemporary works.

### Ibn Sirin, *Dreams and Interpretations*

Ibn Sirin's book, *Dreams and Interpretations,* is by far the most popular Islamic dream interpretation dictionary and is referred to by all other dictionaries. I have discussed in the introduction the question whether Ibn Sirin is actually the original author of all these editions. Certainly, in my experience in the United Kingdom and Pakistan, it is the foremost dream dictionary used in Muslim households. Recently, two anthropology academics visiting Durham also told me it was the most popular book on sale at the largest book fair in Algeria last year.

Ibn Sirin's book draws on the work of the ancient Greek author Artemidorus (1992). Arguably, all subsequent Islamic dream dictionaries are based on the work of Ibn Sirin, except for the work of Phillips. For example, al-Jibaly recommends Ibn Sirin's work above all other dream interpretation books. Indeed, he quotes a text in which Ibn Sirin had "divine support in interpreting dreams" (al-Jibaly 2006: 259), and yet Ibn Sirin apparently interpreted sometimes just one in forty dreams (al-Jibaly 2006: 261) as most dreams are considered meaningless by him. Moreover, on the UK Sunnipath website, an enquirer asks about dream interpretation and is referred to the work of Ibn Sirin (spelling as on website):

09–15–2004, 01:17 AM

Asalamualaykum Warahmatullah,

Can anyone direct me to a Shaikh who can give tafseer [Qur'anic commentary] for dreams, but someone who is known by reputation of giving sound interpretation?

If there was any Shaykh I would direct you to for the interpretations of dreams, then it would be no other then Imam Muhammad Ibn Seerin Al-Basri "Allah bless his soul" [33 AH] 653 AD, also known as Ibn Seerin. He is from amongst the masters in the filed [*sic*] of dream interpretations. Eastern people easily recognise the name of Imam Muhmmad ibn Seerin, who is most honoured for his outstanding knowledge and piety. He is particularly known for his outstanding work *Muntakhab Al-Kalam fi Tafisr Al-Ahlam* (The Key Declamation on Dream Interpretation) which is considered by dream interpreters in the Muslim world as a major source of knowledge that enriched the spirit of readers as well as dream interpreters for the past one thousand years. There is of course the other works of masters on this branch of knowledge which must be credited. Most of these masters (Allah bless their souls) agree upon the basic interpretations, based on their common understanding of the principal references in religious books. Unfortunately as you know these masters are not amongst us today, but we have their works! Imam Ibn Seerin's *Tafsir Al-Ahlam* has been translated into English and is in the bookshops, it is called: *Ibn Seerin's Dictionary of Dreams*.

This is a very thick book and has everything to know about dream interpretation and its position in the Shariah as Fard has already mentioned also has over thousands of dreams explained.

Because of its singular importance, I have studied three different editions of Ibn Sirin's book: London (2000a), New Delhi (2000b), and Karachi (2000c). As can be seen from the publication locations, different versions are widely produced across the Islamic world. Reliance on the

Qur'an and hadiths, word etymology, and use of idiomatic language are core dream interpretation methods. The use of the Qur'an and the hadiths will not be addressed here, but in the words of Philips and al-Jibaly, as they deal with the scriptures in more detail.

Of the three editions, the London edition is more structured: interpretations are placed in paragraphs rather than in single lines. All three editions begin with general principles regarding dream interpretation, which are similar to the other dream interpretation texts studied in this chapter. Then there are many sections containing straightforward and directive interpretations, which are not usually explained with reference to the Qur'an or hadiths. The final sections interpret the meaning of the dreamer reciting different suras from the Qur'an in a dream.

### Yehia Gouda, *Dreams and their Meaning in the Old Arab Tradition*

I have already referred to Gouda's work quite extensively, particularly his summary and formulation of the role of dreams in Islam. Since Gouda summarizes the works of three great Islamic dream interpreters, Ibn Sirin, Ibn Shaheen, and al-Nabulsi, I will not repeat the key dream doctrines such as the threefold classification of dreams, as they are the same as in other works quoted in this chapter. Gouda makes an interesting point that one should substitute "car" and "plane" for "camels" and "donkeys," etc; likewise "sultan" might well become one's "boss"!

### Dr. Abu Ameenah Bilal Philips, *Dream Interpretation according to the Qur'an and Sunnah*

Along with al-Jibaly's work, which I will address below, Philips's book contains the clearest references to the Qur'an and the hadiths. The *Sunnah* refers to the Prophetic example as described in the hadiths; in Shia Islam, the Sunnah also includes the example of the Twelve Imams. While referring to other key interpretative issues in Islamic dream interpretation, Philips's book also contains the clearest exposition of the difference between legislative and general dreams in Islam.

Most Islamic dream dictionaries give directive interpretations often without acknowledging any sources. Philips is critical of this approach and accordingly seeks to embed his interpretations in the narratives and examples of the Prophet Muhammed and some of his followers. As such, his work acknowledges the central importance of the symbolic meanings contained in the Qur'an and the hadiths. Bukhari (1979) and Muslim (1987) contain many examples of prophetic dream interpretations. Also, Philips's work contains sections on Islamic dream theory and practice, such as the threefold typology of dreams as being true, false (from the devil) or unimportant ego (*nafs*) dreams. Philips describes true dreams and waking visions as being the only form of revelation available now to humans following the completion of the Qur'anic prophecy by the Prophet Muhammed. Furthermore, this book includes a section on preparation for sleep, called "etiquette for sleep."

The dream interpretation sections begin with the reminder of the Prophet's common practice of asking his companions about their dreams in the morning: Did any of you see any vision last night? (Philips 2001: 38) Dream interpretation is then distinguished from fortune telling, which is forbidden in Islam. According to one of the Prophet's companions, dreams have a need to be interpreted: "The dream flutters over a man as long as it is not interpreted, but when it is interpreted, it settles. ... and I think he [the Prophet Muhammed] said, 'Tell it only to a beloved friend or one who has good judgement'" (2001: 43). Only good dreams should be interpreted, for otherwise false dreams will confuse or even lead one astray. Interestingly, good dreams are to be interpreted positively as events may be influenced by the interpretation, much like the Western psychological notion of a self-fulfilling prophecy. Philips writes: "Indeed, dreams occur according to how they are interpreted. It is like a man who raises his leg and waits for when to put it down. So, if any of you has a dream, don't relate it except to a confidante or a scholar" (2001: 44).

Only prophets can always correctly interpret a dream (Philips 2001: 46). Moreover, good dreams should lead to action. For example, when someone sees himself doing something "commendable, it is permissible" (2001: 48), to carry out such an act in reality. Here we see the continuing theme of the relationship between manifest dream content and reality events that is such a characteristic feature of Islamic dream theory and practice.

Finally, Philips emphasizes the central importance of the Islamic holy texts for dream interpretation: "The foundation of all Islamic knowledge is revelation contained in the Qur'an and the Sunnah. Since good dreams are also a form of revelation from Allah, any legitimate attempt to interpret the symbolism of dreams should rely primarily on the symbolism found in the Qur'an and the Sunnah" (Philips 2001: 49).

### Sunnah/Hadith Interpretations
Philip's emphasizes that the symbols and metaphors from the hadiths should be used to understand dreams, for example:

> Dreaming of a "rib", refers to a woman as "women are created from a curved rib." (Philips 2001: 51; Bukhari 1979: 7:81, no. 114; Muslim 2:752–53, no. 3468)

Dreaming of a "shirt" refers to "religion," as the Prophet so interprets a dream he had, "While I was sleeping, people were displayed before me wearing shirts, some of which only covered their chests and some of which covered below that. Then Umar ibn al-Khattaab was shown to me and he was wearing a shirt (so long that) he was dragging (it behind him); When the people asked the Prophet how he interpreted it, he replied "It refers to the religion." (Philips 2001: 51; Bukhari 1979: 9:113–14, no. 137)

### Word Interpretation

According to Philips, the Prophet Muhammed also used the meaning of words and names in dreams to assign meaning to the dream. Philips calls this wordplay "analagous deduction." Philips gives as an example of the Prophet's practice: "Last night I (the Prophet Muhammed) dreamt that we were in the house of "Ugbah ibn Raafi," and were brought some Ibn Taab fresh dates. I interpreted it as meaning that eminence in this world will be granted to us, a blessed hereafter, and that our religion has become complete" (Philips 2001: 52). Philips writes that the Prophet "derived the concept of a blessed hereafter (*aaquibah*) from the name Ugbah, he derived eminence (*rifah*) from the name Raafi, and he derived becoming good, i.e., complete (*taaba*) from the name Taab" (Philips 2001: 52).

### Legislative and General Dreams

Philips makes a distinction between these two classes of dreams, i.e., legislative and general dreams, that is not included in many of the Islamic dreamwork books studied. Legislative dreams contain "Islamic legislation or information about the unseen world (*ghayb*)." Philips further states that legislative dreams

> cannot be used to explain dreams occurring after the era of Islamic regulation. Those of their dreams which contained religious practices were validated by the Prophet and thus became part of Islamic law. While, those which addressed events in the future [i.e., concerning heaven or hell and their inhabitants] were confirmed as fact by the Prophet's statements. Consequently, this collection is only for the reader to get an idea of the types of dreams that the Prophet and his companions experienced, as well as some of the unique aspects of divine legislation which came through the dream medium. (Philips 2001: 75)

The history of legislative dreams is not confined to the Islamic world, as Kingsley has argued that the beginnings of Greek law and philosophy came from early Greek shamanic practices (2003).

It is well known in Islam that the *Adhan*, or call to prayer in the mosque, was revealed in a night dream to the Prophet's companion Abdullah ibn Zayd. Philips (2001: 76–77; and verified in the hadith compiled by Sunan Abi Dawood) writes of this momentous event in the history of Islam:

> Abdullah ibn Zayd said, "When the messenger of Allah ordered a bell to be made so that it might be rung to gather the people for prayer, a man carrying a bell in his hand appeared to me in a dream and I asked him, 'O servant of Allah [Abdullah], will you sell the bell?' The man asked, 'What will you do with it?' I replied, 'We will use it to call the people to prayer.' He said, 'Can I suggest for you something better than that?' I replied, 'Certainly.'"

Here follows the full text of the call to prayer, a centerpiece of the Islamic religion, and revealed in a recorded night dream. Then:

> When the morning came, I went to the Messenger of Allah and informed him of what I had dreamt. He said, "It is a true dream, if Allah wills; so get up along with Bilaal and teach him what you saw in the vision, and he should then use it to call people to prayer, for he has a louder and sweeter voice than you have." (Philips 2001: 76–7)

A further legislative dream example in Philips is of information received in a dream by the Prophet concerning Bilaal and his wife ar-Rumaysaa being in Paradise (Philips 2001: 53). Legislative dreams are said to have finished with the Prophet, as major prophecy is understood to have been completed: Muhammed is the seal of the prophets and Islam is understood as being the perfect religion covering all aspects of human existence.

Philips introduces many other examples including legislative dreams in which the Prophet interpreted a "black woman with untidy hair going out of Medina to Mahya'ah, which he interpreted as the spread of an epidemic" (Philips 2001: 79). Philips again refers to how the interpretation uses word analogies: "The relationship between black woman and the epidemic can be deduced from the word *sawdaa* (black), from which the words *soo* (evil) and *daa* (sickness) can be extracted. Her untidy hair represents the outbreak of the evil" (Philips 2001: 78–79). Interestingly, dream interpretation through working with the metaphorical meanings embedded in culturally specific idiomatic language use is commonplace, as I discovered running my own dreamwork groups for my PhD (Edgar 1995; my PhD study was of symbolic dream interpretation practices in three UK dreamwork groups that I co-facilitated in Newcastle-upon-Tyne; there were no Muslim members of the group).

Philips (2001: 79–99) then presents another eighteen legislative dreams of the Prophet from the hadiths. I will summarize some of these in table form:

## Table 1: Legislative Dreams

| Legislative Dream | Interpretation |
|---|---|
| The Prophet dreamed that he was wearing two gold bangles that he was disturbed about (wearing gold jewelry is not allowed for a man in Islam). | The Prophet Muhammed interpreted this as referring to two false prophets who would be killed. |
| The Prophet saw cows being slaughtered. | He interpreted this as referring to the believers who had been killed at the battle of Uhud. |
| Pulling water with buckets from a well. | The Prophet considers this to be referring to his succession, on account of the person present at the well, also pulling water. |
| Seeing "the father of the Ka'b tribe dragging his intestines in the hellfire." | The Prophet interprets this dream image as an originator of idolatry. |
| The Prophet dreams he is using a toothpick and gives it to the elder of two people. | The interpretation concerns respect for elders. |
| Companions were shown that the "Night of Power" would take place in the last seven days of the month of Ramadan. | The Prophet confirms their dreams and says: "Seek it in the last seven days of Ramadan." |
| The Prophet dreams of a palace in Paradise. | Implicitly, this dream refers to the future status of Umar ibn al-Khattab in paradise, for the Prophet Muhammed foresaw him owning this palace. |
| The Prophet has a long dream about the torments of the wicked (liars, adulterers, etc.) in the afterlife of Hell and visits the paradisiacal Garden of Eden where he sees the Prophet Abraham. | So, the dream is interpreted as explicitly showing the heavenly and hellish consequences of different actions in this world. |
| The Prophet dreams of some of his followers dying as fighters in Allah's cause, and "sailing in the middle of the seas like kings." This is reported as a precognitive or "true" dream. The Prophet's companion who is listening asks to be among them, and this is granted. | The true dream needs to be interpreted literally. Philips confirms that the Prophet's companion, Umm Haraam, did go sailing, and after coming ashore, fell down dead. |

I have detailed these core legislative dreams as they provide evidence that there are many accounts in the hadiths that confirm to Muslims the power, authority, and significance of dreams in the Prophetic revelation and have become a source of symbolic interpretation in subsequent Islamic dream dictionaries.

Philips considers general dreams to be dreams that the Prophet interpreted that do not contain legislative material. Hence, the Prophet's symbolic interpretation of these dreams may be used as exemplars for future interpretation, i.e., after the prophetic era. For example, since the Prophet interpreted "milk" as a reference to "knowledge," the dream image of "milk" has been interpreted that way ever since. The dream text of this milk imagery is:

> "While I was sleeping, I was given a bowl full of milk [in the dream] and I drank from it until I noticed its wetness coming out of my limbs. Then I gave it to Umar ibn al-Khattaab." The persons sitting around asked him how he interpreted it and the prophet said, "[It is religious] knowledge." (Philips 2001: 55–56; also Bukhari 1979: 9:112, no. 135)

Like this milk example, Philip (2001: 100–128) sets out a list of symbolic dream interpretations for general dreams. They are referenced from verses from the Qur'an or from the hadiths:

### Table 2: General Dreams

| Dream Symbol | Interpretation | Reference |
|---|---|---|
| Dreaming of eating ripe dates and acquiring them | Symbolizes Allah's granting of provisions, a reminder to pay one's charitable dues or to avoid extravagance | Qur'an: sura *al-An'aam*/The Battlements 1955: 6: v.141 |
| Dreaming of a door | May refer to the "successful completion of a project, or the winning of an argument," cp. Qur'an: "Enter upon them through the gate. For when you enter, victory will be yours." | Qur'an: sura *al-Maa'ida*/The Table 1955: 5: v.23 |
| Dreaming of an egg | May refer to a woman according to the Qur'anic metaphor referring to the "maidens of Paradise": "And they will have with them chaste females with lowered, large, beautiful eyes; delicate and pure, like well-preserved eggs." | Qur'an: sura *as-Saaffaat*/The Rangers 1955: 37: v.48–9 (In 1955 Qur'an "egg" is translated as "pearl.") |
| Dreaming of a flowing stream | May refer to continued rewards for one's good deeds | Bukhari 9:119–20, no. 145 |

| | | |
|---|---|---|
| Dreaming of a silk cloth | May indicate marriage as the Prophet twice dreamed of his wife, Aisha, being borne by an angel to him in a silk cloth and said, "If this is from Allah, then it must happen." | Bukhari 9:115–16, no. 140 |

The symbolic treasure of the Qur'an and the hadiths is then mined to provide rules for dream interpretation that are found in all Islamic dream dictionaries.

## Ahmed Fareed, *Authentic Interpretation of the DREAMS: According to the Quraan and Sunnah*

Fareed's book is a relatively lightweight and derivative dream dictionary. The first part contains the customary Islamic dream theory, which does not at all differ from the other texts considered. Again, the importance of dreams and their interpretations is stated: "The interpretation of dreams is one of the greatest, comprehensive and most useful types of knowledge" (Fareed 2003: 9).

The book contains the usual sections of the different types of dreams, dreams of the Prophet Muhammed, and the importance of the Qur'an and the hadiths as containing examples and metaphors that should be used in dream interpretation. It also refers to Ibn Sirin; for instance, how he interpreted whether the sight of the Prophet Muhammed in a dream pointed to a true dream. From Fareed we learn that Ibn Sirin apparently asked the dreamers to describe the Prophet, in order to see whether the description resembled the authentic descriptions of the Prophet:

> Therefore I shall summarise the description of the prophet. He was very light skinned, with a broad forehead, large deep black eyes, long eye lashes, long thick beard, broad shoulders, and was neither tall, nor short, curly hair reaching to his shoulders, and if he should speak, it would be as if light were coming out from within him. (Fareed 2003: 26)

As with the other texts, "sleep etiquette" seems to be important: preparing for going to bed, prayers, repentance, bed preparation, and sleeping on the right-hand side. Fareed also states that Muslims are enjoined only to tell their dreams to people they love and to scholars. This is referenced by Joseph's story in which he evoked the jealousy of his brothers and which eventually lead to their attempt to kill him (Qur'an: Joseph sura 12.6, and Hebrew Bible, Gen 37–44). From Fareed we also learn that Muslims should never lie about a dream, as this is "one of the worst kind of sin" (2003: 38). This notion is confirmed in Bukhari: "The worst lie is that of a person who claims to have seen a dream which he has not seen" (1979: 12:427). A hadith (Bukhari 1979: 12:427) warns that the punishment for such a sin is to be ordered (presumably in the afterlife) to "make a knot with two barley grains, which he could never do" (Fareed 2003: 49). The book also contains an interesting anecdote that counsels eloquence and tact in interpretation:

> The interpreter should use the best and most eloquent language possible. It was reported that a Caliph called for an interpreter and asked him: "I have seen in a dream that all my teeth fell out." The interpreter said: "All your relatives will die." The Caliph's face changed and was furious; so he called for another interpreter and related his dream to him, the second interpreter said: "If the dream of my Caliph comes true, he will live longer than his relatives." The Caliph was happy and so rewarded him. Both interpretations were correct however, yet the approach was different" (Fareed 2003: 42).

The rest of the book is a straightforward list of dream symbols and their interpretation based on quoted Qur'anic verses and from interpretative examples from the hadiths. Symbols such as egg, rope, cows, shirt, milk, keys, sword, gold, silk, paradise, and door are similarly interpreted as in Philips, though in a shorter form and with less alternatives. Again, Fareed gives the same examples as Philips of interpreting people's names as qualities (called "analogous reasoning" by Philips). Likewise, the example of the woman with unkempt hair and the place of the epidemic is quoted.

In the section "interpreting dreams from the meaning of the proverb" (2003: 92) we find that meaning is found through relating the dream symbols to idiomatic and proverbial language use. Fareed gives an example of a dream in which a jeweler takes part, and the jeweler's presence is interpreted as a reference to the presence of a liar, as in the proverb, "The worst liars are jewelers." Also, digging a hole is "interpreted as deception and cunning," because people say, "to dig one's own grave." Likewise, "dreaming of a long hand," is interpreted as "doing favors" because of the proverb "to lend a helping hand." "Washing hands" is interpreted as hopelessness, because people say: "I wash my hands of you" (2003: 93). The proverbial metaphors of language are used to unravel the dream symbols of the night.

Like in Philips, we also encounter in Fareed the direct use of nature imagery: If you dream of a citrus fruit, you will be praised and admired, as the Prophet Muhammed had compared a believer who recites the Qur'an and acts on it to be like a citrus fruit. Short-lived flowers (e.g., daffodils and narcissus) refer to a short period, and the opposite goes for long-living flowers (e.g., myrtle). Fareed quotes an Islamic dream interpreter, who interprets a wife's dream of being given a narcissus but the other wife being given a myrtle as meaning that her husband would "divorce her and keep his other wife" (2003: 94). Similarly, there is the use of opposites in interpretation: "dreaming of crying is interpreted as happiness, laughter as sadness," love as madness, war as a plague, and poverty as riches and vice versa, etc. (2003: 95).

Then follows a short section on further rules for dream interpretation, full of references to the Prophet's dreams as described in the Qur'an. Are dream messages always to be followed up in reality? The answer seems to be: it depends on the nature of the message. A distinct feature of Fareed's dream interpretation book is a cultural section in which the meaning of the dream is contextualized: different interpretations can occur in different countries. For example, Persians interpret a quince fruit (*safargal*) as "beauty, pride, and relaxation," whereas Arabs believe the fruit points to travel and departure. These cultural differences are linguistically based, since *safar* in Arabic means "traveling" and *jala* means "departure." Similarly, the religion of a people is taken into account when interpreting a dream, e.g., when a dream contains the symbol of an animal not ritually slaughtered, which is a bad omen for a Muslim but a fortunate one for a person of another religion (2003: 98). Context counts.

As we have already seen, similar dreams have different meanings depending upon who dreamed them. Fareed quotes Ibn Sirin who interpreted, via Qur'anic verses, two different peoples' dreams of "giving a sermon." To one person, Ibn Sirin says the dream means that he will go on hajj (pilgrimage to Mecca) while to the other he states that his "hand would be cut off." Ibn Sirin explained his different interpretations of the same symbol: the first person was a good person and therefore he explained the hajj symbol with reference to the Qur'an, "and make *Adhan* (proclaim) to mankind the Hajj" (2003: 99). However, Ibn Sirin didn't like the other person's appearance and subsequently interpreted the symbol according to the verse, "then shouted a crier: 'O you in the caravan surely you are thieves'" (2003: 100).

Fareed mentions another strategy in the rules of dream interpretation: a dream divination often is interpreted as intended for the relative, typically the son, of the person seen in the dream. An example is given: the Prophet seeing that Usaid ibn al-A would be governor of Makkah (Mecca). However, it turned out that his son was appointed. Paradoxically, even though the complete veracity of the interpretation of all the Prophet's dreams is presupposed, this dream holds a secondary meaning to a literal first layer of observation.

## Muhammad Mustafa al-Jibaly, *The Dreamer's Handbook: Sleep Etiquette and Dream Interpretation in Light of the Sunnah*

Al-Jibaly's book is substantially longer and uses more detail and quotes from the Qur'an as well as more Arabic prayers. Nearly half of the book is taken up on sleep etiquette and the "going to bed" preparation. Also, we find the same typology of dreams that we have found in other texts. A little more detail is given on the nature of the true dream. The true dream should have a high impact on the dreamer when awakening. Moreover, the dreamer may awaken suddenly from it. Also true dreams can be forewarning of possible harm and might be admonishment messages about a dreamer's already made errors. Again, in al-Jibaly's book, each of the Prophet Muhammed's dreams from the Qur'an and the hadiths are related and interpreted in the same way as in Philips's book. Philips gives a little more detail, but the key interpretation is almost identical, with the possible exception of the black woman with untidy hair (al-Jibaly 2006: 165; Philips 2001: 78). Al-Jibaly does not interpret the black woman as an "evil disease," an interpretation based upon the meanings of the Arabic word *sawda*. Rather, he understands *sawda* as "prevalent," as that is one of the linguistic meanings of *sawda*. "Woman" is understood as a *fitnah* or trial, because "one of the ways that Allah tries men is through women" (2006: 165). So, al-Jibaly considers the Prophetic interpretation is that of a "prevalent coming harm that had resided in al-Madinah, that had a sinister and ugly nature, and that struck people in all directions, causing them to have a messy and "sick" appearance".

In comparison to other dream books, al-Jibaly gives more detail about some dreams of the Prophet. Also, more emphasis is placed on the Prophet's descriptions of heaven and hell. However, the examples of dreams used to describe these otherworldly realms are the same as the ones used in Philips (i.e., 2006: 88). The two most reliable hadiths, those of Bukhari and Muslim, are the most referred to. Furthermore, the same dreams of the Prophet's companions are presented. Al-Jibaly is clearly opposed to Sufi dream interpretations, arguing that Sufis develop deviant interpretations (2006: 238). However, he does not develop this critique of Sufi dream interpretation further. Also, he resolutely argues against new acts of worship not already taught in the Sunnah being developed upon the basis of dreams and their interpretation.

According to al-Jilaby there are six correct forms of Islamic dream interpretation (2006: 243):

1. Dream interpretation by analogy with the Qur'an
2. Dream interpretation by analogy with Sunnah
3. Dream interpretation by analogy with sayings or poetry
4. Dream interpretation by analogy with tangible facts, e.g., stars are used for guidance
5. Dream interpretation that uses the meanings of names
6. Dream interpretation by means of inversion (the meaning is opposite to the evident one in the dream).

Al-Jibaly also emphasizes the importance of the dreamers' personality, profession, character and piety. Again we see the importance of seasonality in the interpretation of a dream, not just with regard to nature symbols but also with respect to manmade objects and resultant situations. For example, a person wearing thin clothes in winter can be a sign of distress, contrary to their wearing such clothes in summer (2006: 244). Contrary to other dream interpreters, al-Jibaly does not concur that the time in which a dream is experienced is important. However, he does agree with Fareed that a dream event may be applicable not to the dreamer himself, but rather to the dreamer's relative.

In his section on the "etiquettes for a dream interpreter," al-Jibaly advises that only dreams "that have an apparent value as glad tidings, warnings, or guidance, should be interpreted and mixed up medleys" should be avoided (2006: 264). Moreover, in religious matters he regards dream interpretation as being just as significant as giving a fatwa (religious ruling). Interestingly, nature imagery is not always obviously interpreted according to reality. For example, the cedar tree is seen as a symbol of hypocrisy and corruption, while a soft plant or an ear of wheat is thought of as a symbol for a believer who submits to Islam, because such a plant tends to blow in and submit to the wind (2006: 283). Al-Jibaly takes the negative interpretation of the cedar tree as indicating hypocrisy and corruption from the hadiths by Bukhari (1979: 5643–44, 7466). Its interpretation connects the strength of the cedar tree, yet its sudden breakdown, when Allah wills it. The final section of al-Jibaly's book consists of a glossary of dream symbols. This glossary is based upon earlier interpretations of dream symbols.

## Conclusion to Studying Dream Dictionary Books

After studying the aforementioned dream books, a similarity in themes between all books can be observed. First, they all have a common understanding of a threefold typology of dreams: A dream is either 1) a true dream, 2) a false dream, or 3) a meaningless dream. A dream of the Prophet Muhammed, provided he is perceived as complete and the dream message does not contradict the teachings of the Qur'an, is considered to be a true dream. However, Phillips also recognizes the categories of "legislative" and "general" dreams.

Second, interpretation is often based on common experience and understanding of this world's reality. Often dream interpretation books take the manifest meaning of the dream at face value. However, symbolic meaning can be given to the dream content with the help of certain interpretative devices: the etymological root and idiomatic use of a word or name can be important. Also, the linguistic meaning of names and people can help in interpreting a dream. Moreover, the time of night or year in which the dream is dreamed is significant. Furthermore, the spiritual and worldly status of the dreamer is very important and can significantly change the meaning of a dream symbol. Nevertheless, in certain dreams, inversion takes place and a dream symbol must be assigned a meaning opposite of its apparent meaning. Hence, the complexity of such an elaborate set of interpretive devices calls for a trustworthy interpreter. Therefore, dreams in Islam can only be interpreted either by scholars or by persons whom are trusted by the dreamer (usually loved ones).

Third and foremost, dream interpretation books stress the overarching importance of the Qur'an and the hadiths for metaphorical examples from which to make satisfactory symbolic dream interpretations. Therefore, worldly interpretations can be superseded by symbolic meanings derived from the Qur'an and the hadiths. All dream books recount the elevated status the Prophet Muhammed gave to the dream. Hence, each book contains a section on the Prophet's dreams and his interpretations. However, after the example of the Prophet Muhammed, Ibn Sirin is recognized as the foremost dream interpreter in Islamic history. Not only is the dream book attributed to him the most consulted dreamwork text in the contemporary Muslim world, he is also mentioned in all other studied dream interpretation books.

Fourth, it is striking how often the books agree on the interpretation of dream symbols. Partly, this similarity might be clarified by the aforementioned authoritativeness of Ibn Sirin. But above all, all books agree that the metaphorical examples from the Qur'an and the hadiths are the foundational symbolism of dream interpretation in Islam.

꧁ ꧁ ꧁

CHAPTER 8

# A Comparison of Islamic Dream Theory and Western Psychological Theories of the Dream

In one essential respect there is an ontological gap between Islamic and most Western psychological theories of the dream: their differing conceptions of the Self and what Western psychology views as the unconscious. The unknown hinterland of the Self in Islam and also Christianity is deemed to be the house of God, the Godhead, from which the voice of the Lord, the Prophet, and Shatan can all be heard, often in dreams. No such spiritual ontology defines the broadly secularist concept of the hidden worlds of the psyche in Western psychology. Freudian psychology, in particular, obstinately defines all psychic contents as reflections and transformations of daytime reality, "day residues" in the Freudian vocabulary. Yet Western psychology's attempts to create a universal and secular language and structure for the nature of the unconscious have defined the very terms in which someone embedded, particularly in Western culture, now approaches the rather mysterious, and usually confusing, language of the night dream. Perhaps alone in Western psychological theory, the conceptual and applied work of Jung, the famous Swiss psychoanalyst, offers a bridge between these differing schematizations of the unconscious.

In this chapter, I will outline some of the major similarities and differences between Islamic dream theory and major Western theories of dreaming. While acknowledging crucial differences in worldview, such as the ontological difference already indicated, I will seek to show similarities as well as convey their shared respect for the potential wisdom of the dream, as reflected in their differing knowledge traditions. I have already in chapter 1 outlined the core of Islamic dream theory and practice. Now, I will outline core aspects of Western psychological approaches.

## Western Psychological Theories of the Night Dream

I will consider the core Western psychological theories of the dream, particularly Freudian, neo-Freudian, Jungian, and Gestalt, and also the approach of the contemporary dreamwork movement. Freud's pioneering work on the structure of the psyche and the role and function of the unconscious is extremely well known, and many of his insights have passed, not always exactly, into the popular culture of understanding dreams. Freud (1955: 608) proclaimed the interpretation of dreams "the royal road to a knowledge of the unconscious activities of the mind" and saw dreams as being the repository of the unfulfilled and repressed, hence often unknown, wishes and desires of the dreamer.

There is a similarity here between the Islamic theory that most dreams are also egotistical (nafs) dreams. In particular, Freud (1974: 143) distinguished between the manifest content of the dream and its latent content. The manifest content was made up of motifs derived usually from the trivialities of daily experience, which he called the day residue. The latent content referred to the hidden, repressed, and unconscious meaning of these motifs or images that were buried in a distorted form within the manifest content. The transformation or distortion of the latent content of the unconscious takes place through the processes of condensation, displacement, representation, and secondary revision. Dreamwork then became for Freudian analysis the bringing to light, through free association, of the repressed aspects of the Self. Often these repressed aspects referred to incomplete aspects of childhood development, such as the unfulfilled Oedipal wishes of the dreamer, or to a similar traumatic event. Dreams then are "the guardians of the sleep" (Freud 1953: 233), as dreams allow the safe and hidden expression of repressed wishes.

Freud also elaborated upon the important distinction between primary-process and secondary-process thinking. For Kracke, primary-process thought is, "a highly condensed, visual, sensory, metaphorical form of thinking." Secondary-process thinking is defined as conscious, "centred on language and is linguistically communicable" (1987: 38). Dreaming is for Freud, par excellence, primary-process thought that he regarded as a more primitive form of thinking, which also formed the core of myths and fairy tales. In Islamic dream theory, the core distinction is between true, false, and desire dreams. True dreams are often straightforward to interpret: the message is clearly articulated as in an auditory instruction. For instance, a local Muslim drycleaner in the United Kingdom told me of his mother who had dreams of the Prophet, who advised her about how to pray. A textile seller that I met in Peshawar, Pakistan, told me how the Prophet had appeared in a dream and shown him the way to slake the continual thirst he had experienced in his dream, through praying five times a day. Thereafter, he told me, he had been happy.

So, in Islamic theory the manifest dream content can be the same as the latent one. Yet this direct correspondence between what Freudian theory defines as the latent and the manifest content is not always, or even usually, the case in Islamic dream theory, as in the seven fat and thin cows dream of the Egyptian pharaoh interpreted by Joseph and contained in the Joseph sura in the Qur'an (12.6). Also, while in Freudian theory the latent meaning of the dream is usually perceived as a repressed sexual desire and deciphering this latent meaning is part of the purpose of psychoanalysis, such encoded sexual dreams in Islamic dream theory are not considered important, as desire is seen as appropriately regulated through the Sha'ria law, based on the teachings of the Qur'an and the hadiths.

## Revised Psychoanalytical Approaches

While a Freudian perspective is the classical Western twentieth-century perspective on the meaning of dreams, his findings have been substantially developed, particularly in what Fosshage describes as a "revised psychoanalytic model" (Fosshage 1987: 27). In this revised psychoanalytic perspective, the basic distinctions between primary- and secondary-process thought and between the manifest and the latent meanings of the dream have been reevaluated. In this neo-Freudian perspective, dreaming is seen rather as a manifest problem-solving and integrative process that takes place as metaphorical thought. Primary-process thought is, within this more recent model, perceived as being a different but equal form of mentation that is capable of refinement and development during the person's life. Complex mental operations, such as the solving of mathematical problems, can be achieved in dreams (Fosshage 1987: 27). Moreover, the adoption of this model allows for a focus on the manifest content of the dream as being of predominant value for interpretation. No longer is the manifest content considered important solely as a device with which to freely associate in analysis.

Rather, the metaphorical imagery of the manifest content is the most appropriate available representation of the issue or conflict being expressed in the dream. The classic perception of the "real" meaning of the dream being deeply disguised changes then into a focus upon the manifest images and symbols of the dream also. Moreover, the dream is seen as being prospective and possibly future oriented, rather than oriented to the infantile past. It is also adaptational. Dreaming is then a problem-solving and integrative process occurring as metaphorical thought.

## A Jungian Perspective

Jung, like Freud, is a twentieth-century giant in the field of dream interpretation. Jung is important for dream interpretation in several ways. He developed the idea of the collective unconscious, archetypes, and the theory of the dream as compensatory. His technique of "active imagination" is significant as a key method of enabling people to access less-conscious states and arenas of the imagination. With Jung's key theories, we begin to see significant correspondences between Islamic and Jungian dream theory. Interestingly, it is in the Sufi tradition within Islam (Corbin 1966: 406) that the concept of the "imaginal world" is most developed to define a discernible world between that of sensibility and intelligibility. This imaginal world is defined as a world of autonomous forms and images that is apprehended directly by the imaginative consciousness and is held to validate suprasensible perception. Jung famously wrote of the "crucial insight that there are things in the psyche that I do not produce, but which produce themselves and have their own life" (1977: 207). Suffice it here first to recognize the possible apparent genesis of the concept of the imaginal world in the Islamic theory of the visionary dream.

Jung's concept of the "collective unconscious" (1959: 42) underpins the active imagination method, also called imagework, by many contemporary practitioners. The concept of the "collective unconscious" represented Jung's perception that the human psyche contained impersonal and archaic contents that manifested themselves in the myths, dreams, and spontaneous imagery of humans. Jung's idea that all humans contained a common and universal storehouse of psychic contents, which he called "archetypes," is the core model of the unconscious that enables imagework practitioners (Glouberman 1989; Edgar 2004a) to consider the spontaneous image as being potentially a creative and emergent aspect of the Self. So, in Jungian archetypal psychology, we see a holistic and generative theory and method of understanding and opening up of our unconscious contents. Jung's idea, developed from a house dream he had, that all humans contained a common and universal storehouse of psychic contents is in contradistinction to Freud's view of the unconscious as consisting primarily of a personal unconscious. Jung defined the difference thus: "Whereas the personal unconscious consists for the most part of complexes, the content of the collective unconscious is made up essentially of archetypes" (1959: 42).

For Jung, the collective unconscious was a given, something inherited by all people. The Jungian archetypes are the tendencies of the psyche to manifest patterns and forms in certain particular ways. They are not, in themselves, the actual culturally specific representations as perceived in dream and fantasy, though Jung was not always clear about this distinction (Samuels 1985: 33). Archetypes formulated by Jung include the shadow, the anima and the animus, the mother and child, the wise old man, the trickster figure, and the Self. Jung maintained that the archetypes can never be fully known (1951: 109). They have a numinous, awe-inspiring quality, and only their manifestations can be observed in an ordered form in myth and in a more disorganized form in dreams and fantasy. Jung's theory of the archetypes has baffled many psychologists, and certainly empirical definition is difficult. However, taking the example of the anima archetype, Jung (1964: 31) broadly defines this archetype as being the "feminine aspect" of a man. Within this definition, the multifarious representations of the "female" in the dream may represent positive and negative aspects of this feminine self of the male. For instance, a man may contain both representations of the muse as inspiring genius and also that of the siren who can lure men to their downfall. Neither image represents the anima in its totality, but both are aspects that can be recognized and given meaning through imagework and dreamwork. Further, in Jungian theory, the anima can be the principle of relatedness to the unconscious.

Unlike Freud, Jungian dream theory facilitates understanding dream imagery as relating to emerging aspects of the Self. Likewise, most dream theories of indigenous peoples perceive dreams as related to possible futures, a form of divination. Islamic dream theory is likewise future oriented as in the dreams of the Pharaoh that Joseph interpreted. Muhammed is reported in the Qur'an as having a predictive dream of entering the Sacred Mosque at Mecca "in security, your heads shaved, your hair cut short, not fearing" (Qur'an 48.27). A companion of the Prophet, Abdullah b. Zayd, dreamed the *Adhan,* the five-times-daily Islamic call to prayer, at a time when the Prophet Muhammed and his followers were seeking a way of defining their new faith in contradistinction to the calling horn of the Jews and the bell of the Christians. Another aspect of this future relatedness we have discussed here is *Istikhara,* Islamic dream incubation.

Jung saw some dreams as having an anticipatory function, but not a prophetic function as is possible in Islam. He metaphorically described dreams as being a possible sketch of the future but not the oil painting, which would represent the actual future. Yet the end of the Jungian individuation process was the encounter and integration of the archetype of the Self; in his autobiography, Jung describes a climatic dream that came at the end of much soul searching. The dream was set in Liverpool, which he decided represented the "pool of life":

> In the center was a round pool, and in the middle of it a small island. While everything about was obscured by rain, fog, smoke, and dimly lit darkness,

the little island blazed with light. On it stood a single tree, a magnolia, in a shower of reddish blossoms. It was as though the tree stood in the sunlight and was at the same time the source of light. My companion commented on the abominable weather and obviously did not see the tree. They spoke of another Swiss who was living in Liverpool, and expressed surprise that he should have settled here. I was carried away by the beauty of the flowering tree and the sunlit island and thought, "I know very well why he has settled here." Then I awoke. (Jung 1977: 40)

Jung subsequently wrote that

This dream brought with it a sense of finality. I saw that the goal had been revealed. One could not go beyond the center. The center is the goal, and everything is directed toward that center. Through this dream I understood that the self is the principle and archetype of orientation and meaning. Therein lies its healing function.

After Jung's break with Freud, he said that he knew nothing, and then "such a dream comes, one feels it as an act of grace" (Jung 1977: 40).

While Jung partly spent his life studying the meaning of the Imago Dei in humans, he did so as an empiricist of the inner worlds of the psyche, without an apparent commitment to one of the divine highways of belief. In Islam, the true dream, rather like an act of grace, similarly offers as a human goal the concept of the Self, but this Self is a knowledge of God/Allah (Sviri 1997: 26): to know oneself is to know God. Jungian archetypal psychology and Islamic metaphysical theory, both infused with dreamwork theory and practice, share a common goal and pursuit, even if the Jungian approach is without a belief structure and is a form of scientific empiricism as regards inner worlds, as best known through working with dreams. Both approaches perceive awareness of the ego as a part of an awareness of the tremendous possibilities of the self, as potentially realized through dreams.

## Gestalt Therapy

Western psychological theories of the dream are not solely made up of Freud, neo-Freudians, and Jung. The contribution of Gestalt theory and the contemporary dreamwork movement are important as well.

Gestalt therapy was the creation of Fitz Perls (1969). His theory rejected the notion of an unconscious and focused on a concern with the person "getting in touch with the here and now" and "being in touch with their feelings." Dreams in Gestalt theory are "the high road to integration" rather than Freud's "high road to the unconscious" (Houston 1982: 44). Each part of the dream is seen as a part of the person with which he potentially can get in touch through dreamwork. Even an insignificant part of a dream is an opportunity to develop a further emotional integration of the various aspects of the Self. Perls (1971: 27) has written:

> The dream is an existential message. It is more than an unfinished situation; it is more than an unfulfilled wish; it is more than a prophecy. It is a message of yourself to yourself, to whatever part of you is listening. The dream is possibly the most spontaneous expression of the human being, a piece of art that we chisel out of our lives. And every part, every situation in the dream is a creation of the dreamer himself. Of course, some of the pieces come from memory or reality, but the important question is what makes the dreamer pick out this specific piece? No choice in the dream is coincidental. ... every aspect of the dream is part of the dreamer, but a part that to some extent is disowned and projected onto other objects.

Gestalt dream theory and practice is an action approach to re-experiencing the Self in a more complete sense. Hence in Gestalt dreamwork the dreamer is advised to see and actually re-experience each part of the dream as a part of himself. He is asked to identify emotionally with all or part of the dream, very different to Islamic dream practice.

Gestalt theory is often used in dreamwork groups and is a core theory and practice underpinning the contemporary Western dreamwork movement. However, it has no concept of an unconscious Self as such, but rather a focus on unexpressed and unknown feelings; hidden feelings substitute for the hidden worlds of the psyche or as in Islam, the hidden and occasional potential of the true dream.

The dreamwork movement began in the 1970s in the United States as an offshoot of the human potential movement or personal growth movement. At that time, the publication of works by authors such as Garfield and Ullman and Zimmerman both popularized and guided groups and individuals into ways of working with their dreams. The essence of this approach to dreams is that the dream image is an important aspect of the Self and is significant in developing an understanding of Self and the world. Insights that can be revealed through using amplification techniques such as artwork, drama, dance, mask-making, poetry, etc. are buried in the dream. The dreamwork movement is democratic without established dream interpreters. Each dreamer is the expert in their own dream imagery; the group and its facilitator can encourage ways of working with one's dreams. Dreams are seen as letters to oneself, often metaphorically encoded. The dreamwork movement may have no preconceived vision of the Self, and the end point of dreaming and dreamwork, but it shares a common concern across most dream cultures, including Islam, with the issues of dream interpretation and human meaning.

A core difference I have found between Islamic and Western dream theories, particularly those of Gestalt and the dreamwork movement, is in the tension between authoritative and facilitative interpretation, as already noted. Islamic dream interpreters tend to tell the believer what the dream means based on their understanding of the Qur'an and the hadiths, which are perceived to contain all that humans need to know to live well, while certain Western dream interpretative traditions focus on facilitating the dreamer as the expert on his/her dreams.

## Conclusion

Several key differences between Islamic and Western theories of the dream have been noted. Yet, significant similarities are evident also. Both paradigmatic traditions reverence the dream as a potential source of human insight and psychosocial growth. Both consider dreams as relevant, sometimes crucially, to daytime reality and its future possibilities; both traditions are engaged in the core problematic of interpretation, and the relationship between the manifest and latent dream meaning as Freud defined this key distinction. Each tradition is similarly engaged in the issue of how metaphorical and imaginative thinking is related to cognitive understanding of the world and ourselves. Both see the dream as a journey, at least sometimes, into the center of the human condition.

The essence of Islam is surrender to the will of God/Allah. The essence of certainly Jungian psychoanalytical practice is to develop a creative union of the ego with the archetype of the Self, an intuitive connection with the core creative dynamic of the collective unconscious. The garb of words may be different, but there is an affinity, as realized in their respective dreamwork practices, between the two paths.

%&% %&% %&%

# Conclusion

## Conclusions Regarding Jihadist Dream Reports

As I have shown, Sufism is replete with dream narratives of divine import. In militant jihadism, this similarly seems to be the case. Almost all studies of contemporary militant jihadism position the Wahhabi Sunni version of militant jihadism in contradistinction to Sufism. Sufism with its positive attitude to true dreams has shaykhs as mediators with Allah. Sufism sometimes also includes the veneration of saints' tombs. Militant Sunni Islamists reject these aspects of Sufism. Indeed both Islamic outlooks often consider the other to be un-Islamic. What my data and exposition show is that Wahhabist militant jihadists have a similarly high respect for and evaluation of the night dream in Islam. Moreover, they particularly emphasize the inspirational role of the sacred figures in Islamic history when they present themselves in night dreams. However, militant jihadists similarly relate to the manifest content of dreams as Sufis and more mainstream Muslims do. Hence we have encountered Osama bin Laden behaving like a Sufi shaykh when he interpreted the night dreams of his followers. The wisdom of the dream and its interpretation by militant jihadist leaders is comparable with such practices by Sufi shaykhs. Dream interpretation then can perhaps be seen as a unifying aspect in the theology, philosophy, and practice of Islam both historically and contemporaneously.

In chapters 5 and 6, I have analyzed the patterns that inform jihadist dream interpretive narratives. First, jihadists are reported to receive divine inspiration, guidance, and divinatory "news" of future events in this world and the world of hereafter. Second, dream narratives in part legitimate jihadist actions for the dreamers themselves, for their followers, and for the Islamic community, the *Ummah*. Mullah Omar's followers trust him partly because of his reputation for holy dreaming and specifically for his reported strategic guidance received through night dreams. Mullah Omar's belief in such dreams is confirmed particularly by Yusufzai's account of Mullah Omar telephoning him about his brother's precognitive 9/11 dream.

Third, dream visions connect the dreamers with the (mythically) real past of the Prophet Muhammed and his companions, the Golden Age of Islam. As well as this, dreams actually seem to reintroduce this glorious past into the present: the visionary and revelatory world of Islam is reborn today, as dreamers base their inspired jihad upon the "glad tiding" that the Prophet Muhammed said would come through true dreams. This is shown for instance in the quotation from Fouda concerning Binalshibh, who "speaks of the Prophet and his close companions as if he had actually met them." The dream world is experienced as more real than this world, and reality becomes more dreamlike, a veil over the sublime glory of hidden paradisiacal worlds. Dreams can be tastes, divinations, of possible welcome futures. Sacred figures are to be emulated and even identified with, and certainly their words are perceived as divine instruction.

The fourth thread of my argument here is that militant jihadism can be directly authorized by dream content. The classical Freudian distinction between the manifest and latent meanings of a dream is changed. The clearer the manifest communication, the closer to God the dreamer is, as we have seen in many of the dream narratives reported in this book. Mullah Omar is given "instructions" in his dreams as to his military strategy; the US "White House" burns; bin Laden is said to have "executed" 9/11 to avenge the Palestinians. Moussaoui dreams of flying a plane into a tall building; Abu Cheema is welcomed into paradise and the Prophet is heard speaking clearly; the words of Jesus are heard by a Guantanamo Bay inmate; another is "told" he will be released in two years.

However, not all the dream narratives are understood solely through reliance on their manifest meaning. Reid's interpretation of the "full pickup truck" passing him by as referring to his missing the 9/11 attack is an interpretation from a manifest to a supposed latent meaning, as are bin Laden's claiming that his soccer team being dressed as "pilots" and winning against the American team is a good omen and bin Laden's interpretation of the "Egyptian family going about its business" as a reference to Atta.

These narratives clearly show that jihadists understand their dreams within the context of the Islamic worldview. Dreamed sacred figures, for example, are not unreal projections of the unconscious or deeply encoded manifestations of earlier dysfunctional familial experiences, as they would be in Western interpretations, but figures that inhabit the supernaturally real world of Islam and reassert the eternal truths of the Qur'an and the hadiths.

The relationship between dreams and events is another analytic thread running through the narratives. Mullah Omar is called to save his country and introduce Sha'ria. For a while the Taliban did achieve extraordinary success (Burke 2003), which seemed to confirm to his followers his dreamed inspiration. At the time of writing (July 2010), the Taliban again seem to be resurgent against the Coalition. A final thread—that of the Prophetic example of Muhammed's advisory dream before the battle of Badr—is again shown in the dream narratives attributed to Mullah Omar. The battle of Badr in 624 CE was a key battle against the Meccan Quraish tribe. The Muslims were victorious.

In conclusion, charismatic leaders like Mullah Omar offer their dreams as a self-justifying and legitimating device, claiming them to be revelations from beyond this world and containing authorization for radical human action in this world. Such dreams are considered as noumenal assertions of divine will.

Overall, Muslims' understanding of their night dreams can be used as a powerful tool in assessing their worldview and implicit key motivations. The understanding of night dreams offers an entrée into the deepest recesses of Muslims' self-understanding and self-definition.

The militant jihadists' dreams discussed in this book show their reliance upon and sincere belief in the divine power of manifest and interpreted dreams. As a counterbalance, it is important to remember that while dreams and future events are conceptually connected in Islamic dream theory, it is possible that a dream that is perceived to be powerful and directive remains unfulfilled over time. In her seminal study of Sufi initiation dreams in Pakistan, Ewing develops a semiological analysis of dream accounts, which shows how a person who is culturally "open" to the idea of true dreams may redevelop their own narratively expressed self-representations through the impact of powerful dreams and their reflections upon them. Part of her article articulates this perception very well:

> However, the significance of the context of a dream ultimately depends on subsequent events, on how the future actually unfolds. A sufi initiation dream, for example, may have a powerful impact on the dreamer's system of self representations, so that as a result of the dream the dreamer comes to regard him/herself as the disciple of some sufi teacher. But the social salience of a particular self representation will depend upon subsequent events and may shift over time as external conditions change. If the dreamer does not succeed in resolving conflicts by accepting the new self representation, the relevance of both the self representation and the dream may diminish. The dream loses its transformative power. A dream's potentially transformative power, in other words, comes from its ability to give rise to an appropriate self representation and is limited by the dreamer's ability to realize the expectations of the new self-representation in his subsequent life. (1990: 56–57)

Dreams, future events, and emerging self-understanding and self-definition may then be arguably prefigured in night dreams, but there is no causal determination involved. The practice of *Istikhara,* presented in chapter 3, demonstrates this dialogue between dream and reality well. Contingent hypotheses are developed by its practitioners as to the likely outcomes of specific key life decisions. The practice of *Istikhara* can determine future selves, particularly in marriage decisions. For many Muslims, *Istikhara* is a spiritual dream divination practice of almost last resort, when they are faced with a major life decision.

In Islam, the worlds of dream and reality are linked for all humans. Indeed some true dreams are considered to be more real, in terms of deep knowledge, possible prophecy, and divination, than normal human daytime experience. Dreams can be "early warning signals" (Ormsby 2008: 157) of future unwelcome events, and fortunate and dream-wise humans can interpret such signals to avoid danger. In Islam, like in many religions, this world reality is seen as a dream, and death is an awakening. Awareness of and learning to interpret dreams then coincides with learning to understand the deep meanings of events in this world. The two worlds are in tandem and replete with educational meaning and potential. Human life is a metaphorical journey, and dreams are constituted by metaphorical thinking. We walk on earth within a stream of imagery.

In this book we have seen that dreams have several functions or potentialities in Islam. The dream is a way of metaphysical knowledge, divination, and spiritual revelation. Also, it is a practical and alternate way of knowing, which can give information and foreknowledge about invisible worlds. Imaginative inspiration and guidance can be found in dream content, which can provide ethical clarity to action for the individual and the community. Indeed, dreams in Islam can be seen as a potential technology of the sacred, which can give guidance about religious practice for the community and contact with the wisdom of the inner spiritual community. A dream is a founding narrative in Sufism in general: in many biographies of the great shaykhs you can find dreams as revelatory signs of their future greatness. Moreover, dreams can for Islamists contentiously be seen as giving inspiration, legitimation, and information about the lesser jihad of combating the perceived oppressors of Islam.

Gilsenan also neatly summarizes some of the many powerful aspects of the night dream in Islam based on his research in Egypt:

> In dreams began responsibilities. Judgements were made. Commands issued. Justifications provided. Hope renewed. Conduct was commented on by holy figures, by the Prophet himself, by the founding sheik who had died some years before but who appeared with his son and successor.
>
> Dreams were public goods, circulated in conversational exchanges, valorizing the person, authoring and authorizing experience, at once unique

and collective visual, verbal epiphanies. Dreams thus constituted a field of force and framed interchange between the living, and between the living and the only apparently dead. (2000: 611)

## The Imaginative Commonality of Islam

"We are nearer to him than the jugular vein" is a famous Qur'anic verse that expresses the Islamic understanding of the proximity of man to Allah (Qur'an 50.16). Maybe though, the dream is closer still! Hence, anthropologists can through dream reports study how this crucial aspect of the inner Self, the dreaming subject, can significantly affect action and events in this world. As I see it, the various forms and schools of Islam merge unitarily through a shared respect, acknowledgement, and creative relationship with the imaginal or the "unconscious." This perspective can sit alongside other attempts at defining Islam and Muslims (Marranci 2008). "Islam" has been defined as the Qur'an; as the devotional practice of Sha'ria; as a varying set of symbols, concepts, and worldviews (Gilsenan 1982: 19); as a globalized, essentialist cultural system (Geertz 1968; Gellner 1981); as a culturally and historically defined discourse (Gilsenan 1982); as an authoritative discursive tradition based on the Qur'an and the hadiths (Asad 1986); and as the emotional orientation of the Muslim (Marranci 2008). Yet ask a Sufi how he defines Islam, and the answer would be more akin to the unswerving love of and surrender to Allah, as is so well expressed in the great allegorical poem, *The Conference of the Birds*, written around the turn of the twelfth century (Attar 2005).

From my textual studies and ethnographic fieldwork, a commonality emerges across Islam and among many, if not most, Muslims as to the creative and dynamic role of the imaginal source of true night dreams and some human visions, *al-ruya*. Muslims think, feel, and also "see" themselves born of and defined by the prophetic revelation in the Qur'an, which was announced and partly formulated through night dreams. Seeing oneself as Muslim can involve this union of cognition, emotion, and inner and outer sight blending into an existential and defining Self/world regard. This inner visual aspect of "being Muslim" has been largely academically ignored. Yet for the individual Muslim, significant night dreams can confirm and enact the centrality of Allah, the Prophets, revelation, and wisdom pertaining to their particular life struggle, originating and manifesting from the noumenal reaches of the mind and the imaginal, and transmitted and confirmed through the inspirational night dream.

EPILOGUE

# The Marriage of Heaven and Hell[1]

*Imagination, Creativity, and Political Agency in the Inspirational Night Dream in Islam*

In this bold, original, and timely book Edgar captures ethnographically and restores analytically an extremely difficult subject, that of the "inspirational night dream in Islam." Anthropological research on dreams is definitely not a new field (see, for example, Tedlock 1987; Edgar 1995; Mageo 2003; Stewart 2004). Nevertheless, the theorization and analysis of dreams in general, and the "true dream" in particular, remains a difficult and awkward venture. In an earlier article (cf. Kirtsoglou 2010) I have tried to touch upon some of the reasons that make the anthropological analysis of dreams an extremely intricate endeavour. In the present epilogue I will try to locate this difficulty more precisely by commenting further on the relationship between dreams and imagination. I will then argue in favour of a unified approach toward dreams and reality, claiming that the anthropological study of dreams allows us to appreciate the close connection between imagination, creativity, and political agency.

## The Original Sin

The dream is unavoidably associated with human imagination. Some analysts, like Freud, locate the dream in a personal and private unconscious world, while others, like Jung, prefer the concept of a collective unconscious. Edgar here prefers the Jungian approach to dreams because of its similarities to the Islamic tradition that allow him to focus on "the issue of how metaphorical imaginative thinking is related to cognitive understanding of the world and ourselves" (Edgar, this volume). It follows that in order to approach the subject of dreams, we need to firmly establish the importance of imagination and its relation to subjectivity. Imagination is, however, a problematic topic in itself. This is because, as Castoriadis (1995) observes, the central topic of philosophy—almost since its inception—has been the study of mind. From then onward, all the dimensions of human subjectivity that cannot be considered as "falling under the jurisdiction of the Mind" were "attributed to the sub-thinkable, or to beyond-the-thinkable, and to indeterminacy" (Castoriadis 1995: 233; my translation). The radical imagination was thus obscured and treated as abjection, as a simple and pure lack of definition, as belonging to the realm of the superempirical, the transcendental, and the vague (Castoriadis 1995). By consequence, imagination was reduced to a secondary role; it was made to compete against the principles of true and false, good and bad, and beautiful and ugly (which were seen as being externally guaranteed), and it was "expelled to the realm of psychology, or explained away as relating to unfulfilled needs or desires" (Castoriadis 1995: 234; my translation).

In its association with the radical imagination, the dream has also been analyzed as originating in the unconscious, as being a subject that belonged primarily to psychology or psychoanalysis, and—most importantly—it was also made to compete with some externally guaranteed principle of truth. Measured up against the empirical, tangible world of reality, the dream has always come up short. At best, it was to be analyzed as some kind of reworking of waking reality. It either expressed repressed wishes and desires, or it could otherwise be studied from a semiotic approach as a culturally constructed text (cf. Stewart 1997: 878).

The anthropological study of dreams also faces complications that arise from the relation between anthropologist and informant, as well as from the relation between informants and their cultural context. As anthropologists, and precisely because the research process is always "negotiated and tested in an ambiguous and stressful field of interpersonal relations" (Jackson 1998: 5), we are always aware of the possibility that we might need to *not* take at face value what our informants tell us. In his forward to the present book, Lyon provides us with the perfect example of such a case in his comment on a large public feasting event he witnessed while in the field in northern Punjab:

> At the time, I asked the landlord why he chose to do something on such a grand scale and he gave me what I thought was a *playful but deceptive* explanation. He told me that Allah had come to him in a dream and told him to feed his village. Quite frankly, I dismissed the explanation out of hand. It clearly *made no sense and was a very flimsy rationale* upon which to take such a costly and time-consuming decision. Nearly ten years on, I have come to the conclusion that while my analysis of the political significance of

such feasting rituals was both useful and productive, it neglected something rather interesting about a critical element in the underlying inspiration for the decision. (Lyon, this volume; my emphasis)

The reason why Lyon and the majority of anthropologists would be wary of the landlord's explanation relates of course to our Enlightenment-shaped, reason-oriented cosmology, which dictates that whatever happens during dreams does not really exist (cf. Kirtsoglou 2010). Waking reality is the only legitimate source of authentic experience, and in fact we believe that it is what generates dreams. Anything else is a plain violation of human rationality. The anthropologist is then reluctant to seriously consider that a landlord, inspired by a dream, decided to spend money, time, and resources in order to organize a large public feast. What is more, even if anthropologists actually decide to take at face value what an informant tells them, they still hesitate to endorse such a seemingly irrational explanation in a public ethnography. This is what Argyrou (2002) calls the "salvation intent."

Argyrou claims that anthropology "does not so much seek to define Others as to *redefine* them in order to redeem them" (2002: 28). Through examples from the work of Malinowski, Evans-Pritchard, and Levi-Strauss, Argyrou demonstrates how anthropologists became extremely preoccupied with establishing beyond any doubt that the "native" is not prelogical and irrational (2002: 44–51), or at least no more so than the Western man. With reference to dreams, Stewart discusses how Victorian anthropologists evoked the "ability to distinguish purely mental phenomena from real perceptions" as a "prime criterion for having attained civilization" (2004: 76). Victorian evolutionism purported that "those who believed in the reality of dreams lacked a theory of mind" (Stewart 2004: 76) and therefore only "the savage could consider the events in his dreams to be as real as those of his waking hours" (Lubbock 1978 [1870]: 126; cited in Stewart 2004: 76). In order to deal with this apparent problem of native belief in dreams without portraying our informants as prelogical, irrational, superstitious, or backward, anthropologists often resort to treating the dream as a rhetorical device. Thus, our informants might tell us that they acted upon a "true dream," but we conclude that what they actually meant by this was something else. We convince ourselves (and the world) that the true dream must surely be a kind of cultural symbolism, or an excuse, or an evasive maneuver to our persisting questions. Edgar refuses to succumb to this logic and prefers the option of actually trying to ethnographically and analytically capture local beliefs about the true inspirational dream. However precarious this option may be, Edgar does not see dreams just as cultural texts or rhetorical devices. He thus avoids an entirely semiotic approach in favor of a phenomenological appreciation of the dream as experience (cf. Stewart 1997: 878).

The anthropological approach to dreams, however, harbors yet more dangers, for we can never have *direct* access to someone else's dreams. We are then confined to working with someone's narrative story of a dream, never being entirely sure whether the dream actually took place or what happened in it (cf. Kirtsoglou 2010). Our inability to directly share an informant's dream experience violates in a sense the participant-observation dimension of fieldwork. However, as I have argued elsewhere, anthropologists often rely on narratives in order to engage with cultural analysis, and dream narratives need not pose an exception (Kirtsoglou 2010). If we resist the radical break between dream reality and waking reality and accept that dream reality and waking reality influence each other generatively and in a symmetrical fashion, we can then refuse to cast dreams into the realm of the vague and the indeterminate (cf. Kirtsoglou 2010). Whether we believe anthropology to be an art, a science, or a discipline, we cannot accept the arbitrary compartmentalization of the social self and the social mind that the radical separation of dream reality and waking reality entails (Kirtsoglou 2010). We have no apparent evidence that "reality" is what shapes dreams, while—as this book clearly shows—we have ample ethnographic material which demonstrates the opposite. To decide that we do not take this material at face value is an entirely valid decision, but we must remember that it is a capricious decision that *we* made on the basis of *our* refusal to abandon *our* cosmological beliefs in favor of those of others.

## Every Thing Possible to Be Believ'd Is an Image of Truth

As I argued in the previous section, dreams are not just rhetorical devices, cultural texts, or residuals of our waking time. Rather, they need to be analyzed as experiences and as instances of the human imagination. Such a statement presupposes of course that we recover the importance of imagination in the shaping of subjectivity, but before I proceed to comment on that, I would like to briefly inquire into the inspirational jihadist dream. In the story of Mullah Omar recounted in the present book, we learn that "before he attacks some place he dreams, and then in the morning he orders a commander to attack that place" (Arabshahi 1998, in Edgar, this volume). We also learn that Mullah Omar's brother had dreamt of the White House on fire before the attacks on 9/11, without actually knowing that the attacks would happen (Edgar, this volume). Edgar also attests that several Muslims had what they claimed to be prophetic dreams about the events of 9/11. Those dreams involved planes falling on tall buildings, or soccer players dressed as pilots winning a game against the US.

Even if—after considerable theorization—we accept that we should not dismiss our informants' beliefs that dream experiences can guide experiences during waking reality, we still have difficulty accepting that dreams can actually anticipate the future. Such a statement is a direct shot to our system of rational thinking. The anticipatory character of the Islamic dream is even more difficult to swallow than Allah's divine nature. Edgar here advocates two main exegetical lines on the issue of divine inspiration that jihadists report to have received. First, he observes that dream narratives in part legitimate jihadist actions. According to this explanation, "*jihadist* leaders and their followers adopt such dream narratives for propagandist purposes in the knowledge that faithful Muslims believe in the possibility of such divinely inspired night dreams" (Edgar, this volume). Second, he claims that:

> particular dream motifs (such as the Prophet and his companions) are part of a shared visionary world which can connect present day believers with the [mythically] real past, and especially with the imagined early glorious days of Islam, the time of the Prophet himself. Moreover, such true dreams appear to facilitate the re-enactment of this past in the present. (Edgar, this volume)

Edgar is careful to tell us that jihadist dreams need to be understood in the context of the Islamic worldview, according to which "the dream world is experienced as more real than this world, and reality becomes more dreamlike." Thus sacred figures (like that of Allah) are not "unreal projections of the unconscious, or deeply encoded manifestations of earlier dysfunctional familial experiences, like they would be in Western interpretations, but figures that inhabit the supernaturally real world of Islam and reassert the eternal truths of the Qur'an and the hadiths" (Edgar, this volume).

In my attempt to offer a metacommentary on Edgar's analysis here, I am inclined to focus on the second exegetical thread. In the Islamic world, true dreams are not regarded as originating in the unconscious, or as being residuals of reality. They are taken to be as authentic as waking experiences and the figures who appear in them are perceived to be as real as those of waking reality.

In theoretical terms we can accept the continuity between dream reality and waking reality as well as the connection between dream and imagination. What we cannot easily accept is the existence of supernatural beings, gods, and saints, and we do not need to. Allah and the concept of jihad do not exist because people dream of them. Rather, they exist equally in dream reality and in waking reality. They belong to the collective imagination of the Muslim people. Dreaming of them is thus deeply established in the culture, history, and religious cosmology of Muslims, and is analogous to praying to such supernatural beings during waking reality. In our appreciation of the inspirational true dream in Islam, we must disentangle the religious belief in the supernatural from imagination and experience; all are present simultaneously and uninterruptedly in dreams and in reality.

Still, we must solve another puzzle. How is it possible for people who had no prior knowledge of 9/11 to report dreams that clearly seem to anticipate those tragic events? I argue that the answer to the problem of the "anticipatory" nature of jihadist dreams may lie in a rather simple thought. Several concepts and notions, like religion and art for instance, have been born independently in the minds of people across cultures and over the course of history. The idea of setting recognizable symbols of US political and economic dominance like the White House or the World Trade Center on fire is much less complex and a lot more "predictable" than art and religion. This is how Baudrillard commented on the events of 9/11:

> The fact that we had dreamt of this event, that everyone without exception has dreamt of it—because no one can avoid dreaming of the destruction of any power that has become hegemonic to this degree—is unacceptable to the Western moral conscience. Yet it is a fact, and one which indeed can be measured by the emotive violence of all that has been said and written in the effort to dispel it. (2002: 5)

When Baudrillard admits that we have all "dreamt" of this event, he means we have "imagined" it, and even perhaps "fantasized" about it. In the Western[2] cosmological order we accept that we imagine, plan, create, and fantasize in our waking reality because of our own specific ontological suppositions about human subjectivity. In the Islamic cosmology, however, where dream reality and waking reality are not radically separated, it is almost "natural"—if I may—for people to have dreamt of these events in both their sleep and while awake. The attacks of 9/11 did not happen because people have *dreamt* (in their sleep) of them, but because the perpetrators of 9/11, too, had dreamt of them, or imagined them, in their sleep; this is no different than to say that a non-Muslim person had imagined them while awake. Edgar is right to claim that "militant *jihadism* can be directly authorized by dream content." The originality of Edgar's thought lies in the fact that he is careful to explicate the Islamic view of the relationship between dream and reality, thus setting the context for understanding this statement. In a cosmological setting where people see no radical break between dream and reality, the above statement does not invite us to think that jihad leaders (or the pious Muslims who follow them) are irrational, superstitious, and prelogical. Militant jihadism is authorized by dream content in the same sense that any war can be authorized by any belief held in waking reality.

Edgar also claims that—partly at least—such jihadist dream narratives are legitimatizing discourses developed for propagandist purposes. I do not disagree with this line of thought. Jihadist dreams may equally well be rhetorical and legitimizing devices. However, as Edgar's second line of thinking clearly shows, they are most probably not *just* that. Once we circumvent our tendency to measure imagination and dreams against an externally guaranteed truth we realize that the inspirational dream, as it is theorized in this book, touches upon a crucial anthropological preoccupation with political agency. However, in order to appreciate the role and importance of imagination in human creativity, we need to first look the radical imagination in the eye and accept that human subjects are capable of imagining, conceptualizing, and then realizing the true and the false, the good and the bad, the beautiful and the ugly. And we also need to accept that those terms are themselves effects of the radical imagination and not externally guaranteed principles that fell from the sky.

## As I Was Walking among the Fires of Hell, Delighted with the Enjoyments of Genius; Which to Angels Look Like Torment and Insanity

Most people would agree that politics is a dirty business. At the same time, however, our romantic, Rousseauian view of a fundamentally noble human nature imagines the political *vision* to be something righteous and gallant. History and experience, however, provide us with unpleasant and bitter surprises. Not all political visions come to resemble that of Martin Luther King Jr; in fact, very few do.

By examining the notion of the true dream in Islam, and more specifically the jihadist dream, Edgar skates on thin ice. Unavoidably, he negotiates issues like religious fundamentalism, irrationality, and most of all what Loizos calls "a totalizing doctrine of responsibility, a crude, disordered folk-legal doctrine ... [that is] generalizing and collectivist and very hostile to both the idea of *individual* responsibility and to causal and contextual specificity" (1988: 649–50). As I have argued elsewhere, jihad (and terrorism as its extreme expression that saw its culmination in the 9/11 attacks) does not need to be analyzed as a premodern system of accountability (cf. Kirtsoglou 2006). This totalizing doctrine, which predicates that the imagined community of the other is responsible in its abstraction for real or assumed crimes and therefore liable to their consequences (cf. Wilkins 1992: 134), might not be just "a cultural survival of premodern societies" (cf. Dimitrakos 2001: 138). Rather, it could be seen as "an element embedded in the very idea of nation-states as imagined communities who continue to hold each other collectively accountable for the actions of their respective fictive kin-groups" (Kirtsoglou 2006: 72). I do not wish to expand on political systems of accountability here. What concerns me at the moment are the limits of human imagination, and more precisely the lack of such limits.

Political barbarism (or whatever might be seen as political barbarism by different groups of people) is not a new phenomenon and it does not limit itself to "exotic," "premodern," "kin-based," or "native" societies. Genocide, perhaps the ultimate expression of political barbarism, is not even restricted to the fringes of Europe, to places like Serbia, Kosovo, or Armenia. Sadly, and whether we like it or not, Hitler too had a vision. His vision, his *waking dream,* was to exterminate the Jewish population and to establish the ultimate and unequivocal dominion of Germany over Europe and perhaps beyond. I do not know if Hitler was also dreaming of that venture in his sleep. Perhaps he did; it makes no actual difference. What matters here is to establish that political visions are not always noble, because the human imagination stretches boundlessly both toward what we have termed good and toward what we have termed bad. What is more disturbing perhaps is the thought that supernatural figures like Allah play no different teleological role in this process than beliefs in the superiority of a certain race, or of a certain system of social organization. Once war and the killing of other human beings has been conceived and imagined, there can be various reasons for such events actually being realized—all of them equally rational or irrational depending on our point of view, and which value system we have come to worship as worthy of our lives and those of others. Perhaps the most ironic vulnerability of human beings is their tendency to fervently believe in the very things they have invented and imagined—nations as imagined communities (cf. Anderson 1983) being just an example of this and not the most innocent one in human history. By arguing this I do not wish to "redeem" Edgar's informants, or offer justifications for dream-authorized jihad. I merely want to pinpoint that our analysis of what "dream-authorized" or "Allah-guided" is needs not be clouded by the apparent strangeness or assumed irrationality of such concepts, for we can find analogues and homologues in less religious-driven and transcendental contexts. Having established this claim, I now wish to turn to the importance of the radical imagination and dream as an instance of it.

## What Is Now Proved Was Once, Only Imagin'd

I ended the penultimate section with a precarious statement that could easily afford considerable misunderstanding. I claimed that concepts like good, bad, truth, falsity, beauty, and ugliness are themselves products of the radical imagination. By this statement I do not wish to take a position in the debates of moral, aesthetic, or scientific relativism. What I mean is that man *imagined* those concepts in the first place. Such principles are therefore the result of invention, of human creation. To argue the opposite would necessarily mean to accept that they were *given*, presumably by some supernatural being, and thus cast such notions away to the realm of the transcendental. If we agree, however, that all such concepts are the result of the radical imagination, it becomes plainly clear why human imagination cannot in fact be measured up against its own products (i.e., true and false, good and bad, beautiful and ugly); and the same is true for all the expressions of the radical imagination, dreams being one of them.

Dreams cannot be dismissed as false, not real, ugly, or evil, much as they cannot be venerated as true, prophetic (in the sense of carrying messages from another world), good, or beautiful (in the sense of providing us with a measure of goodness or beauty). If dreams cannot produce reality in a one-way manner, then neither can reality produce dreams in this fashion. Both our waking reality and our dream reality are parts of our social, cultural, and historically informed self, and they produce each other much in the same way that they are produced by each other. They are (to borrow a phrase by Bourdieu) structuring structured idioms of human subjectivity and in fact of human *intersubjectivity*. We might dream alone, but the self who dreams is never a solitary and precultural entity. Our culture and social life is itself a product of our imagination and, by extension, also part of our waking reality and our dreams.

The aforementioned idea finds its perfect expression in the work of Castoriadis, especially in his theorization of *vis formandi*, or, as he states:

> ... the acknowledgement of the basic fact that one cannot "explain" either the birth of society or the course of history by natural factors, be they biological or other, any more than by the "rational" activity of the "rational" being (man). From the start of history one sees the emergence of radical novelty, and if we do not wish to resort to transcendental factors to account

for this, we definitely must postulate a power of creation, a *vis formandi*, immanent to human collectivities as well as to individual human beings. ... Language, customs, norms, and technique cannot "be explained" by factors extrinsic to human collectivities. (2007: 72)

The power of creation, the *vis formandi,* is therefore a sine qua non of the human existence and is constitutive of human subjectivity as much as it is constituted by it, but it is also constitutive of the social, cultural, and historical sphere. This dialectic and poetic relationship between the *instituting* and the *instituted* imagination is precisely what makes the dream such an important topic of anthropological enquiry and the present work of Edgar such a significant contribution to anthropological knowledge.

Edgar does not dismiss the inspirational potential of dreams. As a consequence he theoretically implicates himself in the discussion of political structure and agency in a unique manner. His work demonstrates beyond any doubt that the human imagination produces structure as much as it is produced by it, but not always in some obscure and time-consuming fashion. The Islamic dream (of jihad or not) is an instance of spontaneous creation. This is not to say that the dream does not carry in its veins history, myth, and what Smith (1986) would have termed the *ethnie.* The dream is firmly established in the collective imagination of Muslim people and connects the past with the present. It is also shaping that imagination in class-less, status-less, (compare with Mullah Omar), and education-less ways. The ability to influence history becomes (peculiarly, according to Western standards) open to all, for all are the sons and daughters of Allah. This is a process much different from the technohistorical processes that in their necessity for economic and educational elites suited European societies (cf. Gellner 1983; Anderson 1983). The difference between dream-based political agency and political agency during waking reality is that the former (in the Islamic world at least) does not need further legitimization. It is open to all, acute, and effective—and perhaps, because of these very qualities, strange and difficult to accept by the Western mind, which has been trained to acknowledge the truth only when it comes from legitimate (read already legitimized by some other discourse) sources. In reality, however, all kinds of political agency and all kinds of legitimate sources of reality have been at one time or another invented, imagined, and realized, albeit perhaps not as quickly as in the case of dream-based agency.

In its contribution to our understanding of political agency, Edgar's work has consequences for the theorization of agency in general. The dream as an instance of the human imagination proves to be central in the anthropological discussion of subjectivity. In its embodied character it offers itself as a unique context for bringing together different approaches to structure and the role of creativity in shaping it and being shaped by it.

Undoubtedly the Foucauldian view of the subject as the result of a regime of truth has dominated the social sciences in recent years. Inspired by Foucauldian thinking, Butler claims that what we can be "is constrained in advance by a regime of truth that decides what will and will not be a recognizable form of being" (2005: 23). At the same time, however, most theorists are ready to accept that the Foucauldian "regime of truth" does not foreclose agency, since it "does not fully constrain the formation of the self" (Butler 2005: 23). Edgar's analysis of the true inspirational dream in Islam engages with an expanded sense of the self and demonstrates clearly "the dynamism of the psyche" (this volume). The dreaming self is a "self becoming," but it is also a "whole self," never at one with its consciousness (cf. Kirtsoglou 2004); a self where emotions, intuitions, prereflexive subjectivity, and social meaning are finally united. The unfinished, unpredictable quality of dreams allows us to analytically approach nonverbal forms of being: embodied, narrativized, deeply social and historical, but nonetheless more visual and experiential than verbal and semiotic. Edgar's analysis constitutes an answer to McNay's claim that "agency cannot be conceptualized through universal models of recognition" (2008: 11). The true inspirational dream in Islam has been indeed an ethnographically and analytically neglected "indirect route of power," which nevertheless clearly "connects identity formations to the invisible structures underlying them" (McNay 2008: 11).

The inspirational true dream is then a space of subject formation, but also of the formation of the "moral subject" (cf. Butler 2005). Edgar's study thus reveals another dimension of the relationship between power and dreams. Dreams evoke meaning and manage to place social actors in the context of history in unprecedented ways. They clearly manifest what Castoriadis refers to as "ontological creation," the creation of new forms and institutions which nevertheless belong "densely and massively to the socio-historical being" (2007: 73). Allah-guided dreams are then settings and means through which subjects engage in dialogue with their own subjectivity and history. This is an idiom of agency that requires careful anthropological consideration, both for its significance and wider theoretical and analytical repercussions as well as for its originality.

Last but not least, Edgar's insistence in taking his informants seriously provides us with an invaluable methodological lesson and enforces our convictions about the unbreakable continuity between ethnography and theory. Rather than "analyzing his subjects," Edgar engages here in the ethnographic appreciation of new motifs of power, agency, and structure by carefully listening to the voices of his informants, and by not rushing to dismiss their beliefs or mask them with intricate and politically or scientifically correct interpretations. His anthropological intuition and analytical sensitivity resulted in the present book, which is in itself evidence of the fact that "one thought, fills immensity" (Blake 1974).

Elisabeth Kirtsoglou
University of Durham

## Notes

1. The first part of my title is borrowed from William Blake's 1974 ambiguous work, as are the titles of the subsections and the final phrase of the epilogue. More particularly: "Every thing possible to be believ'd is an image of truth" (Blake 1974: xx); "As I was walking among the fires of hell, delighted with the enjoyments of Genius; which to Angels look like torment and insanity" (Blake 1974: xx); "What is now proved was once, only imagin'd" (Blake 1974: xx); and "One thought, fills immensity" (Blake 1974: xx).
2. My use of the term West and Western in this document does not intend to reinforce Occidentalism. It is figurative and does not seek to obscure the internal differentiations of the abstraction we call "Western culture." It rather refers to a system of thought and even more so to the social representation of that system, to our belief that somehow and despite "the differences within," this particular imagined community exists.

## References

Anderson, B. 1983. *Imagined Communities: Reflections on the Origins and Spread of Nationalism*. Lodon: Verso.

Argyrou, V. 2002. *Anthropology and the Will to Meaning: A Postcolonial Critique*. London: Pluto Press.

Baudrillard, J. 2002. *The Spirit of Terrorism*. London and New York: Verso.

Blake, W. [1974] 1994. *The Marriage of Heaven and Hell*. Mineola, NY: Dover.

Butler, J. 2005. *Giving an Account of Oneself*. New York: Fordham University Press.

Castoriadis, C. 1995. *Oi horoi tou anthropou*. Athens: Ypsilon vivlia.

Castoriadis, C. 2007. *Figures of the Thinkable*. Stanford, CA: Stanford University Press.

Dimitrakos, D. 2001. "The Socialism of the Idiots." In *The New World Disorder*, edited by G. Pretenderis. Athens: To Vima-Nees Epoxes.

Edgar, I. 1995. *Dreamwork, Anthropology and the Caring Professions: A Cultural Approach to Dreaming*. Aldershot: Avebury.

Gellner, E. 1983. *Nations and Nationalism*. Oxford: Basil Blackwell.

Jackson, M. 1998. *Minima Ethnographica: Intersubjectivity and the Anthropological Project*. Chicago: University of Chicago Press.

Kirtsoglou, E. 2004. *For the Love of Women*. London: Routledge.

Kirtsoglou, E. 2006. "Unspeakable Crimes: Athenian Greek Perceptions of Local and International Terrorism." In *Terror and Violence; Imagination and the Unimagi-*

*nable,* edited by A. Strathern, P. J. Stewart & N. L. Whitehead, 61–88. London: Pluto Press.

Kirtsoglou, E. 2010. "Dreaming the Self: A Unified Approach towards Dreams, Subjectivity and the Radical Imagination." *History and Anthropology* 21, no. 3: 321–35.

Loizos, P. 1981. "Intercommunal Killing in Cyprus." *Man* 23, no. 4 (December 1988): 63953.

Mageo, J. M. 2003. *Dreaming and the Self: New Perspectives on Subjectivity, Identity and Emotion.* Albany: State University of New York Press.

McNay, L. 2008. *Against Recognition.* Cambridge: Polity Press.

Smith, A. 1986. *The Ethnic Origins of Nations.* Oxford: Basil Blackwell.

Stewart, C. 1997. "Fields in Dreams: Anxiety, Experience and the Limits of Social Constructivism in Modern Greek Dream Narratives." *American Ethnologist* 24, no. 4:877–94.

Stewart, C. 2004. "Introduction: Dreaming as an Object of Anthropological Analysis." *Dreaming* 14, nos. 2–3:75–82.

Tedlock, B. 1987. *Dreaming: Anthropological and Psychological Perspectives.* Cambridge: Cambridge University.

Wilkins, B. T. 1992. *Points of Conflict: Terrorism and Collective Responsibility.* London: Routledge.

# Glossary

*Adhan:* the Muslim call to prayer

*Alam al-Mithal:* non-egoic imaginative/imaginal world

*Al-Haq:* the truth

*al-Hissiyya:* sensible world

*Al-Qhayb:* the unseen universe

*al-quwwa al-musawwira:* form-creating faculty

*al-Ruya:* true dream or vision from Allah

*Baraka:* blessing/grace

*dar al-haq:* the next world

*Dua:* personal prayer

*Ghayb:* unseen world

*Hadith:* sayings and actions of the Prophet Muhammed

*Hafiz:* a person who knows the Qur'an by heart

*Hajj:* pilgrimage to Mecca

*Hanafi:* one of the schools of law in Sunni jurisprudence

*Haram:* forbidden behavior in Islam

*Hulm:* ordinary night dream

*Imam:* leader of congregation

*Isha:* night prayer

*Istikhara:* Islamic dream incubation

*Jihad, greater:* struggle with inner soul

*Jihad, lesser:* holy war against the oppressors of Islam

*Jinn:* lesser spirit beings

*Laylat al-isra wal miraj:* the night of the Prophet's ascent to heaven

*Laylat al-Qadr:* the night of power during Ramadan when the Qur'an was revealed

*Madrasah:* Islamic/Qur'anic school

*Mujahideen:* engaged in jihad

*Murid:* disciple of a shaykh

*Nafs:* lower self, ego, soul

*Pir:* Sufi shaykh

*Salah:* ritual prayer

Salafi: Sunni Islamic movement that follows the *Salaf,* the companions of the Prophet Muhammed; the first three generations of Muslims are revered as being righteous predecessors; closely related to Wahhabi

*Shahada:* Islamic declaration of belief

*Shahid/Shaheed:* holy martyr

*Sha'ria:* Islamic law

*Shatan:* the devil

*Shaykh:* tribal elder/Sufi leader

*Shia:* one of the two main branches of Islam

*Sufi:* religious mystic

*Sunnah:* the Prophet Muhammed's example

*Sunni:* one of the two main branches of Islam

*Sura:* Qur'anic chapter

*Taliban:* primarily Pashtun Sunni Islamist political movement in Afghanistan that governed Afghanistan from 1996 to 2001 and is currently fighting the Western (NATO) coalition forces.

*Tariqah:* Sufi order/path

*Ulema:* religious scholar

*Ummah:* the world of Islam/community of believers

*Wahhabi:* conservative Sunni Islamic group based on the teachings of Muhammed ibn Abd-al-Wahhab, an eighteenth-century scholar from Saudi Arabia. Wahhabism is the dominant form of Islam in Saudia Arabia today; closely related to Salafi

*Zikr:* remembrance of Allah

# References

Adams, K. 2004. "Scriptural Symbolic Dreams: Relevant or Redundant in the 21st Century?" *Sleep and Hypnosis* 6 (3): 111–18.

*Al Ahram*. 2006. issue 800, 22–28 June. http://weekly.ahram.org.eg/2006/801/lil.htm.

Albalagh. 2001. "Istikarah." http://www.albalagh.net/qa/istikharah.shtml (accessed 10 August 2008).

al-Jibaly, M. 2006. *The Dreamer's Handbook: Sleep Etiquette and Dream Interpretation in Light of the Sunnah*. Arlington, TX: Al-Kitaab & as-Sunna Publishing.

Allen, D. 2006. "Hope as Waking Dream." Conference paper given at the American Anthropological Association annual conference. November, San Jose, CA.

Amanullah, M. 2009. "Islamic Dreaming: An Analysis of Its Truthfulness and Influence." In *Dreaming in Christianity and Islam: Culture, Conflict, and Creativity*, edited by K. Bulkeley, K. Adams, and P. Davis, 98–110. New Brunswick, NJ: Rutgers University Press.

Arabshahi, P. 1998. http://www.payk.net/mailingLists/iran-news/html/1998/msg01751.html (accessed 6 September 2003).

Artemidorus. 1992. *The Interpretation of Dreams*, trans. Robert White. Isle of Arran, Scotland: Banton Press.

Asad, T. 1986. *The Idea of an Anthropology of Islam*. Washington, DC: Center for Contemporary Arab Studies.

Attar, Farid al-Din. 2005. *The Conference of Birds*. London: Penguin Books.

Aydar, H. 2009. "*Istikhara* and Dreams: Learning About the Future through Dreaming." In *Dreaming in Christianity and Islam: Culture, Conflict and Creativity*, edited by K. Bulkeley, K. Adams, and P. Davis, 123–36. New York: Rutgers.

Basso, E. 1987. "The Implications of a Progressive Theory of Dreaming." In *Dreaming: Anthropological and Psychological Interpretations*, edited by B. Tedlock. Cambridge: Cambridge University Press.

BBC News. 2006. "Huge Crowds at Pakistani Funeral." http://news.bbc.co.uk/2/hi/south_asia/4768615.stm. 19th July 2007.

Begg, M. 2006. *Enemy Combatant: A British Muslim's Journey to Guantanamo and Back*. London: Free Press.

Bell, S. 2005. *The Martyr's Oath: The Apprenticeship of a Home Grown Terrorist*. Mississauga, ON: Wiley.

Bonney, R. 2004. *Jihad: From Qur'an to bin Laden*. Hampshire, UK: Palgrave Macmillan.

Bringa, T. 1995. *Being Muslim the Bosnian Way: Identity and Community in a Central Bosnian Village*. Princeton, NJ: Princeton University Press.

Brown, M. 1987. "Ropes of Sand: Order and Imagery in Aquaruna Dreams." In *Dreaming: Anthropological and Psychological Interpretations,* edited by B. Tedlock. Cambridge: Cambridge University Press.

Bulkeley, K. 2008. *Dreaming in the World's Religions: A Comparative History.* New York: New York University Press.

Bukhari. 1979. *The Translations of the Meanings of Sahihal-Bukhari,* trans. M. M. Khan. Lahore: Kazi Publications.

Burke, J. 2003. *Al-Qaeda: Casting a Shadow of Terror.* London: I. B. Tauris.

Burridge, K. 1969. *New Heaven, New Earth.* Oxford: Blackwell.

Corbin, H. 1966. "The Visionary Dream in Islamic Spirituality." In *The Dream in Human Societies,* edited by G. Von Grunebaum and R. Callois, 384. Berkeley: University of California Press.

Crapanzano, V. 1975. "Saints, Jnun and Dreams: An Essay in Moroccan Ethnopsychology." *Psychiatry* 38 (2): 145–59.

Dilley, R. 1992. "Dreams, Inspiration and Craftwork among Tukolor Weavers." In *Dreaming, Religion and Society in Africa,* edited by M. C. Jedrej and R. Shaw, 71–85. Leiden: Brill.

Domain of Islam Forum. *http://darulislam.info/forum/archive/index.php?t-113. html.* 19th July 2007.

Donahue, K. 2007. *Slave of Allah: Zacarias Moussaoui vs. the USA.* London: Pluto Press.

Edgar, I. 1995. *Dreamwork, Anthropology and the Caring Professions: A Cultural Approach to Dreaming.* Aldershot, UK: Avebury.

———. 2002. "Invisible Elites? Authority and the Dream." *Dreaming* 12 (2): 79–92.

———. 2004a. *Guide to Imagework: Imagination-based Research Methods.* London: Routledge.

———. 2004b. "A War of Dreams? Militant Muslim Dreaming in the Context of Traditional and Contemporary Islamic Dream Theory and Practice." *Dreaming* 14 (1): 21–29.

———. 2006. The "True Dream" in Contemporary Islamic/Jihadist Dreamwork: A Case Study of the Dreams of Taliban Leader Mullah Omar." *Contemporary South Asia* 15 (3): 263–72.

———. 2007. "The Inspirational Night Dream in the Motivation and Justification of Jihad." *Nova Religio* 11 (2): 59–76.

———. 2009. "A Comparison of Islamic and Western Psychological Dream Theories." In *Dreaming in Christianity and Islam: Culture, Conflict, and Creativity,* edited by K. Bulkeley, K. Adams, and P. Davis, 188–99. New Brunswick, NJ: Rutgers.

Edgar, I., and D. Henig. 2010. "*Istikhara:* The Guidance and Practice of Islamic Dream Incubation Through Ethnographic Comparison." *History and Anthropology* 21 (3): 251–62.

Evans-Pritchard, E. E. 1937. *Witchcraft, Oracles and Magic Among the Azande.* Oxford: Oxford University Press.

———. 1940. *The Nuer: A Description of the Modes of Livelihood and Political Institutions of a Nilotic People.* Oxford: Clarendon Press.

———. 1956. *Nuer Religion.* Oxford: Clarendon Press.

Ewing, K. 1990. "The Dream of Spiritual Initiation and the Organization of Self Representation among Pakistani Sufis." *American Ethnologist* 17: 56–74.

———. 1994. "Dreams from a Saint: Anthropological Atheism and the Temptation to Believe." *American Anthropologist* 96 (3): 571–83.

———. 2006. *Arguing Sainthood: Modernity, Psychoanalysis and Islam.* Durham, NC: Duke University Press.

Fareed, A. 2003. *Authentic Interpretation of the DREAMS: According to the Qur'an and Sunnah,* London: Al-Firdous.

Fisk, R. 2005. *The Great War for Civilisation: The Conquest of the Middle East.* London: Fourth Estate.

Fosshage, J. 1987. "New Vistas in Dream Interpretation." In *Dreams in New Perspective: The Royal Road Revisited,* edited by M. Glucksman and S. Warner. New York: Human Sciences Press.

Fouda, Y. 2003. *Masterminds of Terror: The Truth Behind the Most Devastating Terrorist Attack the World Has Ever Seen.* London: Mainstream Publishing.

Foulkes, D. 1985. *A Cognitive-Psychological Analysis.* London: Lawrence Erlbaum Associates.

Frenkel, Y. 2008. "Dream Accounts in the Chronicles of the Mamluk Period." In *Dreaming in Christianity and Islam: Culture, Conflict, and Creativity,* edited by K. Bulkeley, K. Adams, and P. Davis, 98–110. New Brunswick, NJ: Rutgers University Press.

Freud, S. 1953. *The Standard Edition of the Complete Psychological Works of Sigmund Freud,* trans. J. Strachey. London: Hogarth Press and the Institute of Psychoanalysis.

———. 1955. *The Interpretation of Dreams.* New York: Basic Books.

———. 1955b. "The Uncanny." In *The Standard Edition of the Complete Psychological Works of Sigmund Freud,* trans. J. Strachey, 17: 217–55.

———. 1974. *Introductory Lectures on Psychoanalysis.* London: Pelican.

Garfield, P. 1974. *Creative Dreaming.* New York: Ballantine Books.

Geertz, C. 1968. *Islam Observed.* New Haven, CT: Yale University Press.

Gelder, G. van. 1999. "Dreamtowns in Islam: Geography in Arabic Oneirocritical Works." In *Myths, Historical Archetypes and Symbolic Figures in Arabic Literature: Towards a New Hermeneutic Approach,* edited by A. Neuwirth et al. Stuttgart: Steiner Verlag.

Gellner, E. 1981. *Muslim Society.* Cambridge: Cambridge University Press.

Gilsenan, M. 1982. *Recognizing Islam: Religion and Society in the Modern Middle East.* London: I. B. Taurus.

———. 2000. "Signs of Truth, Enchantment, Modernity, and the Dreams of Peasant Women." *Journal of the Royal Anthropological Institute* 6 (4): 597–615.

Giustozzi, A. 2007. *Qur'an, Kalashnikov and Laptop: The Neo-Taliban Insurgency in Afghanistan.* London: Hurst.

Global Terrorist Alert. 2006. http://www.globalterroralert.com/archive0406.html (accessed 11 August 2006). 19th July 2007.

Glouberman, D. 1989. *Life Choices and Life Changes through Imagework.* London: Unwin Hyman.

Gouda, Y. 1991. *Dreams and their Meaning in the Old Arab Tradition.* New York: Vantage Press.

Green, N. 2003. "The Religious and Cultural Roles of Dreams and Visions in Islam." *Journal of the Royal Asiatic Society* 13 (3): 287–313.

Hansberger, R. 2008. "How Aristotle Came to Believe in God-given Dreams: The Arabic Version of *de divinatione per somnum.*" In *Dreaming Across Boundaries: The Interpretation of Dreams in Islamic Lands,* edited by L. Marlow. Cambridge, MA: Harvard University Press.

Hartmann, E. 2008. "The Central Image Makes 'Big' Dreams Big: The Central Image as the Emotional Heart of the Dream." *Dreaming* 18 (1): 44–57.

Hirschkorn, Phil. 2006. "Shoe Bomber Denies Role in 9/11 Attacks." http://www.cnn.com/2006/LAW/04/21/moussaoui.trial (accessed 11 August 2006).

Hoffman, V. J. 1997. "The Role of Visions in Contemporary Egyptian Religious Life." *Religion* 27 (1): 45–64.

Houston. G. 1982. *The Red Book of Gestalt.* London: The Rochester Foundation.

Ibn Khaldun. 1967. *The Muqaddimah,* trans F. Rosenthal. Princeton, NJ: Princeton University Press.

Ibn Sirin. 2000a. *The Interpretation of Dreams.* London: Dar Al Taqwa.

Ibn (Bin) Sireen, 2000b. *Dreams and Interpretations.* New Delhi: Abdul Naeem for Islamic Book Service.

Ibn Sirin, A. H. 2000c. *Dreams and Interpretations.* Karachi: Darul–Ishaat Urdu Bazar.

Jung, C. 1951. "Foreword to the I Ching." In *I Ching,* trans. R. Wilhelm. Routledge: London.

———. 1959. "Archetypes of the Collective Unconscious." *The Collected Works of C. G. Jung,* vol. 9, part 1. London: Routledge and Kegan Paul.

———. 1964. "Approaching the Unconscious." In *Man and His Symbols.* London: Aldus.

———. 1977. *Memories, Dreams, Reflections.* London: Collins Fount Paperbacks.

Kahana-Smilansky, H. 2008. "Self-reflection and Conversion in Medieval Muslim Autobiographical Dreams." In *Dreaming Across Boundaries: The Interpretation of Dreams in Islamic Lands,* edited by L. Marlow. Cambridge, MA: Harvard University Press.

Kinberg, L. 1994. *Ibn Abi al-Dunya, Morality in the Guise of Dreams: A Critical Edition of Kitab al-Manan with Introduction.* Leiden: Brill.

———. 2008. "Qur'an and Hadith: A Struggle for Supremacy as Reflected in Dream Narratives." In *Dreaming Across Boundaries: The Interpretation of Dreams in Islamic Lands,* edited by L. Marlow. Cambridge, MA: Harvard University Press.

Kingsley, P. 2003. *Reality.* Inverness, CA: Golden Sufi Center.

Knafo, A., and T. Glick. 2000. "Genesis Dreams: Using a Private, Psychological Event as a Cultural, Political Declaration." *Dreaming* 10 (1): 19–30.

Koet, B. 2009. "Divine Dream Dilemmas: Biblical Visions and Dreams." In *Dreaming in Christianity and Islam: Culture, Conflict, and Creativity,* edited by K. Bulkeley, K. Adams, and P. Davis, 17–31. New Brunswick, NJ: Rutgers University Press.

Knudson, R. 2001. "Significant Dreams: Bizarre or Beautiful? *Dreaming* 11 (4): 167–77.

Kracke, W. 1987. "Myth in Dreams, Thought in Images: An Amazonian Contribution to the Psychoanalytical Theory of Primary Process." In *Dreaming: Anthropological and Psychological Interpretations,* edited by Barbara Tedlock. Cambridge: Cambridge University Press.

———. 2003. "Beyond the Mythologies." In *Dream Travellers: Sleep Experiences and Culture in the Western Pacific,* edited by R. Lohmann, 212. New York: Palgrave Macmillan.

Krippner, S., and A. Thompson. 1996. "A 10-Facet Model of Dreaming Applied to Dream Practices of Sixteen Native American Cultural Groups." *Dreaming* 6 (2): 71–96.

Kruger, S. 1992. *Dreaming in the Middle Ages.* Cambridge: Cambridge University Press.

Kuspinar, B. 2008. "The Chief Characteristics of Spirituality in Said Nursi's Religious Thought." In *Spiritual Dimensions of Bediuzzaman Said Nursi's Risale-I Nur,* edited by Ibrahim M. Abu-Rabi, 125–46. Albany: State University of New York.

Lamoreaux, J. 2002. *The Early Muslim Tradition of Dream Interpretation.* New York: State University of New York.

———. 2008. "An Early Muslim Autobiographical Dream Narrative: Abu Jafar al-Qayini and His Dream of the Prophet Muhammed." In *Dreaming Across Boundaries: The Interpretation of Dreams in Islamic Lands,* edited by L. Marlow. Cambridge, MA: Harvard University Press.

Landau, Y. 2008. "Dreams and Dream Interpretation in Said Nursi's I *Risale-I Nur:* Islamic, Judaic, and Universal Resonances." In *Spiritual Dimensions of Bediuzzaman Said Nursi's Risale-I Nur,* edited by I. Abu-Rabi. Albany: State University of New York.

Lines, Andy. 2001. "Sick Videotape Proves bin Laden Was the Evil Mastermind behind the Horrors of Sept. 11," *The Mirror* [London], 14 December.

London *Times.* "Tim Reid, 'Shoe-bomber' Likely to be Jailed for Life." London *Times,* 30 January 2003.

Lyon, S. 2004a. *An Anthropological Analysis of Power and Patronage in Pakistan.* Lampeter, UK: Edwin Mellen Press.

———. 2004b. "'Indirect' Symbolic Violence and Rivalry Between Equals in Rural Punjab, Pakistan." *Durham Anthropology Journal* 12 (1): 37–50.

———. 2005. "Culture and Information: An Anthropological Examination of Communication in Cultural Domains in Pakistan." *Cybernetics and Systems: An International Journal* 36 (8): 919–32.

MacFarquhar, Emily. "The Rise of Taliban." *US News and World Report,* 6 March 1995. http://www.usnews.com/usnews/news/articles/950306/archive_011192.htm. 19th July 2007.

Malcolm, N. 1998. *Kosovo.* London: Macmillan.

Malinowski, B. 1954. *Magic, Science and Religion.* New York: Doubleday.

Marquand, Robert. 2001. "The Reclusive Ruler Who Runs the Taliban." *Christian Science Monitor.* http://www.csmonitor.com/2001/1010/p1s4-wosc.html (accessed 10 August 2005).

Marranci. G. 2008. *The Anthropology of Islam.* Oxford: Berg.

Marsden, P. 1998. *The Taliban: War, Religion and the New Order in Afghanistan.* London: Zed Books.

McElwain, T. 2004. "Sufism Bridging East and West: The Case of the Bektashis." In *Sufism in Europe and North America,* edited by D. Westerlund. London: Routledge.

McGinty, A. 2006. *Becoming Muslim: Western Women's Conversions to Islam.* New York: Palgrave.

Meier, F. 1966. "Some Aspects of Inspiration by Demons in Islam." In *The Dream and Human Societies,* edited by H. Corbin, and R. Caillois. Berkeley: University of California Press.

Mittermaier, A. 2007. "The Book of Visions: Dreams, Poetry and Prophecy in Contemporary Egypt." *International Journal of Middle East Studies* 39 (2): 229–47.

Murshed, I. 2006. *Afghanistan: The Taliban Years.* London: Bennett and Bloom.

Muslim Sahih. 1987. *Sahih Muslim bi-Sharh al Nawawi,* 18 vols. Beirut: Dar al-Kitab al-Arabi.

News24.com. 2004. "Zarqawi: Delinquent to Extremist." http://www.news24.com/world/archives/iraq/dossier/zarqawi-delinquent-to-extremist-20041108 (accessed 11 August 2006).

Newsmax.com. 2006. http://www.newsmax.com/archives/reports/2006/3/9/95852 (accessed 8 November 2006).

Ormsby, E. 2008. "The Poor Man's Prophecy: Al-Ghazali on Dreams." In *The Interpretation of Dreams in Islamic Lands,* edited by L. Marlow. Cambridge, MA: Harvard University Press.

Perls, F. 1969. *Gestalt Therapy Verbatim.* Lafayette, CA: Real People Press.

———. 1971. "Four Lectures." In *Gestalt Therapy Now,* edited by J. Fagan and I. Shepherd. New York: Harper & Row.

Philips, Abu Ameenah Bilal. 2001. *Dream Interpretation According to the Qur'an and Sunnah.* Kuala Lumpur: A. S. Noordeen.

Quinn, S. 1996. "The Dreams of Sheikh Safi al-Din and Safavid Historical Writing." *Iranian Studies* 29 (1–2): 127–47.

———. 2008. "The Dreams of Shaykh Safi al-Din in Late Safavid Chronicles." In *Dreaming Across Boundaries: The Interpretation of Dreams in Islamic Lands,* edited by L. Marlow. Cambridge, MA: Harvard University Press.

*The Qur'an.* 1955. Oxford: Oxford University Press.

*The Qur'an.* 1956. Trans. N. J. Dawood. London: Penguin Books.

*The Qur'an.* London: Everyman, Dent. 1977.

Rashid, A. 2000. *Taliban: Militant Islam, Oil and Fundamentalism in Central Asia.* New Haven, CT: Yale University Press.

———. 2002. *Jihad: The Rise of Militant Islam in Central Asia.* New Haven, CT: Yale University Press.

Reeve, S. 2001. "The Worldwide Net: Is Bombing Effective Against Terrorism?" *Ecologist,* 22 November. http://www.the ecologist.org/archive_article.html?article=256&category=71 (accessed 22 November 2001).

Samuels, A. 1985. *Jung and the Post-Jungians.* London: Routledge.

Sanneh, L. 1979. *The Jakhanke: The History of an Islamic Clerical People of the Sengambia.* London: International African Institute.

Sedgwick, M. 2000. *Sufism*. Cairo: American University.

Shaw, R. 1992. "Dreaming as Accomplishment: Power, the Individual and Temne Divination." In *Dreaming, Religion and Society in Africa*, edited by M. Jedrej and R. Shaw. Leiden: Brill.

Sindawi, K. 2008. "The Image of Ali b. Abi Talib in the Dreams of Visitors to His Tomb." In *Dreaming Across Boundaries: The Interpretation of Dreams in Islamic lands*, edited by L. Marlow. Cambridge, MA: Harvard University Press.

Sirriyeh, E. 2005. *Sufi Visionary of Ottoman Damascus: Abd al-Ghani-Nabulusi 1641–1731*. London: Routledge.

Sviri, S. 1997. *The Taste of Hidden Things*. Inverness, CA: Golden Sufi Center.

———. 1999. "Dreaming Analysed and Recorded: Dreams in the World of Medieval Islam." In *Dream Culture*, edited by D. Shulman and G. Stroumsa, 252. London: Routledge.

Taylor, J. 1992. *Where People Fly and Water Runs Uphill: Using Dreams to Tap the Wisdom of the Unconscious*. New York: Warner Books.

Tedlock, B. 1987. "Dreaming and Dream Research." In *Dreaming: Anthropological and Psychological Interpretations*, edited by B. Tedlock. Cambridge: Cambridge University Press.

*Time Asia*. 2000. "'We Are Against Terrorism,' Online-only interview with Taliban supreme leader Mullah Muhammed Omar." http://www.time.com/time/asia/magazine/2000/0221/afghan.omar.html. 19th July 2007.

Trimingham, J. 1971. *The Sufi Orders in Islam*. London: Oxford University Press.

Tulku, T. 1999. "Lucid Dreaming: Exerting the Creativity of the Unconscious." In *The Psychology of Awakening*, edited by G. Watson, S. Batchelor and G. Clayton, 271–83. London: Rider.

Ullman, M., and N. Zimmerman. 1979. *Working with Dreams*. Wellingborough, UK: Crucible.

*USA Today*. 2006. http://www.usatoday.com/news/nation/2006-04-20-moussaoui _x (accessed 8 November 2006).

Vaughan-Lee, L. 1998. *Catching the Thread: Sufism, Dreamwork and Jungian Psychology*. Inverness, CA: Golden Sufi Center.

Werbner, P. 2003. *Pilgrims of Love: The Anthropology of a Global Sufi Cult*. London: Hurst.

Westerlund, D. 2004. "Introduction: Inculturating and Transcending Islam." In *Sufism in Europe and North America*, edited by D. Westerlund. London: Routledge.

Zahab, M. 2008. "'I shall be waiting for you at the door of Paradise': The Pakistani Martyrs of the Lashkar-e Taiba (Army of the Pure)." In *The Practice of War: The Production, Reproduction and Communication of Armed Violence*, edited by A. Rao, M. Böck, and M. Bollig, 133–60. Oxford: Berghahn Books.

# Index

Secretary of State
like military